Teaching Caribbean Students

Teaching Caribbean Students: Research on Social Issues In the Caribbean and Abroad

Editors:
Tony Bastick
Austin Ezenne

Department of Educational Studies, University of the West Indies, Kingston, Jamaica

Copyright © 2003 by Department of Educational Studies,
University of the West Indies,
Kingston,
Jamaica.
All rights reserved.

Teaching Caribbean Students: Research on social issues in the Caribbean and abroad/
Tony Bastick, and Austin Ezenne editors.
p. cm.
Includes bibliographical references.
ISBN: 976-632-046-2
1. Education - Caribbean, English-speaking. T. Bastick, Tony; A. Ezenne, Austin
LB1028.25. C27 T42 2003   371.2

CONTENTS

INTRODUCTION *(vii)*
  Maxine Henry-Wilson
  Minister of Education, Youth and Culture for Jamaica.
FOREWORD *(ix)*
  Zellynne Jennings
  Head of the Department of Educational Studies, University of the West Indies, Mona, Jamaica.
EDITORIAL *(xiii)*
  Tony Bastick and Austin Ezenne
  Department of Educational Studies, University of the West Indies, Mona, Jamaica.
EDITORIAL CONSULTANTS *(xv)*

CONTRIBUTING AUTHORS *(ixx)*

PART 1. SOCIALLY SENSITIVE PEDAGOGIES

CHAPTER 1.
  Pages 3 - 30
  Domain-Specific Modern Language Course Developments for Caribbean Integration.
  Béatrice Boufoy-Bastick
  Department of Modern Languages, University of the West Indies, Mona, Jamaica.
CHAPTER 2.
  Pages 31 - 70
  Creole Interference or Linguistic Elasticity?
  Ingrid Waldron
  Ontario Institute for Studies in Education, University of Toronto, Canada.
CHAPTER 3.
  Pages 71 - 88
  Use of Case Method in Educational Administration
  Austin Ezenne
  Department of Educational Studies, University of the West Indies, Mona, Jamaica.

CHAPTER 4.
> *Pages 89 - 116*
> Situated attainment: Measuring under achievement in Jamaica
> **Tony Bastick**
> Department of Educational Studies, University of the West Indies, Mona, Jamaica.

CHAPTER 5.
> *Pages 117 - 160*
> El Colectivo Tonguas: The Development of a Bilingual, University-level Creative Writing and Performance Poetry Extracurricular Program in the Puerto Rican Context
> **Loretta Collins**
> University of Puerto Rico, Río Piedras, Puerto Rico.

PART 2.
ADAPTING TO SCHOOL AND SOCIETY

CHAPTER 6.
> *Pages 163 - 214*
> Identity Development of Caribbean Girls in Canadian Schools.
> **Beverly-Jean Daniel**
> University of Toronto, Ontario Canada.

CHAPTER 7.
> *Pages 215 - 248*
> Caribbean Student Speakers' Education and Experiences in American Schools: A Constant Struggle with Varied Results
> **Clarissa N. West-White**
> Florida Memorial College, USA.

CHAPTER 8.
> *Pages 249 - 284*
> Racism, Resistance and Resilience: The 3Rs of Educating Caribbean Students in a Canadian Context
> **Brenda McMahon**
> Department of Theory and Policy Studies in Education, University of Toronto, Canada - and
> **Denise Armstrong**
> Ontario Institute for Studies in Education, University of Toronto, Canada.

CONTENTS

CHAPTER 9.
Pages 285 - 316
Dominican Adolescent Immigrants' Experiences with Schooling
Shana R. Grossman
George Mason University, USA.

PART 3.
ATTITUDE IN THE CLASSROOM

CHAPTER 10.
Pages 319 - 344
Disruptive Behaviour Inside A Jamaican Classroom
Loraine D. Cook
Department of Educational Studies, University of the West Indies, Mona, Jamaica.

CHAPTER 11.
Pages 345 - 386
Learning Patterns of Caribbean Boys in the Secondary School
Hyacinth Skervin
University of Cincinnati, Ohio, OH, USA.

CHAPTER 12.
Pages 387 - 402
Does disruptive classroom behaviour make adolescent Caribbean students more popular or less popular with their peers?
Tony Bastick
Department of Educational Studies, University of the West Indies, Mona, Jamaica.

CHAPTER 13.
Pages 403 - 432
Reading Comprehension, Attitudes to reading and Locus of Control beliefs of African-Caribbean students: A Jamaican-UK study.
Jossett Smikle
Department of Educational Studies, University of the West Indies, Mona, Jamaica.

CHAPTER 14.
    Pages 433 - 456
    An Analysis of Jamaican Technical High School Students'
    Attitudes to Technical and Vocational Education
    Anita Thomas-James
    University of Technology, Jamaica - and
    Kola Soyibo
    Department of Educational Studies, University of the West
    Indies, Mona, Jamaica.

NOTES ON CONTRIBUTORS
    Pages 457 - 467

INTRODUCTION

MAXINE HENRY-WILSON, MP
Minister for Education, Youth and Culture, Jamaica.

Interwoven in the issues and findings of the research essays in this collection are two recurring themes; the identification of challenges posed in preparing Caribbean students to be positive actors in the new global network and the isolation of challenges posed in developing these global relations. Of course, both themes are part of the same dual reality, which is "Try as we might the Caribbean cannot escape the demands of globalisation. We are a part of globalisation and we cannot escape it."

Over recent years, many of our teachers in the Caribbean have been recruited to work in metropolitan centres in North America and Europe (primarily England). In many instances they have been placed in the centres with Caribbean communities. These teachers can, therefore, benefit from the findings of these research papers and better deal with the patterns of language use, crises identification and other unique situations faced by our students abroad.

The content of this publication should therefore be a "must read" for all our teachers - to give them new insights and direct information on what they are confronting and what approaches they need to take.

The foresights of the editors, and the rigorous research of the authors, have come together to provide us with this invaluable publication. To all we say "thanks."

FOREWORD

ZELLYNNE JENNINGS
Head, Department of Educational Studies,
University of the West Indies, Jamaica

Nearly two decades ago a Caribbean educator exploring educational research in the English – speaking Caribbean wrote that "in many instances, the concerns and topics that are foremost in research are those that are current in Western intellectual communities and not necessarily those that are relevant to life in the Caribbean" (Miller 1984:181). But the world is much more complex than it was twenty years ago. It has become more 'global' and countries have become borderless in the sense that their nationals are not confined within the limits of their boundaries. And so we speak of the Caribbean Diaspora. Concerns which are relevant to the experiences of students in the Caribbean also touch the lives of those who have made their homes in Canada, Europe, The United States of America and anywhere else in the world. This book is very timely in that it addresses some of these concerns.

An issue that has engaged the minds of Caribbean language educators for many years is that of how to teach Standard English to Creole speakers. Craig (1996), for example, highlights the differences of opinion between those in the Caribbean who favour a native language English-teaching approach as opposed to those who advocate teaching English as a second language. In this book, Ingrid Waldron challenges the concept of Creole interference as an explanation for the language problem of 'Black British' children. These are children of Caribbean heritage , born and raised in Britain or born in the Caribbean and brought up in Britain. Waldron favours a bidialectal approach which recognises the 'linguistic elasticity' of these children. Clarissa West –White also deals with the language issue as one of the challenges which face children schooled in the United States who hail from the Caribbean islands, including Haiti.

Beverley ¬Jean Daniel highlights the problem of racialised identity development amongst African Caribbean girls in Canadian schools. In the context of globalisation, identity as an issue takes on added significance. The search of African –Caribbean girls in Canada for an identity and a sense of knowing who they are as Black Women in a sense symbolises the search of people in the Caribbean for their unique identity. Daniel's chapter also takes up the issue of race – an area in Caribbean education where it seems angels fear to tread. And yet so many of our children who make their homes abroad become victims of 'system racism'. McMahon develops the issue and highlights how this manifests itself in low test scores, and high drop out rates among Black Caribbean students in Canada.

Another issue taken up in this book is that of the underachieving male. Much has been written on this in the Caribbean; for example, the *Marginalization of the Black Male by Errol Miller* (1986). Other Caribbean researchers have contended that the underachievement of boys in our schools can be explained more in terms of

FOREWORD

their under participation in schools (Bailey 2000) and that factors such as parental occupation, pre-school attendance and the type of school attended are more powerful explanations of underachievement than the sex of the child (Kutnick 2000). Two chapters in this book add to this continuing dialogue. Tony Bastick operationally defines underachievement so as to distinguish it from low ability and reports research that validates the basic assumptions of the concept. Hyacinth Skervin examines learning behaviours in the classroom that can be associated with gender identities in male students and she discusses the types of learning experiences for which boys have a preference.

What is evident therefore is that the issues that face our students in the Caribbean are also causes of concern in other parts of the world where our students make their homes. This is what makes this book readable and appealing to a wide audience -from university undergraduate and graduate students to the ordinary person in the street who has an interest in the fate of Caribbean students in schools at home and abroad. What is interesting is that the book showcases the multilingual background of the Caribbean people – English, Spanish and French-speaking.

But what is the teacher to make of all this research? A number of the writers in this book offer suggested approaches to teaching which may well prove to be valuable to the teacher. However, one should perhaps here be reminded of the definition of curriculum put forward by Stenhouse (1993: 223) as " a way of translating any educational idea into a hypothesis testable in practice. *It invites critical testing rather than acceptance*"(my emphasis). Stenhouse at the time was writing on the *Teacher as Researcher* and he concluded as I conclude here that " a research tradition which is accessible to teachers and which feeds teaching must be created if education is to be significantly improved" (ibid: 233). This book is one that is creating such a research tradition.

REFERENCES

Bailey, B. (2000). School failure and success: A gender analysis of the 1997 General Proficiency Caribbean Examinations Council (CXC) Examinations for Jamaica. *Journal of Education and Development in the Caribbean* Vol. 4 No.1 (1-18)

Craig, D. (1996). English Language Teaching :Problems and Prospects in the West Indies. In: Craig, D (Ed) *Education in the West Indies: Developments and Perspectives 1948-1988* ISER: Mona

Kutnick, P. (2000). Girls, boys and school achievement: critical comments on who achieves in schools and under what economic and social conditions achievement takes place – a Caribbean perspective. *International Journal of Educational Development* Vol. 2,No.1 65-84

Miller, E. (1984). *Educational Research: The English Speaking Caribbean* Ottawa: IDRC

Stenhouse, L. (1993). The teacher as research. Hammersley, M (Ed) *Controversies in Classroom Research.* Buckingham, Open University Press: 223-234

EDITORIAL NOTE

TONY BASTICK &
AUSTIN EZENNE
Department of Educational studies,
University of the West Indies, Jamaica

This peer-reviewed research publication of the Department of Educational Studies, at the University of the West Indies in Jamaica, identifies characteristics that define teaching and learning of Caribbean students both within the Caribbean region and throughout its Diaspora. The research presented here results from experts' analyses of experiences, data, policy and programmes concerning the education of Caribbean students studying in Caribbean centres around the world. It speaks to both the many difficulties and successes experienced by students, teachers and policy makers. It is intended primarily for educators, researchers and administrators who are seeking new perspectives on the difficult and competing necessities of educating for both cultural relevance and international accreditation, for both integration and identity, for both globalisation and the maintenance of national values, and for both social assimilation and appreciation of our social differences. The purpose is to inform good practice and future policies, and to guide educational research on the continuing challenges of teaching and learning to develop the full potential of our Caribbean students.

While these texts represent the rich cultural and linguistic diversity of our expert contributors, the views expressed are not necessarily those of the Editors or the Department of Educational Studies.

EDITORIAL CONSULTANTS

We greatly appreciate the extensive contributions from our editorial consultants who represent the current state of knowledge on social issues affecting the teaching of Caribbean students. They have carefully analysed the many complex and important issues that have been researched and generously offered insights, support and suggestions that have added immeasurably to the quality of this book.

DR. JOSEPHINE A. BEOKU-BETTS
Women's Studies Center, Florida Atlantic University, Boca Raton, FL, USA

DR. GLORIA BURKE
Department of Education, University of the West Indies, Mona, Jamaica, West Indies.

DR. JUNE GEORGE
Department of Education, UWI, St. Augustine, Trinidad, West Indies.

DR. JOHN M. GONZÁLEZ
Department of English and the Center for Mexican American Studies, The University of Texas at Austin, TX, USA.

HOWARD E. HERRNSTADT
    Director, YourBusinessEditor, Cleveland, Ohio, OH, USA.

DR. MILES ANTHONY IRVING
    Department of Educational Psychology, Georgia State University, GA, USA.

DR. ARNOLD HARRICHAND ITWARU
    Director, Caribbean Studies Program, University of Toronto, ON, Canada.

ELIZABETH A. JANSEN
    Institute of Child Development, University of Minnesota, MN, USA.

PROFESSOR PETER KUTNICK
    Education Research Centre, University of Brighton, UK.

DR. BARBARA MATALON
    Institute of Education, University of the West Indies, Mona, Jamaica, West Indies.

TOM MCARDLE
    Senior Director Planning and Project Development Division, HEART/NTA, Kingston, Jamaica, West Indies.

EDITORIAL CONSULTANTS

DR. GLENDA M. PRIME
>Morgan State University, Baltimore, Maryland, MD, USA.

DR. MARCIA RAINFORD
>Department of Educational Studies, University of the West Indies, Mona, Jamaica, West Indies.

DR TONY SEWELL
>School of Education, University of Leeds, Yorkshire UK.

DR. PATRICK SOLOMON
>Faculty of Education, York University, Toronto, ON, Canada.

DR. DAVID SUTCLIFFE
>Universitat Pompeu Fabra, Barcelona, Catalonia, Spain.

DR. APRIL TAYLOR
>University of Southern California, Los Angeles, CA. USA.

DR. ALISSA TROTZ
> Institute for Women's Studies and Gender Studies, New College, University of Toronto, Canada.

DR. JENNIFER WILLIAMS
> Community College of the Cayman Islands, George Town, Grand Cayman, West Indies.

DR. MELANIE ZIMMER-GEMBECK
> Griffith University, Gold Coast Campus, Queensland, Australia.

CONTRIBUTING AUTHORS

BÉATRICE BOUFOY-BASTICK
Department of Modern Languages, University of the West Indies, Mona, Jamaica, West Indies.

INGRID WALDRON
Ontario Institute for Studies in Education, University of Toronto, Ontario, ON, Canada.

AUSTIN EZENNE
Department of Educational Studies, University of the West Indies, Mona, Jamaica, West Indies.

TONY BASTICK
Department of Educational Studies, University of the West Indies, Mona, Jamaica, West Indies.

LORETTA COLLINS
English Department, University of Puerto Rico, Río Piedras, Puerto Rico.

BEVERLY-JEAN DANIEL
University of Toronto, Ontario, ON, Canada.

CLARISSA N. WEST-WHITE
Florida Memorial College, Miami-Dade, FL, USA.

BRENDA MCMAHON
Department of Theory and Policy Studies in Education, University of Toronto, Ontario, ON, Canada.

DENISE ARMSTRONG
Ontario Institute for Studies in Education, University of Toronto, Ontario, ON, Canada.

SHANA R. GROSSMAN
George Mason University, Fairfax, Virginia, VA, USA.

LORAINE D. COOK
Department of Educational Studies, University of the West Indies, Mona, Jamaica, West Indies.

CONTRIBUTING AUTHORS

HYACINTH SKERVIN

University of Cincinnati, Cincinnati, Ohio, OH, USA.

JOSSETT SMIKLE

Department of Educational Studies, University of the West Indies, Mona, Jamaica, West Indies.

ANITA THOMAS-JAMES

University of Technology, Jamaica, West Indies.

KOLA SOYIBO

Department of Educational Studies, University of the West Indies, Mona, Jamaica, West Indies.

TEACHING CARIBBEAN STUDENTS

PART 1.

SOCIALLY SENSITIVE PEDAGOGIES

CHAPTER 1.

Pages 3 - 30
Domain-Specific Modern Language Course Developments for Caribbean Integration.

Béatrice Boufoy-Bastick
Department of Modern Languages, University of the West Indies, Mona, Jamaica

CHAPTER 2.

Pages 31 - 70
Creole Interference or Linguistic Elasticity?

Ingrid Waldron
Ontario Institute for Studies in Education, University of Toronto, Canada

CHAPTER 3.

Pages 71 - 88
Use of Case Method in Educational Administration

Austin Ezenne
Department of Educational Studies, University of the West Indies, Mona, Jamaica.

PART 1

CHAPTER 4.

Pages 89 - 116
Situated attainment: Measuring under achievement in Jamaica

Tony Bastick
Department of Educational Studies, University of the West Indies, Mona, Jamaica.

CHAPTER 5.

Pages 117 - 160
El Colectivo Tonguas: The Development of a Bilingual, University-level Creative Writing and Performance Poetry Extracurricular Program in the Puerto Rican Context

Loretta Collins
University of Puerto Rico, Río Piedras, Puerto Rico.

DOMAIN-SPECIFIC MODERN LANGUAGE COURSE DEVELOPMENTS FOR CARIBBEAN INTEGRATION

BÉATRICE BOUFOY-BASTICK

ABSTRACT

A major challenge of 21st century Education for the Caribbean is to support an ever-increasingly interconnected globalised economy. Universities in the English-speaking Caribbean are meeting this challenge through courses, graduates and research that enhance the strengthening of economic, political and diplomatic ties in the region. The emergence of the Caribbean as an integrated political and economic trading unit now makes foreign language communication an inescapable necessity for all Caribbean university students, professionals and decision-makers so as to fit in this new globalised trade-reliant politically-interrelated order. To this end, Caribbean institutions have initiated modern languages programs in the three official languages of the region, namely English, French and Spanish. The objectives of these Caribbean linguistic initiatives starkly differ from traditional language programmes offered in Departments of Modern Languages at Caribbean universities. The traditional approach which focused on language and literature study has switched towards developing communicative skills in specific domains with the intent to prepare university students, professionals and decision-makers to function adeptly and efficiently in an integrated trilingual Caribbean.

This paper examines current language policy initiatives in the Caribbean and describes three novel modern language courses designed for non-linguist undergraduates at the University of the West Indies and the University of Technology in Jamaica.

INTRODUCTION

The increasing globalisation of trade, regional CARIFORUM/CARICOM economic integration and the creation of the Association of Caribbean States (ACS) have made it imperative for Caribbean students, professionals and decision-makers to acquire a functional knowledge of, at least, two of the three official languages of the Caribbean. To this effect, Caribbean economico-political organisations and tertiary educational institutions have recognised the urgency of linguistically competent trans-Caribbean leaders and they have instigated the development of innovative communication-based domain-specific modern language courses. This paper briefly outlines the major language policy initiatives at the macro political level aimed to foster an emergent integrated pan-Caribbean trilingual region. The then paper looks at the development of modern language university course innovations and describes two examples of a domain-specific modern language course delivered at the University of the West Indies and the University of Technology in Jamaica.

PAN-CARIBBEAN MODERN LANGUAGE COURSE INITIATIVES FOR SPURRING REGIONAL INTEGRATION

Caribbean political and educational decision-makers strive to strengthen ties between the regional institutions of the anglophone, francophone and hispanophone Caribbean island states. A major issue in strengthening ties was to overcome the difficulty to communicate in a linguistically diverse region. This linguistic diversity is exhibited in the use of three international languages of wider communication, namely English, French and Spanish, together with a multiplicity of creole languages. Caribbean leaders acknowledged the importance of maintaining this linguistic diversity, and in particular the significance of promoting the three international languages for the Caribbean to participate fully in the globalised economy. They are now committed to promoting *plurilingualism* among Caribbean citizens in a *multlingual* Caribbean reigion – this distinction between plurilingualism and multilingualism made by the Council of Europe emphasises that : "le premier concept est utilisé pour les individus, le second pour les sociétés" (the first concept is used for individuals, the second for societies) (Puren, 2001, p. 97).

Several modern language policy initiatives testify this support to a trilingual Caribbean, in particular the implementation of four funded higher education projects: (i) the introduction of the Caribbean Universities Level (CULP) programme, (ii) the establishment of a Caribbean Universities Network, (iii) the ACS common curriculum for teaching the official languages of the Caribbean and (iv) the Centres of Excellence.

(I) EU-FUNDED CARIBBEAN UNIVERSITIES LEVEL (CULP) PROGRAMME

INNOVATIVE PAN-CARIBBEAN MASTERS' PROGRAMMES

The CULP was established under the Caribbean Regional Indicative Programme of the 7th European Development Fund (EDF). The main objective of the CULP is "to support the creation of a Caribbean capability to help meet the demand by public and private sector institutions in the region for trained professional staff able to deal with the transnational development challenges of the future" (Terms of Reference, CULP). This objective is to be "achieved through the establishment of regionally integrated Masters courses in key applied disciplines to be delivered in five participating universities" (ibidem). Three universities are located in Dominican Republic, namely Universidad Católica, Pontificia Universidad Madre y Maestra (PUCMM), Universidad

Nacional Pedro Henríuez Urena (UNPHU) and two in the English-speaking Caribbean, at the three campuses of the University of the West Indies (UWI) and the University of Technology, Jamaica. The university of Quisqueya, in Haiti, participates in this educational initiative although no MA course is delivered at this campus. Each university mentioned above offers a MA course in a specific discipline, hence the choice of campus is determined primarily by the field of study and not by the language of instruction.

BUILDING ON CARIBBEAN PLURILINGUALISM FOR EXPERT TRANS-CARIBBEAN UNIVESITY EDUCATION

This pan-Caribbean trilingual approach to postgraduate education is a challenge to be faced by both lecturers and students. On one hand, lecturers teach to a linguistically and culturally diverse student population with different educational backgrounds. On the other hand, students study and research in a foreign language and their attainments are expected to be comparable with those of native speakers. To this end, MA-targetted language courses were developed and students whose mother-tongue is not the language of instruction are required to take a three-month intensive immersion language course prior to starting their Masters studies. The language training component of the CULP Masters has two objectives. The first objective is to prepare students to have a functional knowledge of the target language which enables them to communicate judiciously both orally and in writing in usual social and educational contexts. The second objective relates to their specific domain of study, that is to say, language instruction aims to impart domain-specific lexical registers pertaining to the students' area of specialisation - International Business, Natural Resource Management, Agricultural Diversification, Caribbean Tropical Architecture. Thus these intensive language training courses have a common language core aiming to develop communicative competence, and a domain-specific language component aimed to impart a specialist language base. The common core is taught using conventional foreign language (FL) teaching approaches and focuses on the linguistic content. By contrast, the specialist FL courses focuses on thematic content. As Kahn explains: "Dans ce cas, ce n'est pas la logique de la langue qui l'emporte mais la logique du domaine ou de la branche d'activités" (In this case, it is not the logic sequencing of the language which prevails but that of the domain or the branch of activities) (1993, p. 147). In other words, the domain-specific foreign language component is thematically-, as opposed to grammatically-, structured (Moirand, Bouacha, Beacco & Collinot, 1992). This non-grammatical thematically-structured course design requires a content-directed approach as opposed to a language-based one; it starkly deviates from the conventional foreign language teaching approach used in the foreign language core component.

The CULP Masters programmes are innovative university initiatives intended to facilitate Caribbean integration between anglophone, francophone and hispanophone students (Johnson, 1997). These MA courses evidence the determination of Caribbean educational decision-makers to integrate the wide-ranging expertise of Caribbean's linguistically diverse scholars in keeping with Caribbean integration policy. CULP is a seminal trans-Caribbean higher education initiative highlighting the importance for the Caribbean to build on its linguistic diversity and multi-facetted professional experience for trilingual inclusion. The contribution of the CULP to Caribbean university integration paved the way to the elaboration of the emergent Caribbean University Network.

(II) ESTABLISHMENT OF A CARIBBEAN UNIVERSITIES NETWORK (CUN)

The Caribbean Universities Network (CUN) is another university led initiative towards trilingual-based Caribbean integration. It differs from the Association of Caribbean Universities (UNICA) as it stresses the necessity to develop an integrated plurilingual Caribbean university network. CUN is a regional university project modelled on the Association of European Universities (CRE) and the Association of Latin American Universities (AULA). This project involves French- and Spanish-speaking universities, as well as the English-speaking universities, the Univerisity of the West Indies and the University of Technology, Jamaica. The significance of this project for integration is both educational and academic. The educational significance is that it is intended to facilitate the future movement of students within linguistically-diverse Caribbean universities. The academic significance is that it seeks to promote the design and implementation of anticipated regional university-led research projects. CUN demonstrates the major role Caribbean universities play in fostering Caribbean integration which can only be achieved by supporting trilingual university programmes. These programmes are reliant upon solid FL courses whose purpose is to train students to use their second language effectively in domain-specific contexts for a state-of-the-art pan-Caribben university education.

(III) THE ASSOCIATION OF CARIBBEAN STATES (ACS)

The linguistic diversity of the Caribbean is also a chief concern of the Association of Caribbean States (ACS). To this end, ACS is developing a common curriculum for teaching the official languages of the Caribbean. This curriculum was earmarked as one of the ACS priorities in 1998 and it is intended to provide the basis for intensive teaching of French and Spanish to English-speaking professionals. It is the urgency to train English-speaking leaders and decision-makers to function competently and effectively in the increasingly interconnected Caribbean which guided the decision to design a French and Spanish curriculum which language trainging institutions in ACS member states and Associate Members could implement for use. The ACS initiative further demonstrates the widespread determination to progress towards a trilingual integrated Caribbean.

(IV) CREATION OF TRILINGUAL CARIBBEAN CENTRES OF EXCELLENCE

The ambitious 'Centre of Excellence' project was a French initiative. It was proposed by the French embassy in Jamaica in 1999 and received official approval by the French Ministry of Foreign Affairs in October 2000. This project was designed to train Caribbean postgraduate professionals engaged in the two key Caribbean economic sectors, namely Tourism and Management, to operate using the three official languages of the Caribbean. It aimed at the "development of plurilingualism with professionalism in the Caribbean" (ACS/1999/S&T.IV/WP/004). The project was enthusiastically received by the two universities in Jamaica, UWI (the regional university) and UTech (the national university), and by high level management training institutions. However, this project was discontinued as funding for a mandatory feasibility study was not available.

These four region-wide initiatives are cited to evidence the recognised demand from Caribbean governments to train linguistically-competent professionals to work in the globalised trilingual Caribbean. Similar economically-driven FL course developments have been instigated at some Caribbean universities. The next section reports on three chronologically-presented course developments designed for non-linguists: (i) UWI reading course, (ii) the UWI-UTech FL course for the Hospitality Industry and (iii) the UTech FL course for Food Service Management. These courses attest the diversification of FL course offerings at tertiary level and the increasing demand for specialised domain-specific modern language courses.

DOMAIN-SPECIFIC MODERN LANGUAGE COURSE DEVELOPMENTS IN THE CARIBBEAN

A major effect of globalisation is the necessity for professionally mobile Caribbeans to acquire the linguistic and socio-professional skills to interact effectively with their Caribbean partners (Morris, 2000). This necessity has given rise to innovative modern language course developments in several Caribbean tertiary institutions. These courses bear significant similarities with domain-specific modern language courses, commonly referred to as 'languages for special purposes', which have been developed in Europe and North America since the early 1970's (Lehmann, 1993, p. 40; Stern, 1983, p. 110). The rationale for languages for special purposes in Europe was to ensure linguistic democracy (UNESCO Linguapax, 1997), in particular to prevent "la domination d'une langue sur les autres" (the domination of a language over others) (Lehmann, 1993, p. 62). The rationale for domain-specific modern language courses in the Caribbean is both economic and political. The aim is to facilitate trade relations and to foster Caribbean regional integration. This aim has been endorsed by the two Jamaican universities, the University of the West Indies (UWI) and the University of Technology, Jamaica (UTech) where novel French and Spanish language courses have been specifically designed for non-linguist undergraduate students. This section focuses only on French and Spanish courses and looks at three course developments: (i) UWI Reading course, (ii) UWI-UTech course for the Hospitality Industry and (iii) UTech course for Food Service Management.

(I) DIVERSIFYING UWI FOREIGN LANGUAGE OFFERINGS: A FIRST ATTEMPT

Commercial and political exchanges within Caribbean island states developed rapidly over the last decade. These exchanges highlighted the necessity for today's Caribbean graduates to exchange printed materials and have access to scientific literature (Stern, 1983, p. 464) in their particular fields. It was expected that this would broaden the range of expertise available in the region and give the Caribbean an economic advantage – a view commonly held in economically developed countries (Lerat, 1995; Lepetit, 1997). This expectation prompted the design of a first foreign language (FL) course for non-language specialists: The Foreign Language Reading Course. This course, which is offered by the Department of Modern Languages and Literatures at UWI, has two course options: the French Reading course (F10R) and the Spanish Reading course (S10R). Both language options focus on the development of one language skill and "restricts the goal of language teaching to training in reading comprehension" (Stern, 1983, p. 460). The reading method has long been established and had its advocates in the early 1920's (Bond, 1953; Coleman, 1929; West, 1926). In particular, it is an effective method for teaching self-effacing Asian and Arab students, who value the written word (Boufoy-Bastick, 1997; Pennycook, 1992; Pennycook, 1994; West, 1926) and disregard spoken communication. By contrast, learning through reading may present a challenge to some Caribbean students whose root culture is anchored in orality and expressed in the 'word' (Brathwaite, 1984). The 'word', however, is a fundamental Caribbean cultural expression and this cultural aspect weighs heavily in the choice of texts selected for reading study – these include French texts of cultural interest on francophone Caribbean islands and African countries. This first Caribbean-targetted FL reading course was the first step towards diversifying FL offerings at UWI.

(II) UWI-UTECH COURSE FOR THE HOSPITALITY INDUSTRY: A NOVEL DEVELOPMENT

BACKDROP TO THE DEVELOPMENT OF THE FL COURSE FOR THE HOSPITALITY INDUSTRY

Tourism industry is a key income-generating economic sector in Jamaica (Narcisse, 2000, p. 209). The importance of supporting the development of this expanding competitive economic sector was soon recognised by the emergent progressive University of Technology, Jamaica (UTech). To this end, UTech approached UWI to provide foreign language training for their Hospitality and Tourism Management (HTM) undergraduates. An agreement was signed betweeen the two univerities and foreign language instruction began at UWI in September 1998 as part of a new joint UWI-UTech degree. Under the signed UWI-UTech agreement, the Department of Modern Languages and Literatures, UWI, accepted HTM students from UTech on their existing French and Spanish language courses. HTM students were expected to attend two years of FL instruction, that is (i), F02A/S01C (Beginners' French/Spanish I) and F02B/S01D (Beginners' French/Spanish II) the two-semester beginners' course in French/Spanish in the first year, followed by (ii) F111 (1st year of the French Language year-long course) or S11A&B (Spanish Language I), the first year language components of the French or Spanish degree courses. At the outset, it was felt that these language courses did not respond to the professional needs nor did they use the cognitive strengths and experiences of professionally and industrially oriented students (Clowes, 1994; Gremmo, 1997; Swales, 2000). The F02/S01 pre-degree courses were designed primarily as feeder courses for other FL degree courses and to provide necessary solid lexical and grammatical skills necessary for undertaking undergraduate FL study. This linguistic purpose did not serve the domain-specific language needs of HTM students; needs such as the acquisition of relevant linguistic registers appropriate to the tourism industry and the building of communicative socio-professional competence in HTM-related contexts (Makita-Discekici, 1998, p. 76). The lack of HTM-relevance of traditional FL courses prompted the Department of Modern Languages and Literatures, UWI, to design two-year-long parallel French and Spanish courses for Hospitality students with the intent to prepare them to work in trilingual Caribbean work contexts.

DESIGNING A FL COURSE FOR THE HOSPITALITY INDUSTRY

Thus F10H/S10H (French/Spanish for the Hospitality Industry I) and F11H/S11H (French/Spanish for the Hospitality Industry II) were developed and introduced in the first year and F20H/S20H (French/Spanish for the Hospitality Industry III) and F21H/S21H (French/Spanish for the Hospitality IV) in the second year. The first 10H/S10H cohorts were enrolled in September 1999 and the first F20H/S20H cohorts in September 2000.

The aims of UWI-UTech HTM FL courses are twofold and satisfy both the formal objectives of traditional Caribbean university FL instruction delivered at UWI and the professionally-oriented objectives of the emergent technological university in Jamaica, that is UTech – a dilemma for FL instructors (Dlaska, 1999; Malcolm, 1993). These Caribbean FL courses use a mixed pedagogical methodology (Barton & Salmon, 2000; Debyser, Massacret, Pacthod & Thierry, 1996; Kahn, 1993; Lowe-Dupas, 1995); they combine the teaching of a grammatically-sound base necessary for further FL study with the development of functional language competence necessary for working in a Caribbean-wide tourism industry (Yalden, 1987; West, 1992). The duration of the UWI-UTech FL courses is two years, that is they consist of four 3-credit constituent semester-long courses. Language instruction is delivered weekly in three 2-hour classes, of which one hour is designated for active listening practice and content-rich video-based work (Mason, 1997, p. 16) in the UWI language laboratory. Each of the four

French and Spanish courses is assessed by 2 in-course tests in listening, reading and writing (50%) and a final examination (50%) in speaking, reading and writing.

The introduction of Caribbean tourism-specific French and Spanish language courses prompted an interest in making professionally-oriented FL courses also an integral part of UTech undergraduate courses – a policy move also supported by other progressive universities worldwide (Johnson, 1997, pp. 26-27). In keeping with this, the Department of Liberal Studies at UTech undertook to develop and to offer discipline-targetted FL courses to the five UTech faculties. The first UTech FL courses were thus introduced in January 2001 on the degree course for Food Service Management (FSM) delivered by the School of Hospitality and Tourism Management. The design of these Caribbean FL courses is radically different from traditional university FL courses in both subject content and teaching methodology. They also further deviate from the UWI-UTech FL Hospitatlity courses as they prioritise the development of oral/aural skills – these being the linguistic skills which students are likely to use predominantly when in FSM employment. The FSM language courses described below are resolutely profession-targetted with well-defined communication-specific objectives.

(III) INITIATING DOMAIN-SPECIFIC FL COURSES TO MEET SOCIO-PROFESSIONAL DEMANDS IN THE CARIBBEAN

As part of its response to, and promotion of, pro-social and positive economic changes in the Caribbean, the University of Technology, Jamaica, undertook to develop innovative FL courses which would equip students to operate successfully, and communicate appropriately, with their future non-English-speaking Carribbean trade partners. To this end, the design of innovative French and Spanish communication courses was initiated and these FL courses were introduced gradually - either as integral components or as electives - on selected UTech professionally-oriented degree courses. A major FL course development is the introduction of the FSM FL communication courses delivered by the Department of Liberal Studies.

DESIGNING CONTENT-RELEVANT FSM FL COMMUNICATION COURSES

The School of Hospitality and Tourism Management, UTech, was the first to manifest a strong interest in including FL instruction on their degree courses – as discussed in section (ii). HTM reiterated their support for the inclusion of a two-semester course in French and Spanish, corresponding to 105 hours of language instruction each. To this end, the first professionally-oriented FSM domain-specific modern language courses were specifically designed to meet the demands of a thriving pan-Caribbean FSM industry. Like similar FL courses delivered in technological universities overseas the main objective was to train a pool of functionally competent FSM communicators (Debyser, Massacret, Pacthod & Thierry, 1996; De Vries, Herman & Long, 1997; Lepetit, 1997; Lerat, 1995; Moirand, Bouacha, Beacco & Collinot, 1992). Achieving communicative competence was the objective which directed the design of the FSM FL courses in terms of content and teaching methodology.

FSM CONTENT-DEFINED FL COMMUNICATION COURSES

The FSM FL courses at UTech differ from many other domain-specific FL courses. A major difference is the primary focus on the development of speaking and listening skills. The rationale for prioritising oral/aural proficiency is work-relevance (Henning & Slater, 2000): Speaking and listening are the skills used by Caribbean practising FSM professionals. Reading and writing skills are developed as much as they support language acquisition.

Secondly, the FSM FL course content is thematically structured and its structure reflects the variety of FSM task-based situations. Each FSM theme introduces a specific FSM lexical register using a wide range of simulated and stimulating FSM work experiences (Berns, 1984; West, 1992); that is language is presented in contextualised FSM work-relevant sequences (Schrum & Glisan, 1994). However, the development of FSM linguistic proficiency is only one facet of FSM communicative competence and it is developed integratively with socio-professional competence. FSM students are sensitised to the social norms and professional specificities of the FSM sector.

In other words, from Salmon's activist perspective (2000, p. 68), the FSM FL communication courses are geared to train competent FL users to display appropriate linguistic, social and professional skills.

FSM TEACHING METHODOLOGY

The pedagogical methodology used to promote FL competence is purposefully communicative. The emphasis is on language use rather than on formal language study (Beeching, 1997; Dolle & Willems, 1984; Lowe-Dupas, 1995; Larsen-Freeman, 1986; Mangin, 1996; Oxford, 1989; Salmon, 2000), that is on teaching the language rather than teaching about the language. Considering that the students are being prepared to relate to visitors to their own countries (the local sistuation), it uses a Situated Language Teaching methodology "which presents language in situations..." - albeit not only - similar to those the learner may encounter in the foreign country" (Boufoy-Bastick, 2000, p. 90). Teaching geared to achieving FSM FL competence is fundamentally practical and it aims, first, at the development of pseudo-communication acts using a situation-based approach. This necessitates the use of lists of speech acts, functions and notions, giving meanings to impart elementary 'survival' exchanges. Lexical register building activities use language-in-context sequences (Berns, 1984, p. 5; Gerngross & Puchta, 1984), Direct Method strategies, utilising realia (Diller, 1975; 1978) and Total Physical Response (TPR) techniques (Asher, 1981), involving students in executing FSM domain-specific commands during their comprehension stage, then encouraging them to give relevant FSM commands and making requests during their productive stage. A major feature of FSM language teaching is that it relies primarily upon simulation and role-play activities to impart key situational phrases and to promote effective culturally and linguistically appropriate social and professional communication (Prestel, 1995). The use of dramatisation reinforces language internalisation and also increases motivation through enjoyable activities that provide essential insights into what is, and what is not, culturally appropriate in relevant French and Spanish FSM situations.

EVOLVING TEACHING METHODOLOY TO PROMOTE FSM PROFESSIONAL COMPETENCE

FSM teaching methodology shifts from a narrower situation-based approach to a broader task-based approach over the two semesters.

The initial situation-based teaching methodology used in semester 1 is geared to prepare FSM students to deal competently, both professionally and linguistically, with common FSM situations. The major pedagogical outcome of semester 1 courses is to instil survival FSM-related language behaviours and to prepare FSM students for further language acquisition in semester 2. These survival language skills are expected to promote the students' confidence in using the language appropriately in selected FSM situations.

By contrast, the pedagogical outcome of semester 2 FSM FL courses is to enable students to deal with novel FSM situations. This is achieved through increasingly more 'formal' communicative language teaching methodology which shifts from semester 1 *situation-based teaching* towards *task-based teaching*. This task-based approach necessitated preparing a taxonomy of tasks suited for each FSM language competency level. Another aspect of the second semester FSM FL courses is that they acknowledge the primacy of effective verbal communication in FSM contexts. Effective communication is hence enhanced through discrete functional grammar teaching. The inclusion of some formal grammar teaching in FSM interaction-based pedagogy has two purposes: a linguistic and an educational purpose. Linguistically, it facilitates accuracy in communication acts through semantic and syntactic clarity. Educationally, it empowers students to become autonomous FL speakers by strategically providing the tools necessary for further language development – a major consideration in an emerging globalised Caribbean.

These innovative university FL courses are evidence that modern departments or centres have become "leaders in globalization of the campus" (Johnson, 1997, p. 26).

The emergence of the Caribbean as an increasingly economically and politically integrated region has impacted considerably on tertiary education. Universities are given the mandate to prepare future Caribbean leaders and decision-makers to function competently and adeptly in an interconnected trilingual Caribbean. To this effect, Caribbean organisations and universities have designed modern language courses geared to facilitate professional communication between English, French and Spanish speakers. This paper first reported on four Caribbean language development initiatives aimed to train linguistically competent professionals in the three official languages of the Caribbean. Then, the paper described three novel foreign language university course developments at UWI and UTech, Jamaica. In particular, the paper overviewed the innovative pedagogical approach used in designing and teaching the domain-specific French and Spanish courses for UWI-UTech Hotel Tourism Management and UTech Food Service Management undergraduates – e.g., the methodological emphasis on using domain-specific lexical registers, relevant content-based simulated situations and non-formalist language teaching.

The significance of domain-specific modern language courses for Caribbean economic integration and trade globalisation is increasingly recognised by other economic sectors and university departments and this has led to the further development and introduction of French and Spanish domain-specific courses for engineering and business students.

REFERENCES

Asher, J. (1985). The total physical response (TPR): Theory and practice. In H. Winitz (Ed.) *Native and Foreign Language Acquisition* (pp. 324-331). New York: The New York Academy of Sciences.

Barton, J. & Salmon, H. (2000). Foreign language teaching strategies and students' performance in Spanish. In T. Bastick (Ed.) *Education Theory and Practice* (pp. 71-88). Kingston: Department of Educational Studies, UWI.

Beeching, K. (1997). French for specific purposes: The case for spoken corpora. *Applied Linguistics 18*(3), 374-394.

Berns, M. S. (1984). Functional approaches to language and language teaching: Another look. In S. Savignon and M. S. Berns (Eds.) *Initiatives in Communicative Language Teaching. A Book of Readings* (pp. 3-21). Reading, MA: Addison-Wesley.

Bond, O.F. (1953). *The Reading Method: An Experiment in College French.* Chicago: Chicago University Press.

Boufoy-Bastick, B. (1997). Using language policies to highlight and contrast the values that shape multicultural societies: Examples from Singapore and Australia. *Australian Journal of Education 41*(1), 59-76.

Boufoy-Bastick, B. (2000). Perspectives on situated language teaching (SLT) methodologies: A view from within. In T. Bastick (Ed.) *Education Theory and Practice* (pp. 89-106). Kingston: Department of Educational Studies, UWI.

Brathwaite, E.K. (1984). *History of the Voice: The Development of Nation Languages in Anglophone Caribbean Poetry.* London: New Beacon.

Carter, B. (1998). Fostering learner autonomy among mature language learners. *Caribbean Journal of Education, 20*(1), 02-116.

Clark, J. L. (1987). Classroom assessment in a communicative approach. *British Journal of Language Teaching 25*(1), 9-19.

Clowes, P. (1994). What are the language needs of industry. *Language Learning Journal 9*, 22-25.

Coleman, A. (1929). *The Teaching of Modern Languages in the United States*. New York: Macmillan.

Debyser, A., Massacret, E., Pacthod, A. & Thierry, A-M. (1996). *Analyse de méthodes français langue étrangère. 1: Français à objectifs spécifiques*. (Analysis of methods for French as a Foreign Language. 1: French for Specific Purposes). Sèvres: CIEP.

De Vries, Jr., Herman, J. Long, R. (1997). The EUROTECH module: A curricular innovation for German instruction. *Foreign Language Annals, 30*(3), 369-377.

Diller, K.C. (1975). Some new trends for applied linguistics and foreign language teaching in the United States. *TESOL Quarterly, 9*, 65-73.

Diller, K.C. (1978) *The Language Teaching Controversy*. Rowley, Mass: Newbury House.

Dlaska, A. (1999). Suggestions for a Subject-Specific Approach in Teaching Foreign Languages to Engineering and Science Students. *System, 27*(3), 401-17.

Douglas, D & Selinger, L. (1992). Analyzing oral proficiency test performance in general and specific purpose contexts. *System 20*(3), 317-328.

Gremmo, M-J. (1997). Matériaux d'enseignement et apprentissage de langue: les options didactiques des "modules de français pour les professionnels du tourisme" (Instructional materials and language instruction:

Teaching options for "French modules for tourism professionals). *Mélanges, 23.*

Henning, S. & Slater, J. (2000). *On-Site French Language and Quebec Culture Training for Business and Indu*stry. ERIC ED446437.

Hall, C. (1993). The direct testing of oral skills in university foreign language teaching. *IRAL 31*(1), 23-38.

Hughes, T. (1996). Developing listening and speaking skills in the intermediate business Spanish class. Paper presented at the 14th Annual Conference *on Languages and Communication for World Business and the Professions.* Ypsilanti, MI, April 11-13, 1996.

Johnson, R. (1997). Foreign language departments as leaders in globalization of the campus. *ADFL Bulletin 29*(1), 26-27.

Kahn, G. (1993). Différentes approches pour l'enseignement du Français sur objectifs spécifiques. (Different approaches for teaching French for specific purposes). In D. Lehmann (Ed.) *Objectifs spécifiques en langue étrangère.* (Specific Objectives in Foreign Languages) (pp. 144-152). Vanves: Hachette FLE.

Larsen-Freeman, D. (1986). *Techniques and Principles in Language Teaching.* Oxford: Oxford University Press.

Lehmann, D. (Ed.) (1993). *Objectifs spécifiques en langue étrangère.* (Specific Objectives in Foreign Languages). Vanves: Hachette FLE.

Lepetit, D. (1997). Le Francais des affaires: Problèmes et perspectives. (Business French: Problems and Perspectives). *Canadian Modern Language Review 53*(4), 648-676.

Lerat, P. (1995). *Les langues spécialisées.* (Specialised Languages). Paris: PUF

Lowe-Dupas, H. (1995). Business French or French business? What do we teach and what do we call it? Paper presented at the 13th Annual Eastern Michigan University Conference on *Languages and Communication for World Business and the Professions.*Ypsilanti, MI, April 6-8, 1995.

Makita-Discekici, Y. (1998). Hotel employees' Japanese language experiences: Implications and suggestions. *Journal of Language for International Business 9*(1), 76-83.

Malcolm, I. (1993). Languages for specific purposes and degree studies: Are they compatible? Paper presented at *the 28th Annual Meeting of the Southeast Asian Ministers of Education Organization Regional Language Center Seminar*, Singapore, April 19-21, 1993.

Mangin, G. (1996). Le Français des affaires: Approches méthodologiques (Business French: Methodological Approaches*). Le Français dans le Monde 284*, 60-62.

Mason, K. (1997). And now for our feature presentation: Using films for contextualized language learning. *Mosaic, 5*(1), 16-19.

Moirand, S., Bouacha, A., Beacco, J-C. & Collinot, A. (Eds.) (1992). Parcours linguistiques de discours spécialisés: colloque en Sorbonne les 23-24-25 septembre 1992. *Sciences pour la communication, 41.*

Morris, B. (2000, July 20). Education must be agile. *The Gleaner*, July 20, 2000. Excerpt from the University of Technology first Chancellor at his installation on July 12, 2000.

Narcisse, C. (2000). Social integration and disintegration – The Caribbean experience. In K. Hall and D. Benn (Eds.) *Contending with Destiny* (pp. 204-236). Kingston: Ian Randle Publishers.

Omaggio Hadley, A. (1993). *Teaching Language in Context*. Boston: Heinle & Heinle.

Oxford, R. L., et al. (1989). Language learning strategies, the communicative approach, and their classroom implications. *Foreign Language Annals, 22*(1), 29-39.

Panella, C. (1998). Meeting the needs of international business: A customer service-oriented business language course. *Journal of Language for International Business 9*(1), 65-75.

Pennycook, A. (1992). *The Cultural Politics of Teaching English in the World*. Unpublished doctoral dissertation, OISE, University of Toronto.

Pennycook, A. (1994). *The Cultural Politics of English as an International Language*. London: Longman.

Puren, C. (2001). Compte-rendu de la journée de réflexion sur le plurilinguisme. *Les Langues Modernes, 95*(4), 96-99.

Prestel, D. (1995). Situational role-play as a basis for a business Russian program. *Journal of Language for International Business 6*(2), 26-37.

Salmon, H. (2000). Two contrasting foreign language teaching orientations. In T. Bastick (Ed.) *Education Theory and Practice* (pp. 57-70). Kingston: Department of Educational Studies, UWI.

Schrum, J.L. & Glisan, E.W. (1994). *Teacher's Handbook: Contextualized Language Instruction*. Boston: Heinle & Heinle.

Stern, H.H. (1983). *Fundamental Concepts of Language Teaching*. Oxford: Oxford University Press.

Swales, J.M. (2000). Languages for Specific Purposes. *Annual Review of Applied Linguistics, 20*, 59-76.

UNESCO (1997). *Linguapax.* UNESCO etxea.

Yalden, J. (1987). *Principles of Course Design for Language Teaching.* London: Cambridge University Press.

Wenden, A. (1987). Incorporating learning training in the classroom. In A. Wenden and J. Rubin (Eds.) *Learner Strategies in Language Learning* (pp. 159-168). London: Prentice Hall.

West, J. (1992). The Development of a Functional-Notional Syllabus for University German Courses. *CLCS. Occasional Paper No. 32.*

West, M.P. (1926). *Learning to Read a Foreign Language: An Experimental Study.* New York: Longmans, Green & Co.

BÉATRICE BOUFOY-BASTICK

CHAPTER 2

CREOLE INTERFERENCE OR LINGUISTIC ELASTICITY? EXAMINING THE PATTERNS OF LANGUAGE USE AMONG BLACK CARIBBEAN STUDENTS IN BRITAIN

INGRID WALDRON

ABSTRACT

This paper examines the various ideologies in the British educational system that have influenced how the Creole language has been perceived by educators, linguists, scholars, and the community at large from the 1960's up until today. It traces the two main theories on the legitimacy of Creole as a valid and distinct linguistic system capable of expressing thought: the deficit theory and the difference theory. Scholars and educators who adhere to a deficit view of the language see it as an unsystematic and corrupted version of standard British English and as incapable of preparing Black British children for academic achievement and social mobility (this paper uses the term "Black British" to refer to Black people of Caribbean heritage who reside in Britain and were born either in Britain or the Caribbean). Difference theorists, on the other hand, argue that Creole is a separate and distinct language with its own rule-governing system and is merely different to standard British English, not inferior.

I look at how the concept of *Creole interference* that was used in the 1970's and early 1980's when Caribbean immigrant children were first entering the classroom, inappropriately blamed the Creole language for the difficulties that Black British children were having in learning standard British English. I posit, instead, that it may be more appropriate to characterize the speech patterns of these children as one of *linguistic elasticity* because it describes the ease, flexibility, and dexterity with which many Black British children traverse a linguistic continuum that includes both standard British English and Creole. I also use the concept to articulate the influence that various social determinants have on the speech patterns of these children.

Finally, I offer the bidialectal approach as one effective means by which teachers can take effectively utilize the language elasticity displayed by their students as a bridge in learning standard British English.

INTRODUCTION

The educational underachievement of Black British youth has long been a matter of concern and debate. Since 1971, when the Department of Education and Science began to look at the educational achievement of immigrant Caribbean children, statistics have continued to show that their reading standards, as well as those of children of Caribbean heritage who today, more often than not, were born in Britain remain lower than those of White British children and other immigrants and that they are over-represented in non-selective schools and lower academic streams (Association of Teachers of English to Pupils from Overseas, 1970; Bagley, 1979; Edward, 1986; Gillborn, 1990; TUC Report, 1996).

Contributing to the underachievement of some of the immigrant Caribbean students at that time and some of those born in Britain today are the difficulties that they encounter in acquiring the rules of standard British English. These difficulties have been said to arise out of mismatches between the grammatical and phonological rules of standard British English and Creole. These students' unfamiliarity with the rules of standard British English may significantly affect its transmission and acquisition, resulting in what some educators have called *Creole interference*. Interference was said to lead to difficulties in reading, writing, and speaking because the grammar of these children fail to correspond to the text that they are presented with, resulting in difficulties in pronunciation, grammar, and vocabulary. Interference was also said to affect these children's spelling ability and their recognition of words. Moreover, their comprehension was thought to be based on their own framework of reference sounds that are based on Creole. Consequently, they were thought to transfer the grammatical and vocabulary rules of Creole to their speech. Past studies have demonstrated that the reliance on testing in standard British English may considerably underestimate the language skills of Black British children. Roberts (1988, p. 185) identified the following major areas of difficulty in English grammar for Caribbean children:

1. Use and forms of the verbs *be, have,* and, *do* as verbs, as well as auxiliary verbs.
2. Subject-verb concord.
3. Inflections in verbs, nouns, and pronouns.
4. Negation.
5. Use of prepositions.
6. Use of subordinating conjunctions.
7. Differences between *there, they,* and *their.*
8. Pronunciation- and structure-influenced spelling.

Wheldall and Joseph (1985/1986) found that although heavy reliance on formal standardization testing in the Standard resulted in poor examination results for these children, they demonstrated superior performance when Jamaican Creole grammatical features were substituted. In addition, the poor performance that these children displayed when standard British English was used may have had much to do with the reliance on verbal tests over written tests.

The term Creole interference, which, as I indicated earlier, had been used in the past by scholars who adhered to a deficit view of the language, is problematic because it blamed the language of Black British people, an integral part of their cultural identity and self-concept, for their academic difficulties. It may be more appropriate to state that it is the clash of two distinct linguistic systems (English and Creole) that creates learning problems for these children, as well as an intolerant school system that has been resistant to acknowledging the language as a viable means of expression. Using studies from the 1970's up until today, this paper provides an historical overview of the attitudes and response by educators, linguists, and scholars to the validation of Creole as a distinct and viable language and to its integration into classroom learning. Mailloux (1989) states that:

> "...Ideologies - such as capitalism and socialism, abolitionism, and White supremacy - are sets of beliefs and practices serving particular socio-political interests in a specific historical context...(p. 60).

It is within this context that I wish to discuss how socially constructed ideologies of "good" and "bad" languages have resulted in the Creole language being perceived as a substandard, bastardized, and inferior form of standard British English. In any given society, the language that is deemed superior will be that which is defined and spoken by the group that holds power within a particular socio-political moment. Moreover, although the notion that there exists a standard form of English has yet to be proven, the social construction or mythical conception of standard English as the yardstick against which all other language varieties are measured is simultaneously empowering and oppressive depending on your membership in or exclusion from the dominant group in society. So, although I use the term "standard British English" and "standard American English" throughout this paper to refer to so-called Received Standard British English and Received Standard American, it is important to point out that there is no single agreed-upon variety of either language.

This paper begins by examining the diverse viewpoints that deficit and difference theorists hold about Creole and the implications for pedagogy, policy, and curricula. In the second part of this paper, I flesh out the concept of linguistic elasticity by examining the social determinants that influence the speech patterns of Black British children. I conclude this paper by offering the bidialectal approach as one that can make effective use of the linguistic elasticity of Black British children as a resource in language acquisition.

Although I make use of American and British studies in this paper, it is important at this juncture that I make a major distinction between the British experience and the American one in discussing standard English language acquisition among Black British children and African American children. Unlike some African American children whose language is similar to their parents (who may be American-born), many Black British children (most of whom were born in Britain) live in home environments where they may speak a language that is different from that of their parents who may have been born in the Caribbean and who may have more Creole features in their speech.

Consequently, elasticity may be a greater facet of the linguistic repertoire of Black British children than of African American children since they may be called upon to code-switch more often by adapting their speech to parents and other family members, their teachers, as well as their peers and friends. This code-switching may entail adapting their speech patterns to the standard British English used by their teachers and peers in the classroom, the Creole spoken by their parents and family members, and to the combination of a local variety of English and any variety of Creole found in the various Caribbean islands (e.g. the London/Jamaican speech pattern described by Sutcliffe (1982)). Moreover, the language of these children will undoubtedly be influenced by the variety of Caribbean peoples who have immigrated over the years to Britain and who speak a variety of Creole languages. By contrast, although regional differences make it impossible to argue for one variety of African American English (AAE), the differences between these varieties are not as wide as the differences between the different varieties of Creole in the various Caribbean regions. In the following section, I provide a historical overview of the prevailing attitudes that educators and scholars in the United States and Britain have held about the viability of Creole as both a language with its own distinct, rule governing system and as having the capacity to express and communicate rational thought.

DEFICIT OR DIFFERENCE?: BLACK BRITISH ENGLISH AND IMPLICATIONS FOR POLICY, CURRICULUM, AND PEDAGOGY

The Creole that is spoken today by the peoples of the British West Indies is the end result of a pidgin transformed into a more complex and flexible language. Pidgin languages arose out of the need for a common means of communication between slaves of diverse African tribes in the Caribbean during the slave trade in the 17th and 18th centuries. British slave masters, fearing conspiracy and revolt, separated slaves who spoke a common language as a result of their membership in the same tribe. This pidginized variety of the master's tongue facilitated communication among slaves and between master and slave. According to Hall (1966, p. xii), two conditions must be met before a language can be considered a true pidgin:

1. There must be a sharp reduction in its grammatical structure and vocabulary; and
2. The resultant language must not be the native language of its speaker.

The final stages of the use of the pidgin language involved heavy interlading of words and constructions from standard British English. The paradox of Creole lies both in its similarity to and distinctiveness from the grammatical and phonological rules of standard English. The debate over whether Creole should be considered a separate and valid language distinct from standard British English or merely a substandard variant of it has to do with it being the product of two originally separate linguistic systems: African and British English.

Using research conducted in Britain and the United States from the 1970's up until the late 1980's , this section provides an historical analysis of two opposing theories on the speech patterns of Black children within the context of political and social climates that changed from liberal and socialist to right wing and conservative. These two theories are: 1) the deficit theory and 2) the difference theory. Interestingly, many of the studies I use in this paper from three decades ago still have relevancy today since many of the issues pertaining to linguistic diversity have, unfortunately, not progressed significantly since that time.

I cite studies that examine the situation in the late 1960's and early 1970's when Caribbean immigrant children were entering the British school system with little familiarity with (White) standard British English. It was at this time that the American linguist Labov (1972) published his important work that argued that the language of African American children in working-class and ghetto areas should not be considered a deficit but a distinct and separate language with its own rule-governing system. It was also at this time that Bernstein in Britain (Baratz, 1970) made a case for the existence of marked differences between middle-class and working-class children in their speech patterns, stating that the latter used language that was more grammatically simple and rigid and that had a narrower lexical and syntactical range. Although Bernstein did not refer to Black British people specifically, it is a fact that the working-class in Britain consists of a large proportion of Black British people.

An opposing socialist view emerged at this time in Britain commencing in the late 1960's up until the mid-1970's, followed by a liberal pluralist view that influenced activities like Harold Rosen, Michael Rosen, and John Richmond of the London Education Authority (LEA) to advance the prestige of Creole. Unfortunately some of these efforts were undermined in the late 1980's and the 1990's in Britain as the political climate in Britain became increasingly right wing with educational policy following suit and politicians seeking to hold on to an imaginary White British identity that was felt to be under attack by immigrants and people of colour.

Moreover, the Black population in Britain and, consequently the composition of students in the classroom, was undergoing a gradual transformation as the first generation of British-born Black children were being replaced by second-generation British-born children. Unlike their immigrant counterparts years earlier, many of these students used Creole in the classroom and elsewhere, not because they were unfamiliar with standard or local British English, but because it was conscious choice to hold on to a cultural identity that was being constructed by politicians and the media as a threat to British nationhood.

Deficit theorists like Bernstein (Baratz, 1970) in England and Orr (1987) in the United States blamed the unsystematic structure of Black children's home language for creating interference in acquiring the grammatical and phonological rules of standard English. They saw as urgent the need to eradicate Creole from the speech patterns of Black children and to replace it with standard English. Difference theorists like Labov (1972) in the United States and Edwards (1979 a; 1979 b; 1986) in Britain, on the other hand, saw the speech patterns of these children as being merely different to standard English and as a valid and distinct language in its own right, capable of expressing and communicating the thoughts and ideas of its speakers. They argue that it is the responsibility of the educational system to acknowledge and validate the language of Black children and to use it as a resource for teaching standard English.

CREOLE AS A DEFICIT

Gordon (1981) described the deficit theory in relation to language in the following way:

> Any hypothesis that seeks to explain differential educational attainment to any significant degree in terms of the intrinsic nature of two fundamentally different varieties of language used by schoolchildren, both at the commencement of their school careers and subsequently; and seeks to explain the unequal social distribution of educational attainment in terms of which social groups are deemed to speak one of the two varieties, rather than the other (p. 60).

The linguistic deficit theory, which emerged in the late 1960's in the United States and Britain (when a new wave of Caribbean immigrants emigrated to Britain) viewed the speech patterns of African American ghetto children and the working-class Jamaican community in Britain as an impediment to success, inadequately preparing them for academic achievement, employment, or social mobility. The inability of these groups to acquire and express the grammatical and phonological rules of standard English was attributed to their exclusive use of what was considered to be a "low variety" language that was thought to result in retarded linguistic development (Gordon, 1981).

I agree, however, with Foster (1997) who said that:

> The reason that African American English has drawn such fire is not because it is inferior, but because it is spoken by Black people (p. 11).

Discussions about the inferiority of non-standard forms of English (e.g. those spoken by African Americans and Black British people) essentially masked what was an inherently racist discourse that gave impetus to long-held stereotypes about the intellectual and cultural inferiority of Black peoples. Although 'substandard' is a term that is avoided by linguists, educators, and others when referring to African American English (AAE) and the Creole spoken by many Black British people, it is clear from the research conducted by deficit theorists that long-held negative perceptions and stereotypes about the inferiority of Black culture and intelligence have a powerful influence on how many people view the speech patterns of Black British people and African Americans.

The deficit view attributed the differences in educational attainment between middle-class and working-class groups to the relationship between language and social class and blamed the socialization practices of working-class parents on the underdeveloped standard English language skills of Black children (Gordon, 1981). In the United States, the argument was that African American children in urban ghettos suffered deficiencies in language because they received little verbal stimulation at home and were not exposed to standard English (Labov, 1972). The supposedly unsystematic structure and functionally inadequate nature of their language was attributed to limited mother-child interaction, environmental noise in urban ghetto areas, and sensory deprivation (Baratz, 1969a). In addition, their inability to discriminate auditorally was attributed to the impoverished state of their verbal expression (Harrison and Trabasso, 1976).

In Britain, Bernstein's theory on codes centered on the existence of a high and low variety of language (Baratz, 1970). Bernstein pointed to the marked differences between middle-class and working-class speakers in their orientation toward the verbal channel. He argued that the language of the working-class speaker was *restricted*, short, grammatically simple, and rigid and was characterized by a narrower lexical and syntactical range and the use of non-verbal channels. Consequently, the speech of these children was said to consist of unfinished sentences, short commands, and a limited use of adjectives. Conversely, the *elaborated* codes used by middle-class speakers were said to be characterized by a wider lexical and syntactical range, as well as an explicitness in verbal ability. These speakers were thought to use accurate grammatical order and syntax, complex sentence construction, and a high level of prepositions and impersonal pronouns (Edwards, 1979 b).

Robinson (1965) argued that the inability of working-class children to use the elaborated code may have more to do with a lack of opportunity than with lack of access. He acknowledged that there were significant and distinct socio-cultural variables between middle-class and working-class speakers that influenced their propensity to use a specific style of speech. Robinson also found that the tendency for working-class children to use either code was determined by how familiar they were with a particular issue under discussion, with the restricted code being used in informal and unstructured conversation and when children were uninformed on a particular topic. He found that the expectation that they would use restricted code also prompted these children to use it with their peers.

Robinson's study (1965) supported Bernstein's findings (Baratz, 1970) that argued that working-class children had a less varied vocabulary than middle-class children. But, unlike Bernstein, he argued that this was partly due to the fact that they were not frequently called upon to use the full extent of their vocabulary. And, unlike Bernstein, Robinson argued that working-class and middle-class children operated with similar codes. His study found that both groups used elaborated code when they wrote formal letters, which required a wider syntactical and vocabulary range than required in informal writing. Similarly, Edwards (1979 b) found that the greater formality needed for writing than speaking was reflected in the presence of elaborated code in the written work of working-class children and its absence in their oral work.

Labov (1972) attacked Bernstein's theory for failing to provide a proper linguistic specification for the central concept of codes. He argued that Bernstein's pronouncements about the existence of code differences among middle-class and working-class speakers may simply be due to stylistic preferences among speakers who circulate in environments that are more or less conducive to certain styles of communication, whether they be informal or formal. Baratz (1970) and Stubbs (1976) also took issue with Bernstein's theory for not providing any conclusive evidence for the existence of codes, as well as for his failure to provide any evidence for cognitive deficits among speakers whose language is characterized primarily by restricted code use.

Perhaps the deficit theory was most powerfully illustrated by the anti-Ebonics movement that came to the fore in 1996 in Oakland, California as a result of actions taken by African American teachers and educators in the Oakland Unified School District to pass a resolution recognizing AAE (or Ebonics) as the dominant language that many students in that district speak. The result was that anti-Ebonics legislation was passed by several states challenging the notion of AAE as a legitimate language.

The deficit view, which drew parallels between the Creole-standard contrast and Bernstein's contrast of restricted-elaborated codes as it relates to social class to explain the supposed cognitive deficits of Black children, was reflected in educational policy, curricula, and pedagogy between the late 1960's and the 1980's that argued for the complete eradication of Creole from the language of Black children.

DEFICIT THEORY AND ITS IMPLICATIONS FOR EDUCATIONAL POLICY, CURRICULA, AND PEDAGOGY

The belief that the linguistic problems of immigrant Caribbean children in Britain were due to cognitive deficiencies initially resulted in many schools placing these children in schools for children with mental retardation and learning disabilities. Unlike Asian immigrants who were given special language classes, the Local Education Authority (LEA) did not make special arrangements to teach standard British English to Caribbean immigrant children. Moreover, since the LEA did not acknowledge Creole as a language in its own right, seeing it as a dialect of standard British English,

Caribbean children were not given monolingual status. Caribbean students were consequently put in a precarious position because the LEA incorrectly presumed that they understood and would gradually acquire the rules of standard British English because of its superficial similarities to Creole. As a result, a second language policy was never developed for Caribbean children (Edwards, 1986).

It is often difficult for some Black children to master the fundamental rules of standard British English if they have not achieved a level of competence in their own language. Moreover, their cognitive development will be restricted if their teachers prevent them from using their own language to process meaning. It has also been suggested that teachers who refuse to incorporate Creole into their teaching practices stunt the formation of abstract concepts by Creole speakers.

According to Lander (1981), ignorance about Creole, as well as the pressure placed on Black children to learn standard British English often fosters low self-confidence in these children, which can negatively affect school performance. Similarly, Edwards (1979b) found that teachers who constantly correct Creole features in Black children's speech communicate to these children that their language and culture is unacceptable and inferior. This tendency to hyper-correct the child may also cause the child to read for accuracy and not for meaning. Difference theorists have advocated for linguistic egalitarianism and bidialectalism as a means to validate the speech patterns of Black British people and to foster more culturally sensitive and inclusive classroom environments that nurture academic achievement.

CREOLE AS DIFFERENT

According to Williams (Gordon, 1981):

> Like the proponents of the deficit position, the difference theorists agree that the poverty child is failing in our schools and that something has to be done. But where the former would focus much of the remediation upon the child's apparent unreadiness for school, the difference theorists tend to accuse the school of unreadiness (p. 99).

Difference theorists like Labov (1972) and Edwards (1979 a; 1979 b; 1986) have long focused on the defects of an educational system that has failed to respond to linguistic diversity in the school environment. Labov (1972) recognized that AAE is a distinct and separate system that differs systematically from standard American English in regular and rule-governed ways. He argued that if AAE was indeed a separate and distinct language from standard American English, the strategies used to teach English as a foreign language would have to be used with African American children and the monolingual status of these children would then have to be acknowledged in the same way that it is for immigrants for whom English is a second language.

However, Labov (1972) contended that since many of the rules of AAE are similar to those of other English dialects, it should be considered part of this single system. Baratz (1969b) found that when the non-standard language of African American working-class children was used as a criterion of "correctness", White children performed more poorly than Black children. They also had as much difficulty producing non-standard sentences as Black children had in producing standard English. These findings suggested that educational tests that assess knowledge using standard American English as a criterion of cognitive ability may not reflect the full capabilities and potential of Black children.

Such evidence (i.e. Baratz's) suggests quite strongly that the presence of certain speech modes does not impair the cognitive ability of African American children. In fact, Labov (1972) found that the home and social environments of African American working-class and ghetto children was quite conducive to linguistic development and that they received considerable verbal stimulation and heard more well-formed sentences than middle-class children. He also rejected the notion that a "culture of poverty" produced severe linguistic deficits in these children since these children "have the same basic vocabulary, possess the same capacity for conceptual learning, and use the same logic as anyone else who learns to speak and understand English" (p. 201).

It is critical, then, that Black children in Eurocentric societies not be pressured into abandoning their language when they enter the school environment. Rather, it is urgent that the educational system demonstrate respect for their language by developing pedagogical approaches, curricula, and policies that reflect a commitment to language diversity and that appreciate how the linguistic elasticity inherent to the speech of these children can be a valuable resource in teaching standard forms of English.

DIFFERENCE THEORY AND ITS IMPLICATIONS FOR EDUCATIONAL POLICY, CURRICULA, AND PEDAGOGY

According to the difference view, the schools objective should be to provide Black British children with the linguistic and verbal skills to compete on equal terms in society, whilst simultaneously acknowledging, respecting, and preserving their linguistic heritage. In the late 1960's and mid-1970's, the socialist view influenced activities by the LEA to advance the prestige of Creole and to encourage teachers to adopt more tolerant attitudes toward Creole (Hewitt, 1989). In the mid-1970's in Britain, the liberal pluralism view encouraged teachers to learn and understand the diverse languages spoken by their students and to foster classroom environments that provided a safe space for students who wished to speak in their native tongue. Special provisions were made to employ specialist teachers to take on the responsibility of language teaching in schools where there was a considerable proportion of Caribbean children.

With the advent of the repertoire approach in the 1980's, Black British students were encouraged to communicate in a range of different languages whilst developing their verbal skills in standard British English so that they could compete on equal terms with other students. Moreover, although there was consensus that all students should be provided with instruction in standard British English, it was felt that it should not be a prerequisite for learning English, mathematics, and other academic subjects (Berdan, 1981). The objective of the repertoire approach was to use a curricular approach that incorporated and made effective use of Creole and standard British English by allowing the child to master his own language before gaining competence in the latter. In the following section, I discuss some of the most significant social determinants for the linguistic repertoire and the linguistic elasticity displayed by Black British children.

LINGUISTIC ELASTICITY: SOCIAL DETERMINANTS FOR SPEECH PATTERNS AMONG BLACK BRITISH CHILDREN

Blacks in Britain demonstrate a kind of linguistic elasticity that is a reflection of their experiences living in two speech communities. I use the term *elasticity* to connote the capacity that this group has for traversing a linguistic continuum that finds a Creole with few features of standard British English at one end, standard British English at the other end, and other varieties of English sandwiched in between. Unlike the term Creole interference which negatively portrays the speech patterns of Black British people as deficient, problematic, and as a deterrent for acquiring the rules of standard British English, the term elasticity makes positive reference to their speech patterns by highlighting the skill and dexterity that Black British have in being able to alternate between two distinct linguistic systems.

Although this section of the paper provides an historical overview of the linguistic behaviour of Black British children and focuses on the situation from the early 1970's until the late 1980's, many of the issues have relevance today as well as important implications for educational curriculum, pedagogy, and policy. It is important to point out here that the speech patterns of Black British children and the response by schools to them has changed significantly since the late 1960's and early 1970's when immigrant Caribbean children began entering the school systems. It was at this time that debates arose between those scholars who adhered to a "deficit view" of Creole and those who embraced a "difference view" of the language.

As scholars began conducting more research on the speech patterns of these children (many of whom were now being born in Britain) in the early 1980's, they found that Black children who used Creole in the classroom did so consciously and not because they were unfamiliar with or lacked the skills to use standard British English. Sutcliffe (1982) was one of the first scholars to discuss the elastic nature of the speech patterns of Black British people in the 1970's and early 1980's, characterizing it as a rapid switching from one part of the continuum to the other. He also found that Black British people have a linguistic repertoire that is functional within a specific social network, enabling them to modify and adapt their speech depending on who they are speaking to and the environment that they are in. He found that Black British people in London were able to speak standard British English or an English close to the English of British-born Whites, as well as a London/Jamaican consisting of features of both the standard/local variety of British English (i.e. London) and of a Jamaican variety of Creole that was only slightly modified from that of their parents, in the case of Jamaicans.

It is this notion of linguistic elasticity that forms the basis to this paper and that I wish to elaborate on further in this section. Several studies found that the elasticity that Black British children display in their speech patterns is significantly determined by five main socio-cultural factors: 1) social class; 2) whether the child or his parents immigrated from a rural or urban area of a Caribbean country; 3) whether the speaker was born in Britain or the Caribbean; 4) the specific Caribbean country that the child's family immigrated from; 5) gender; and 6) the extent to which the speaker affiliates with Caribbean culture and peoples.

Two distinct varieties of the Creole that is spoken in the Caribbean can be distinguished, both of which are influenced by social class and whether an individual came from an urban or rural environment in the Caribbean. Middle-class urban dwellers tend to speak a Creole language which differs systematically (but only slightly) in a number of areas from standard British

English and working-class urban dwellers speak a language with substantial Creole features and which differs maximally from standard British English.

Although middle-class Black children who emigrated from an urban area in a Caribbean island in the period between 1950 and 1975 (when large numbers of Caribbean people immigrated to Britain) spoke with a recognizable Caribbean accent, their language was clear and comprehensible, displaying many features of standard British English. Linguistic interference may not have been a feature of these children's school experience since they may have been unable to speak or understand Creole, (Schools Council Working Paper 29, 1970). The children who may have encountered a considerable amount of linguistic interference in that period were those who emigrated to Britain from a rural working-class family in the Caribbean. These children may have spoken a Creole that consisted of few features of standard British English and that may have been incomprehensible to their teachers. It may have also made the acquisition of standard British English difficult (Schools Council Working Paper 29, 1970).

The second issue that has a significant bearing on the speech patterns of Black British children is the length of residency in Britain. It goes without saying that the longer that these children reside in Britain, the more likely they will adopt features of standard British English from White classmates, friends, and the media and, consequently, the more likely their speech will reflect features of standard British English. This issue, however, may hold less significance for Black British children today, most of whom are born in Britain. For most of these children, unlike those in earlier periods, issues like social class and whether their parents were urban or rural dwellers in the Caribbean have no or little bearing on their ability to speak standard British English. British-born Black children today can speak both the standard British English of their White British counterparts, as well as the Creole spoken by their parents (if their parents were born in the Caribbean). What distinguishes these children from the children who immigrated to Britain in the late 1960's, early 1970's and the 1980's is that the former had encountered difficulties learning and understanding a language (standard British English) that was different from their own and the latter's use of Creole is a conscious choice.

Also having an impact on the speech patterns of Black British children is the specific Caribbean country from which their parents immigrated from. Britain has seen a diverse group of Caribbean groups immigrate to its shores over the past few decades, resulting in a heterogenous Black British population speaking several varieties of Creole. I would like to point out here that my use of the term "Creole" refers to the many varieties of Creole spoken among Black British people and not to a singular, unitary, and monolithic Creole language.

The research also suggests that gender has a significant bearing on the propensity for Black British children to use Creole features in their speech. Hewitt (1989) found that Black British boys tend to use more Creole features in their speech than girls. He argued that Creole served a dual purpose for these boys: 1) it provided them with a sense of identity and solidarity as young Black men of Caribbean or Jamaican heritage and 2) it was viewed and used as a form of resistance to a racist and authoritarian school system. Edwards (1986, p. 56) identified linguistic differences between male and female speech patterns and found that these differences were further compounded by whether these children socialized in single sex or mixed group settings.

Green (1985) and Coultas (1989) found that since Black British girls were less likely than Black British boys to have relationships with teachers that were fraught with conflict, they were less likely to engage in anti-authority and resistance activities and, consequently, less likely to use Creole in their speech. Similarly, a study done by Mac an Ghaill (1988) documented resistance activities among youth subcultures in the British school system in the late 1980's. Many of the Black British boys were members of a subculture called the Rasta Heads that was involved in various anti-authoritarian activities in the school environment as a way to deal with conflictual relationships with teachers. Mac an Ghaill found that the members of this group used Creole features in their speech to communicate with each other outside the classroom environment and that when these boys spoke Creole in the classroom, it was usually done as a means to thwart the authority of their teachers.

Finally, the speech pattern of Black British children will also be greatly influenced by the extent to which they identify or affiliate with their culture. Since the issue of language is intimately tied to the issue of identity and heritage, attempts to undermine and suppress the language of groups who are already marginalized because of their race, culture, and class is especially punitive. Edwards (1986) stated that language and cultural identity are strongly linked and play a significant role in the speech patterns of Black British youth. She found that young people who used Creole features in their speech were those who affiliated with other Creole speakers, were critical of White British society, and who underachieved in school.

For many Black British youth, Creole has long acted as a form of resistance to a hostile and racist British society and has come to symbolize group solidarity and unity. Harrison and Trabasso (1976) argued that a long suppressed rage at the social and racial injustices that Caribbean people have suffered in Britain since they began emigrating to Britain in the 1950's resulted in many Black British children displaying a resistance to learning and using what they considered to be "the language of the oppressor" (i.e. standard British English).

These findings, many of which hold true today, continue to have important implications for pedagogy, curricula, and policy. Educators who respond to Black British children as one homogenous mass, despite these distinctions and variations, will not be able to adequately identify or respond to the diverse needs of Caribbean students or to customize their pedagogical approaches to resolve their academic difficulties. In the following section, I examine how teachers can teach standard English in a way that respects, affirms and maintains the speech patterns and communication styles of Black children. The objective, then, would be to take advantage of the elastic nature of these children's communication style by expanding it to include standard English, therefore, providing them with the opportunity to traverse a wider linguistic community.

MAKING A CASE FOR A BIDIALECTAL APPROACH TO TEACHING STANDARD BRITISH ENGLISH

In a controversial ruling in 1996 and 1997, the Oakland School Board of California advocated for African American children to be considered "language minority students" because their native dialect (AAE or the more commonly used term Ebonics) was considered a "language barrier" to their full integration and participation in the school. The Oakland resolution demanded that federal bilingual education funds support its Ebonics program, despite the fact that the Ebonics program called for language maintenance, whereas federal bilingual education funds are earmarked only for transitional, not maintenance programs.

The resolution drew comparisons between African American children and other children whose primary languages were not English (Asian Americans, Latino Americans, Native Americans), arguing that bilingual education principles should apply to African American children under the Bilingual Education Act (Dennis, 2000). It also challenged perceptions of these students as having a speech pathology or impairment, as being "linguistically disabled", or as needing to be placed in special education programs. Baugh argued that the term language minority did not fully capture the situation of these students and proposed, instead, that the term "students for whom standard English is not native" was more appropriate.

At this juncture, I would like to identify some of the main distinctions between bilingualism and bidialectalism. Bilingual people (e.g. many Hispanics in the United States and Catalans in Spain) have the ability to speak two completely different languages; bidialectal individuals (e.g. many Black British people), on the other hand, have the capacity to code switch or shift dialects or styles within a single language or speech continuum. For example the speech patterns of many Black British people span a broad linguistic continuum that is comprised of one or more Creoles, so-called standard British English, as well as other regional English dialects (Baugh, 1999).

Baugh (1998, p. 298) suggested that schools develop an annual linguistic census that provides teachers and school administrators with a linguistic profile of their students so that they can develop policies that respond to the individual needs of learners. He identified three linguistic divisions derived from the linguistic background of students in the American educational system: 1) students who are native speakers of standard English; 2) students who are native speakers of non-standard English; and 3) traditional "limited English proficiency" (LEP) students for whom English is not native. Although Baugh (p. 284) argued that the term "limited English proficiency" (LEP) may most closely describe African American students who comprise a subset of other linguistic minorities who are not native speakers of standard English, he emphasized that African American students are neither traditional LEP students nor native speakers of standard English. Consequently, he argued that since African Americans belong to a unique language category, schools should develop pedagogical approaches, curricula, and policies that effectively respond to their unique needs.

The categorical programs in Hawaii that support bidialectal education for Hawaiian students may be a useful model for helping to resolve the educational difficulties of African American students and Black British students since these groups share similar linguistic histories and situations (Baugh, 1998, p. 294). Similar to African Americans and Black British people, Hawaiians faced the pidginization, creolization, and eventual suppression of their language; these three groups were also "involuntary caste-like" minorities; and finally, these groups have a history of poor academic achievement. Hawaiians have sought to resolve the language difficulties of their students by pressuring the federal government to provide educational support to native Hawaiians and by stressing the value of a bidialectal approach to education that acknowledges and supports their native language.

Although territories like Trinidad and Tobago and Jamaica have sought to implement changes to language policies by reorienting the language curriculum in accordance with developing methodologies, fundamental changes cannot occur without fundamental changes in attitudes about Creole (Robertson, 1996). But, although the general consensus in the Caribbean is that the educated Caribbean person must have access to a language of international currency (e.g. English), there are also those who believe that the promotion of Creole, the dominant language of the nation, contributes to a healthy and positive national spirit and pride.

Roberts (1993, pp. 12-14) suggested that an "integrative approach" (like the bidialectal one) that integrates Creole into schools may be an effective method for teaching English because it gives students the confidence to use the full range of their linguistic ability in their speech and writing. Similarly, Simmons-McDonald (1996, p. 137) argued that Creole speakers may be effectively and successfully taught to develop skills in standard English if they are encouraged to develop communicative competence and literacy in their native language first. He stated that the transition to standard English may be easily facilitated once language skills in the native language are fully developed and the students have acquired the linguistic and cognitive competence necessary to make the transfer.

Using a bidialectal approach to teach standard English requires that teachers become familiar with the features and rules of Creole so that they can design and effectively implement instructional techniques that use the speech patterns of their students as a bridge to teaching standard English. As first put forth by Feigenbaum (1970), a contrastive technique where standard English phonological and syntactic features are compared to those of the student's speech pattern may be effective because it enables students to observe how their linguistic features differ from those of standard English. The objective would be to help students identify the distinctions between their communication styles and standard English using the speech and language of radio and television broadcasters and characters in books as a reference point.

It is also important that teachers help students identify the distinctions between their communication style and the language used in the classroom by stressing to them the appropriateness of language use in certain situations. Several contrastive techniques have been posited by scholars as particularly effective. Perez (2000) stated that the word discrimination drill using the rules of standard English and the child's speech pattern allows children to use the contrastive methodology in a more natural context. In this method, students are asked to differentiate between stimulus patterns presented by the teacher that are characterized by a combination of standard English and their own speech patterns by indicating whether they are "same" or "different". For example, the teacher would present a sentence in standard English and immediately follow it with the same sentence translated into the speech pattern of her students and students would indicate whether both sentences are the same or different. A variant on this method would be the translation drill where the teacher asks students to translate standard English patterns into their speech pattern and then translate their speech pattern into standard English.

Tompkins and McGee (1983) also described an approach that uses children's literature to teach standard English. This involves the teacher reading the book to the students and asking them to repeat the syntactic pattern once the pattern has been established. In addition, the students practice repeating the standard English pattern by saying the pattern in their own speech style and then using the standard English form.

Despite the success of some of these studies, some researchers argue that foreign language methods do not yield positive results. Dennis (2000) argued that these methods are only effective with small, highly motivated students who are being taught by well-trained teachers. McWhorter (1997) also argues that teaching African American students English as a foreign language is ineffective because the speech patterns of these students are not different enough from standard English to be blamed for their poor reading scores. He also argued that since students in Switzerland, Japan, Finland, and Germany (whose languages are much further from the standard English than AAE) are taught in the standard without the use of transition methods, imposing these methods on African American children is inherently racist because it suggests that they are not as intelligent as White children. Moreover, he states that these methods fail to acknowledge the elastic nature of the speech patterns of African American children who hear standard English from birth alongside AAE and consequently have the ability to code-switch between AAE and standard English. McWhorter contends that these children do poorly in school, not because they are unfamiliar with standard English but because they live in inner-city environments fraught with poverty, poor school quality, and other pathologies.

Although I disagree that teaching standard English as a foreign language should be abandoned altogether, I agree with McWhorter's contention (1997) that immersion is perhaps the most important component to a bidialectal approach because it seeks to use children's own speech patterns as a bridge to learning standard English and because it exposes them to English at home, in the classroom, and in society in general. It is a fact that many people are unable to speak a foreign language despite years of classroom teaching and are often only able to become fluent in that language when they immerse themselves in that language in a foreign country.

It follows then that some Black British children and African American children who are exposed daily to standard English in schools will be able to acquire standard English in the same way that they acquired AAE or Creole - through daily exposure at home and with their peers. It is important, as McWhorter states, to make standard English a part of these children's souls and a language that they live and breathe on a daily basis. This can be facilitated if teachers validate these languages as being able to express thoughts and meanings in the same way that standard English can and allow these children to speak their languages in the classroom whilst simultaneously being immersed in instruction in standard English. In this way, children will be able to express themselves in standard English gradually and naturally in the classroom, thereby further expanding and enhancing the already elastic nature of their speech patterns.

CONCLUSION

In conclusion, this paper argued that Black British students (and for that matter, Black students in other Euro-Western societies) will be more successfully able to expand their speech patterns to include standard

British English if a more holistic approach to learning were used that include some aspects of foreign language teaching, immersion, and an awareness and respect for the linguistic competencies of these students. Schools must abandon the outdated notion of standard English as the only viable medium of instruction in the classroom, especially since it has failed to provide Black children with adequate proficiency in standard English. Teachers and other educators must begin to view the speech patterns of Black children as an asset to language acquisition instead of a hindrance. The impressive linguistic elasticity displayed in these children's ability to code-switch at will or unconsciously has yet to be truly recognized and utilized as an important resource in language learning. In addition, more critical analyses must be conducted on ideology and the politics of knowledge production as they pertain to the social construction of language. Most importantly, however, a holistic approach must recognize that school failure for many Black children is a complex issue that is not only about language but also about living in racist Euro-Western societies where a large proportion of Black peoples are confined to impoverished inner-city areas that severely undermine any academic potential that they may harbour. Although in no way am I saying that Blacks should not see as crucial, the acquisition of standard varieties of English (as well as other languages) as an important aspect of becoming culturally competent in an increasingly globalized world, what I refer to as "the myth of social mobility" for Black people who speak so-called standard English is just that, a myth. The reality is that the ability to speak a standard variety of English will have little or no bearing on the social, economic, and educational attainment of Black peoples if they continue to be subjected to race, culture, and class-based discrimination. It is ultimately the responsibility of the educational system to take a leadership role in transforming attitudes and facilitating changes that result in the equality of opportunity for all groups, regardless of race, culture, class, and linguistic predisposition.

REFERENCES

Association of Teachers of English to Pupils from Overseas (ATEPO) (Birmingham Branch) (1970). *Work Group on West Indian Pupils Report.*

Bagley, C. (1979, March). A comparative perspective on the education of Black children in Britain. *Comparative Education, 15 (1)*, 63-81.

Baratz, J.C. (1969a). A bidialectal task for determining language proficiency in economically disadvantaged Negro children. *Child Development, 40 (3/4)*, 889-901.

Baratz, J.C. (1969b). Teaching reading in an urban Negro school system. In J.C. Baratz & R. Shuy (Eds.), *Teaching Black children to read* (pp. 92-116). Massachusetts: Centre for Applied Linguistics.

Baratz, J.C. (1970). Educational considerations for teaching standard English to Negro children. In R.W. Fasold & R.W. Shuy (Eds.), *Teaching standard English in the inner-city* (pp. 20-40). Massachusetts: Centre for Applied Linguistics.

Baugh, J. (1998). Linguistics, education, and the law: Educational reform for African American language minority students. In M. Salikokos, J.R. Rickford, G. Bailey, & J. Baugh (Eds.), *African American English: Structure, history, and usage* (pp. 282-301). London: Routledge.

Berdan, R. (1981). Black English and dialect-fair instruction. In N. Mercer (Ed.), *Language in School and Community* (pp. 217-236). London: Edward Arnold Publishers.

Coultas, V. (1989). Black girls and self-esteem. *Gender and Education, 1 (3)*, 283-294.

Dennis, B. (2000). Ebonics and the Politics of English. *World Englishes, 19 (1)*, 5-15.

Edwards, V.K. (1979a). *Language and disadvantage.* London: Edward Arnold.

Edwards, V.K. (1979b). *The West Indian language issue in British schools: Challenges and responses.* London: Routledge and Kegan Paul.

Edwards, V.K. (1986). *Language in a Black community.* Avon: Multilingual Matters.

Feigenbaum, I. (1970). The use of non-standard English in teaching Standard: Contrast and comparison. In R.W. Fasold & R.W. Shuy (Eds.), *Teaching standard English in the inner-city* (pp. 87-104). Massachusetts: Center for Applied Linguistics.

Foster, M. (1997). Ebonics: The Children Speak Up. *Quarterly of the National Writing Project, 19 (1)*, 7-8; 10-12.

Gillborn, D. (1990). *Race, ethnicity, and education: Teaching and learning in multi-ethnic schools.* London: Unwin Hyman.

Gordon, J.C.B. (1981). *Verbal deficits.* London: Croom Helm.

Green, P.A. (1985). Multi-ethnic teaching and pupils' self-concepts. In L. Swann (Ed.), *Education for all: Final report of the committee of inquiry into the education of children from ethnic minority groups* (pp. 48-53). London: HMSO.

Hall, R.A. (1966). *Pidgin and Creole languages.* London: Cornell University Press.

Harrison, D. & Trabasso, T. (1976). *Black English: A seminar.* New Jersey: Lawrence Erlbaum Associates.

Hewitt, R. (1989). Creole in the classroom: Political grammars and educational vocabularies. In R. Grillo (Ed.), *Social anthropology and the politics of language* (pp. 126-144). London: Routledge.

Labov, W. (1972). *Language in the inner city: Studies in the Black English vernacular.* Philadelphia: University of Pennsylvania Press.

Lander, S. (1981, February). The written English of second-generation West Indians. *First Language, 2 (1),* 67-73.

Mac an Ghaill, M. (1988). *Young, gifted, and Black: Student-teacher relations in the schooling of Black youth.* Milton Keynes: Open University Press.

Mailloux, S. (1989). *Rhetorical Power.* Ithaca, NY: Cornell University Press.

McWhorter, J.H. (1997, summer). Wasting Energy on an Illusion: Six Months Later. *Black Scholar, 27 (2),* 2-4.

Orr, E.W. (1987) *Twice as Less.* New York: Norton.

Roberts, P.A. (1988). *West Indians and their language.* New York: Cambridge University Press.

Roberts, P.A. (1993). *Affective factors in the use of Creole in the classroom: The resolution of a paradox.* Paper presented at SPCL Conference, Amsterdam.

Robertson, I. (1996). Language education policy (1): Towards a rational approach for Caribbean states. In P. Christie (Ed.), *Caribbean language issues old and new: Papers in honour of Professor Mervyn Alleyne on the occasion of his sixtieth birthday* (pp. 112-119). Barbados; Jamaica; and Trinidad: The Press University of the West Indies.

Robinson, W.P. (1965). The elaborated code in working-class language. *Language and Speech, 8,* 243-252.

Schools Council Working Paper 29 (1970). *Teaching English to West Indian children: The research stage of the project.* London: Evans Brothers Ltd.

Simmons-McDonald, H. (1996). Language education policy (2): The case for Creole in formal education in St. Lucia. In P. Christie (Ed.), *Caribbean language issues old and new: Papers in honour of Professor Mervyn Alleyne on the occasion of his sixtieth birthday* (pp. 120-142). Barbados; Jamaica; and Trinidad: The Press University of the West Indies.

Stubbs, M. (1976). *Language, schools, and classrooms.* Second Edition. London: Methuen.

Sutcliffe, D. (1982). *British Black English.* Oxford: Basil Blackwell.

Tompkins, G.E. & L.M. McGee (1983). *Launching Nonstandard Speakers into Standard 79 (3), 237240.*

TUC Report. (1996, July 8). *The Guardian Newspaper,* p. 4.

Wheldall, K. & Joseph, R. (1985/1986). Young Black children's sentence comprehension skills: A comparison of performance in standard English and Jamaican Creole. *First Language, 6,* 149-154.

CHAPTER 3

USE OF CASE AND CASE METHOD IN TEACHING AND LEARNING OF EDUCATIONAL ADMINISTRATION

AUSTIN EZENNE

ABSTRACT.

A case as it is used in educational administration consists of an educational event, a person, a situation, a problem or an administrative scenario. A case is usually presented with enough contextual details to help a reader to develop an understanding of the situation depicted in an educational setting or scene.

Three levels of case are frequently used in educational administration and these are cases at the macro or systemic, meso and micro levels of the educational system and the school organisation. The case analysis procedures emphasize critical thinking and the use of theories from the foundation disciplines of philosophy, psychology, sociology and educational administration in making decisions on issues raised in the cases.

The use of cases and case method in the study and practice of educational administration is a method of organising subject matter so that students can better understand the issues involved in the cases. Issues raised in the cases are similar to the issues which occur in real-life situations in educational administration. The study of cases help students learn the skill of decision-making, which is vital to the study, and practice of educational administration.

INTRODUCTION

The use of cases and case method in educational administration comprise a way of organising subject matter so that the student will better understand issues involved in a particular case under study. Cases are very much in use in the teaching and learning of educational administration because they help to instruct aspiring and practising administrators. This is also true because the concepts, paradigms and specific ideas and information presented in the case are similar to the real and practical context in which educational administrators operate. The use of cases in the study of educational administration involves making a number of decisions on the case under study, just as the educational administrator in a school situation is expected to make some decisions about school programmes. Because of this, it is believed that the use of cases and case method in the study of educational administration contributes to better decision-making, especially in educational organisation. Lunenburg and Ornstein (1996) stated that decision-making is important to all educational administrators because it pervades all administrative functions such as planning, organising, staffing, directing, conducting and controlling. The authors also defined decision-making as a process of choosing a course of action among alternatives.

Because of the importance of decision-making in educational administration, administrators must develop decision-making skills since they make many decisions that affect their organisation. The quality of the decision made by the administrator affects the effectiveness of organisations in achieving their set goals. Drucker (1993) contended that there are six steps in the classical decision-making process which are: defining the problem, analysing the problem, developing alternative solution to the problem, deciding on the best solution, converting decision into effective action and lastly maintaining and assessing the results of the decisions made. The decision-making process is therefore a rational activity, which is important to educational administration for the achievement of the goals of the educational organisation.

THE MEANING OF A CASE AND A CASE METHOD

A 'case' is a particular example of a phenomenon, which may consist of an event, a person, a situation or a scenario. In educational administration, a case consists of a particular example of administrative phenomenon. The case is usually presented with enough contextual details so that the reader can develop an understanding for what is being depicted.

In medicine, a patient is usually described as a 'case' and in law; a plaintiff may have a 'case' against the defendant pending in the court of law. A case history of a person or a matter in the court of law will contain details of the physical, emotional, mental, social and biographical characteristics which will enable the lawyer or doctor to make informed decisions about the problem or matter under study. Similarly, in the study of educational administration a case may be a detailed description of an educational system or a matter within the system. For example, the Jamaican educational sector or system, and cases at this level are said to be at a 'Macro level'. Cases at the systematic level of the organisation are said to be at the macro level, those cases at the school level are at the 'meso level', while those at the classroom level are said to be at the 'micro level' of individual interaction.

At the macro level, cases may arise from a government policy statement on the educational system as a whole. At the meso level, cases can arise from the school situation, from the Parent-Teacher Association or from the Ministry of Education. At the micro level, cases may arise in the classroom, from teacher-student interaction or from student-student interaction. Cases are very often the true representation of real issues or cases, and these representations can help the educational administrators to develop skills for evaluating the decisions in practice. These three levels are illustrated in Figure 1.

Figure 1: Three levels of cases used in educational administration.

```
                          ┌─────────────────┐
                          │   THE SOCIETY   │
                          └────────┬────────┘
                                   │
                                   ▼
1. ┌──────────────────┐   ┌──────────────────────────┐
   │ The macro or     │   │ --Educational system     │
   │ systematic level │──▶│ --Political system       │
   │ of organisation  │   │ --Economical system      │
   │                  │   │ --Family system          │
   └──────────────────┘   └──────────────────────────┘
                                   │
                                   ▼
2. ┌──────────────────┐   ┌──────────────────────────────┐
   │ The meso level   │   │ --Ministry of Education      │
   │ of organisation  │──▶│ --Schools & school boards    │
   │                  │   │ --Parent-Teachers Association│
   │                  │   │ --Teachers Unions            │
   └──────────────────┘   └──────────────────────────────┘
                                   │
                                   ▼
3. ┌──────────────────┐   ┌──────────────────────────────┐
   │ The micro level  │   │ --Classrooms                 │
   │ of individual    │──▶│ --Teacher-Pupil interaction  │
   │ interaction      │   │ --Pupil-pupil interaction    │
   │                  │   │ --Teacher-teacher interaction│
   └──────────────────┘   └──────────────────────────────┘
```

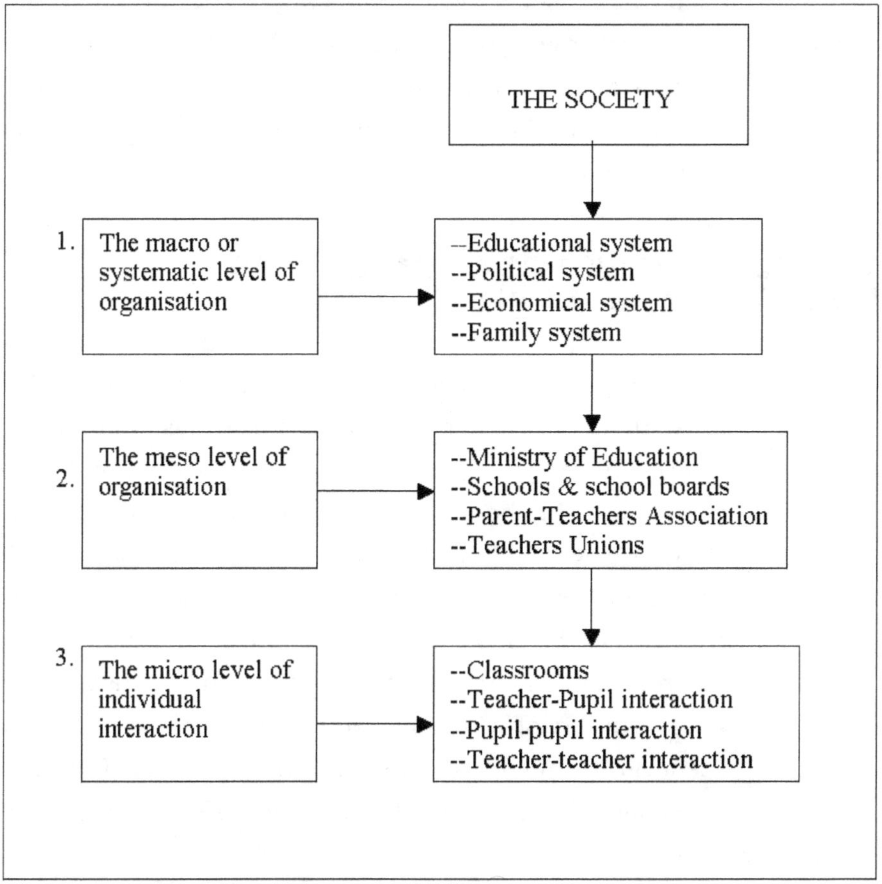

Adapted from Mohammed J. (2001)

Cases at the macro level of the organisation may be long and more complex than cases at the other two levels. In some courses of study in educational administration many cases are used at the meso and micro levels of interaction.

The 'case' is used essentially as an instructional tool. For example a case is circulated to students in an educational administration class to encourage discussion, debates and reflections resulting in informed decision-making. There are steps and procedures that are applied to the case when it is used as an instructional tool and those steps comprise the case method.

THE CHARACTERISTICS OF CASES USED IN EDUCATIONAL ADMINISTRATION

Cases used in the study of educational administration have certain characteristics that tend to make them typical in administrative settings. Mohammed (2001) suggested some characteristics, which make the case typical in the study of educational administration. Cases are derived from real-life situations and they usually depict practical experiences from the educational system, the school, the classroom or from the school-community environment. A case is also context-bound. That is, it is a description of a specific situation, phenomenon or a scenario. Therefore, any discussion or analysis of the case must consider the context from which the case is derived.

Many cases used in the study of educational administration have central issues, and discussions are concentrated on the central issues in the cases. In many situations, decisions are made on the central issues in the case or a critique of decisions already made is required. Important decisions made on the central issues in the case must be related to the relevant foundation theories, which underpin practice in the educational administration discipline. Cases promote thinking, reasoning and debating with peers and colleagues, before decisions making on critical issues in the case is taken. These activities help the educational administrator to develop reflective attitude, which is vital for decision-making in educational organisations.

EXAMPLE OF CASES AND PROBLEM AT THE MACRO, MESO AND MICRO LEVELS OF INTERACTION

Cases at the macro level usually describe situation and scenario in the educational system at the national or international level. A case can be illustrated by a true position or a picture of a similar scenario can be depicted.

The following case at the macro level reflects some of the effects of teachers' low income and poor working conditions in Africa, the Caribbean and Latin America.

A PROBLEM AT THE MACRO LEVEL ON TEACHERS' LOW INCOME IN AFRICA, CARIBBEAN AND LATIN AMERICA

Cuts in teachers' incomes result in low morale in the teaching profession, and reduced motivation and effectiveness, with serious implications for school quality in the developing world such as Africa, the Caribbean and Latin America. As a result, teachers may be forced to take on second jobs or activities, which lead to increased absenteeism and reduced time for class preparation, correction of papers and being available to students. The erosion of incomes also leads to trained teachers leaving the profession especially those in core subjects such as the sciences, mathematics, languages and technical subjects.

Due to lower wages and poor working conditions, the attractiveness of teaching as a career has been considerably reduced. UNESCO's Statistical Year book (1991) indicates a declining proportion of students enrolled in teacher training at the second level of education. Between 1980 and 1989, enrolment in teacher training as a percentage of the total enrolment declined from 7.2 to 6.6 percent in Africa and from 4.1 to 3.2 percent in Caribbean and Latin America.

In many developing counties, an option used to cut back on teacher costs has been to increase the proportion of young, inexperienced and temporary teachers, with the effects of reducing the average salary paid. Using untrained teachers in developing countries where large numbers are already without adequate qualification for teaching is unlikely to contribute to the quality of the educational system. In many African and Caribbean countries, as well as in Latin America, many well-trained teachers have been leaving teaching for other professions. Many well-trained teachers have also migrated to developed countries such, as the United States and the United Kingdom were teachers' salaries are high and the working conditions are better. In Costa Rica, and in Latin America for example high school graduates without adequate training have gradually replaced better-educated teachers. At the secondary level, these high school graduates represented 23.9 percent of the teaching force in 1990 (UNESCO Statistic Year book1991). Primary and secondary education is free in Costa Rica and is guaranteed by the state to all citizens (Hutchinson and Lewin 2001). While primary and tertiary enrolment rates are comparatively high, secondary enrolment rates are lower than those in many developing countries at similar levels of development.

QUESTIONS ON TEACHERS' SITUATION IN DEVELOPING COUNTRIES

Answer the following questions on the above passage.

1. Why are teachers' incomes in developing countries low?
2. Why has the attractiveness of teaching as a profession been reduced in recent times especially in developing countries?
3. What should governments do to improve the quality of teachers in developing countries?
4. How can governments of developing countries reduce teacher turnover?
5. Suggest what should be done to reduce the proportion of high school graduate teachers in the school?
6. How can the Costa Rican government improve the enrolment rate at the secondary school level?

A SAMPLE OF A CASE AT THE MESO LEVEL OF THE SCHOOL ORGANISATION

You are the principal of Stony Hill primary school, a wealthy sub-urban primary school in St Andrew Parish, Jamaica. Students' enrolment increased by 25 percent during the past five years and this increase has occurred primarily in grades four to six.

The present facilities of the school cannot accommodate the increased student population for the next academic year starting in September 2002. You have earlier discussed this problem with both the school board and the Ministry of Education Youth and Culture. During your meeting with the stakeholders, some options were discussed which included: merging with a nearby sub-urban primary school, which has experienced a decline in enrolment, or introducing a double shift in your school, or renting one of the buildings from a nearby basic school. You are expected to recommend one option to the Ministry for implementation.

Answer the following questions on the case.

1. If you are the principal of Stoney Hill primary school, which of the three options would you prefer and why?
2. Which of the three options would present a minimal organisational problem and why?
3. Identify the problems that are presented by each of the three options?
4. What factors are responsible for the increase or decrease in enrolment in your school in the last five years?

EXAMPLE OF A CASE AT THE MICRO LEVEL OF INTERACTION (JENNIFER AND SALLY'S CASE.)

In the rural elementary school where Jennifer taught, resources were thin. Teaching assistants, students' interns, and adult volunteers were scarce, and she couldn't arrange schedules for older students to help the younger ones.

But help was exactly what Sally, a fourth grader in Jennifer's class most needed. A bright child, well meaning and engaging, Sally had limited social skills. Getting along with others was difficult for her. In cooperative activities, she lapsed into wilful, manipulative behaviours. It didn't take a trained psychologist to see that she needed more direction than other students.

What Sally needed was an adult's full-time attention – attention that Jennifer, in charge of 23 other students simply couldn't give. Like many teachers, Jennifer focused heavily on team-based work, and increasingly, she noted that whatever team Sally worked on got into difficulties and lost focus. They never met the objectives. One group even avoided working with Sally, and others were ready to follow suit. Yet, Sally was making progress, however slowly in working with others.

So, Jennifer had a dilemma. Should she continue allowing Sally to participate fully, even if her group suffered as a result? Or should she remove Sally from cooperative learning activities so that the groups can progress faster? Most importantly, what conceptual framework could she use to weigh these two mutually exclusive courses of action?

(Kidder & Born, 1998 p. 38)

CASE ANALYSIS AT THE MICRO LEVEL OF INTERACTION (JENNIFER & SALLY'S CASE)

This case, which is at the micro level, could be used to illustrate the importance of case analysis in the case method. Before you start the case analysis, you should re-read the case. Then you apply the steps of case analysis to the case, by answering the following questions.

Question 1. What does the case require us to do?
Answer. In this case, we are been called upon to help the teacher to make a decision about how best to seek the interest of both Sally and the rest of the class.

Question 2. What do you consider to be the central issue?
Answer. The central issue was the dilemma the teacher faces about the right of the individual student (Sally) Vs the group (Sally's class). Anything decision the teacher makes will have negative consequences for either Sally or the group. Yet schools are supposed to cater for the well being of all children especially in the classroom.

Question 3. What are the secondary problems in the case?
Answer. The secondary problem relate to the lack of classroom resources. Because of the poor rural situation of the school, sound curricular activities or support initiatives such as guidance counselling, individual interaction or media resources are not available for solving Sally's problems.

Question 4. What evidence supports our idea as to the central issue?

Answer. The case makes it clear that the well being of the other students is affected by Sally's slow progress in classroom. However, Sally seems to be slowly improving in interpersonal skills in working with the group. The dilemma of the teacher is how to deal with what is right for both Sally and her group or class.

Question 5. What are the alternative solutions to the dilemma?

Answer. Critical thinking will lead to the following suggestions

i. Keep Sally in the class and deal with problems as they arise.
ii. Keep Sally in class but do something different
iii. Send Sally out of class to pursue other learning activities.
iv. Send Sally out sometimes.
v. Stop cooperative activities altogether.

In these five alternatives, there are advantages and disadvantages for both Sally and her class. The teacher has a critical decision to make in selecting the best alternative solution to the problem in her class. The teacher should be able to select the option that has the maximum advantage and minimum disadvantages for both Sally and the class. Alternative (i) appears to be better than the other alternatives. In this case, cooperative learning can continue when Sally is in the class, she will then grow steadily and slowly in interpersonal skills. Alternatives (ii to v) raise issues about the stability of the school curriculum, differences in the learning ability of students in school and social and psychological problems facing students in the schools. A typical example is the case of Sally, which, due to neglect by the teacher, starts having a felling of low self esteem. She would also lose the ability of working with other students. These problems are meant to be solved by the school.

THE CASE METHOD

A case is central to the case method and the case method advocates the use of cases in the training of educational administrators. The case method of teaching emphasizes the application of theory to practice and it is superior to the traditional lecture method of teaching. The case method can also be used to translate the concept of the foundation disciplines and the theories of educational administration to practical scenarios in the field. This helps the learner to visualise practical problems, which the educational administrator faces from time to time.

In the classroom, a teacher can develop and circulate a case to a class of students, who are asked to read and study the case and later generate a discussion on the case. The students will analyse the case in detail, and then present various views, which generate debates and discussions on the primary and secondary issues raised in the case. The steps of case analysis adopted from Ash Baugh and Kasten (1990) are as follows:

1. Read the case thoroughly to decide on what you are supposed to understand, which may be to make a decision, how to evaluate a decision already made what to suggest or recommend and how to solve the existing problem. Then:
2. Identify the central or primary issues or problems in the case.
3. Identify the secondary issue(s) in the case.
4. Identify evidence on primary and secondary issues.
5. Develop alternative solutions through brainstorming.
6. Evaluate the alternative solutions proposed.
7. Identify a substantive body of theory for example, from the foundation areas or administration theory that could inform and support your position.
8. Select the alternative that is most likely to solve the problem or bring about the desired change, or suggest a better option.
9. Make be a plan for the implementation of your decisions.
10. Write a case report.

All the above steps may not apply to every case because the structure and circumstances of the cases vary. The steps provide a general guideline for case analysis. Educational administrators are expected to develop skills in weighing alternative courses of action before deciding on a better option to choose. The case usually highlights the dilemma facing educational administrators in decision making in educational organisations.

APPLICATION OF THEORY IN DECISION-MAKING DURING CASE ANALYSIS

The decisions made in educational matter should be justified by their relationship to the substantive concepts and theories of foundation areas and educational administration. This is an important step in case analysis procedure. For example, the philosophical study of ethics is important to schools and the practice of educational administration. Many school curricula are well grounded in ethics and the concept of ethics is always applied in decision-making in school organisations. Many ethical principles are used in schools in teaching and learning, in the various school relationships and in dealing with discipline in general in school organisations.

Psychology is another important foundation discipline related to education. In the psychology of education, learning theories suggest certain strategies that have been found to promote learning. Psychological theories also throw some light in the understanding of the personality of the students, teacher and educational administrators as well as parents. Students and teachers may have psychological and emotional problems, which affect their schoolwork and their behaviours in the school.

The school exists in the society and the culture of each society affects the school in that society. The societies have groupings and these affect the behaviour of teachers and student .in the school. Students and teachers may belong to different socio-economic groups, have different cultural backgrounds and may have different religious beliefs. All these differences impact on the behaviour of students in schools.

The school administrator is always confronted with problems of effective decision-making in the school and teachers and supervisors are constantly evaluating him or her on his or her decision-making ability. The role of the principal and his or her leadership effectiveness are subjects of discussion at all times in the school organisation.

CONCLUSION

Cases and case methods are used for organising subject matter of a discipline so that we can better understand the issues involved. In recent times, cases are used in the study of educational administration especially for aspiring and practising administrators. This is because the specific and contextual information presented in a case, are usually very similar to the real practical world in which the administrator operates. In the study of a case, the student has to make certain decisions on the issues involved.

The case method advocates the use of cases in the training of educational administrators. It is a well thought out teaching method that is felt to be far superior to the traditional lecture method of teaching. The case is central to the case method, and recently, the case has been recognised as a means of translating the foundation and the administration theories into practical phenomena. The use of cases in the study of educational administration contribute to a better and more informed decision-making in the practice of educational administration.

REFERENCES

Ashbough, C. R. Kasten, K. L. (1990). "Procedures in case Analysis " In Educational leadership: Case studies for reflective practice. New York: Longman. p 8-13.

Coombs, P.H. & Hallak, J. (1987). Efficiency of Productivity. In cost Analysis in Education. Washington D.C.; World Bank Report.

Drucker, Peter F. (1993). Management: Task, Responsibilities & Practice. New York: Haiper Collins.

Jones, S. O. (1998). Cases on Issues and Problem in Educational Management. Kingston: Canoe Press.

Hutchinson F. and Lewin K. M. (2001). Secondary Education Financing in Costa Rica: Recovering the Initiatives. Paris. UNESCO and International Institute for Educational Planning. (I.I.E.P.).

Kidder, R. M. Born, P. L. (1998). "Resolving ethical dilemmas in the classroom". Educational Leadership, 56(4) p38-41.

Lunenburg F. C. and Ornstein A. C. (1996). Educational Administration Concepts and Practices 2nd Edition, California: Wadsworth Publishing Company.

Mohammed, J. (2001). Current Issues in Educational Administration. Bridgetown, Barbados: The University of the West Indies.

Reimers, F. & Tiburcio, L. (1993). Education, Adjustment and Reconstruction. Option for change. Paris: UNESCO.

UNESCO Statistical Year book (1991 & 1996). Paris: UNESCO.

CHAPTER 4

SITUATED ATTAINMENT: MEASURING UNDER-ACHIEVEMENT IN JAMAICA

TONY BASTICK

ABSTRACT

Under-achievement, particularly among Caribbean male students, is a current concern for teachers throughout the Caribbean and abroad. This chapter operationally defines 'under-achievement' so as to distinguish it from low ability. This allows under-achievement to be identified and measured, even in high-performing students. It allows social, personal and educational factors influencing under-achievement to be identified, and allows effects resulting from under-achievement to be more objectively researched in new and helpful ways in the Caribbean and abroad. This chapter reports research with nine classes of Grade 9 students in Jamaica (N=321) that validates the basic assumptions of the concept. It also reports empirical results using the concept that show how teachers' attitudes contribute to underachievement in Jamaica and how chronic underachievement socially and emotionally affects their students.

INTRODUCTION

If all else were equal within a classroom, we might expect that children's intelligence would be a strong determinant of their attainment. However, there are often other factors that come into play that considerably reduce the correlations between I.Q. and Attainment so that, in a particular classroom situation, a student's actual academic attainment may be more or less what we might have expected based on his or her I.Q. scores. 'Situated Attainment' is a within-class concept that allows us to explore why teachers award some students higher or lower grades than their intelligences might warrant. Situated Attainment allows us to distinguish between low ability students and students who are underachieving.

Situated Attainment (SA) is an application to the normal classroom of an I.Q.-Achievement Discrepancy technique used in Special Education to identify students deserving of special resources (Donovan & Cross, 2002). A student's Situated Attainment (SA) is operationally defined here as the difference in ranks between the grade awarded to the student by the teacher and the student's intelligence quotient. Situated Attainment is the difference between Rank by Grade (RG) and Rank by IQ (RIQ) within the class: SA=RG-RIQ. When students attain over their IQ expectation, their SA is positive. When students attain below their IQ expectation, their SA is negative. It was postulated that teachers' and students' value judgements are made mainly relative to class norms so that using the class as the unit of analysis (CUA) would reveal relationships that were less obvious when the individual was used as the unit of analysis (IUA) or the school was used as the unit of analysis (SUA).

For this initial exploration of the concept, nine classes of Grade 9 students were selected, one from each of nine schools (N=321). These students were, allowing for two missing values, 127 males and 192 females of average age 14 years 5 months. They responded to an attitude questionnaire and a sub-set of culturally and psychometrically appropriate I.Q. questions from the standardized General Ability Tests 2 (GAT-2), which predominately consists of I.Q. questions covering the main domains of Intelligence testing. The students' half-year test results, from which their Grades are derived, were also recorded. The I.Q. scores were calculated and within each class, the students' I.Q. scores and their grade attainments were ranked so that their SAs could be calculated.

The theoretical assumptions of using CUA, SUA and IUA were supported, and further analysis using the SA metric showed that teachers were not gender biased in their grading of males and females relative to their IQs. The SA analysis, however, revealed teachers' extreme grading bias with respect to student's age and a bias towards student's attitudes. It revealed the negative effect of continued underachievement on students' self-esteem and showed that student dissatisfaction with low grades was due to underachievement rather than lack of ability.

SITUATIONAL FACTORS THAT AFFECT GRADES AWARDED BY TEACHERS

Teachers' attitudes can affect both the quality of work produced by students and affect how they grade the work that is produced. Teachers' grading practices vary greatly and, particularly when incorporating alternative assessments, are likely to involve more subjective value judgments (Frary, Cross & Weber, 1993; Plake & Impara, 1993). Teachers' grading is a mostly private practice that Brookhart, refers to as "..hodgepodge grade of attitude, effort, and achievement" (1991, p. 36). For example, the literature reports that teachers' grading is affected by the student's temperament (Holbrook, 1982), how independent, tidy and attractive a student is (Clifford, 1975; Ross & Salvia, 1975), and the teacher's personal relationship with the student (Pedulla, Airasian & Madaus, 1980; Doherty & Conolly, 1985). Interestingly, it is not necessarily the attractive students who are over-graded. For example, Sparacino and Hansell (1979) found a negative correlation between physical attractiveness and Grade Point Average.

Because grades are so dependent on teachers' values, researchers have chosen to use more 'objective' standardized measures for comparisons across classes and schools. Wentzel (1993) noted that grades reflect the social-emotional context of the classroom, such as teacher preference. In her 1993 study "Does Being Good Make the Grade? Social Behavior and Academic Competence in Middle School" Wentzel found that pro-social behaviour was a strong predictor of grades, but not standardized scores. Similarly, Schaefer and McDermott (1999) found that grades were significantly related to social behavior whereas standardized test scores related significantly only to IQ scores. Bennett, Gottesman, Rock, and Cerullo (1993), indicated that grades were influenced by gender and teacher perceptions of behavior. In a longitudinal study (Feldhusen, Thurston & Benning (1970) with 384 least 'socially approved' third and sixth graders, positive social skills were found to correlate with grades over a 5 year period. Malecki (1998) also found that ratings of students' social skills predicted academic achievement in the following term.

Teachers' grade evaluations may be influenced by many situational factors. For example, Yarborough and Johnson (1980) found that girls' superior language and spelling achievement, coupled with their affective advantages, could be mistaken for superior reading skills. This is consistent with Hartley, (1982) who also found that teachers rated girls's reading higher than boys'. This teacher gender bias towards girls has been found even when girls and boys have the same reading ability (Ross & Jackson, 1991).

There have been many and varied conformations of Rosenthal's and Jacobson's classic 1968 study showing how teachers' perceptions of children influenced the their judgements (Babad, 1993; Brophy, 1983; Jussim, 1986, 1989; Weinstein, 1993). Race, ethnicity and SES are such factors that have been found to influence teachers' judgement of children (Baron, Tom & Cooper, 1985; Hall, Howe, Merkel & Lederman 1986). In a 1983 metastudy of 16 research results, Dusek and Joseph concluded that race and social class were major influences on teachers' judgements. This was confirmed in an experiment by McCombs and Gay (1988) who manipulated information on students' race, class and IQ to influence teachers' (n=80) evaluations of pictures of a White child and an Hispanic child.

The many situational factors that affect the grades awarded by a teacher makes such grades more suitable for comparison with other in-class grades awarded by the same teacher and less appropriate for wider comparison.

ARGUMENTS FOR THE 'CLASS' AS THE UNIT OF ANALYSIS

If all else were equal, we might expect that students' IQs were good predictors of their in-class grades (Lassiter, 1995; Poteat, Wuensch & Gregg, 1988; Rodriguez, Prewitt & Joseph, 1990). Interestingly, many measurement courses use concocted IQ and Grade data, or data from an academically homogeneous groups, for correlation exercises that illustrate the expectation that IQ and Grades are correlated. However, although there is a large literature on the use of standardized measures to predict future grades, such as the use of IQ and SAT scores to predict College grades (Bridgeman, Mccamley-Jenkins & Ervin, 2000; Carvajal & Pauls, 1995), there is comparatively little literature reporting significant correlations between individuals' standardized measures and in-class grades across multi-school populations. In practice, situational variables can intervene to enhance or degrade performance, so that the grade percentage attained on a particular assignment may be higher or lower than that predicted by academic ability alone (Boulon-Diaz, 1992; Cuppens, 1967; Konarzewski, 1993; Sternberg, 1996). It is of some concern to educationists to identify situational variables that might act systematically to reduce grade scores of individuals or groups to levels below those justified by their abilities. 'Situated Attainment' is a within-class metric that describes the difference between expected and actual within-class performance. It may be used to identify cases where situational variables may have intervened to influence performance scores, positively or negatively, and it may be used to explore the nature of these influences.

Children and teachers naturally norm their educational value judgements in the context of their class, as their extensive time and involvement within their class environment can be expected to have a dominant influence on their evaluative experiences. For example, for socio-pedagogic reasons of motivation, self-esteem and accountability a teacher of a class students who are very below the academic average is unlikely to award assignment percentage grades to the whole class that are correspondingly very low. Similarly, a teacher of a class of students who are very above academic average is unlikely to award assignment grades to the whole class that are correspondingly very high. Hence, by taking the individual as the unit of analysis we would not expect to find that standardised academic ability and teacher awarded grades would correlate highly across school populations of varied academic standards. However, taking the class as the unit of analysis we would expect to find a correlation between students' relative academic standing within the class and the grades awarded to students by the teacher of the same class. An early study of this kind was attempted by Krueger in 1939 and subsequent within-class studies have found strong associations between standardized measures of academic attainment and grades (Fisher, 1995).

Following this logic, it may be expected that within-class metrics could be more useful for exploring some socio-pedagogic issues than using the individual or school as the unit of analysis. 'Situated Attainment' (SA) is such a class-based metric.

Situated Attainment is the difference between grade rank and IQ rank within the class. It can have many possible uses. A positive SA indicates the student's grade was higher than would be predicted by their relative IQ. Negative SAs indicate under grading or under performance. Using SA we can separately identify under performance and underachievement. These words are defined here as: Under performance results in a standard below some group norm comparison (e.g. below average), and underachievement results in a standard below that predicted by the student's academic ability. Where a grade is given for a short term assignment, a negative SA can be used as feedback to show that the student can be expected to produce better work. If a grade represents a combined mark over some longer period of time, such as an end of year grade, the student's consistently lower than expected achievement is likely to have become evident to his or her peers. Such negative SA may then indicate serious underachievement which may be associated with peer related social, personal or behavioural problems (Goergi, 1972).

OPERATIONAL DEFINITION OF SITUATIONAL ATTAINMENT

Situated attainment (SA) is the difference between how a student is ranked in-class by IQ and by assessment Grade (the grade awarded for work done, e.g. as a percentage, not year Grade as in k-12). SA=RG-RIQ where SA is Situated Attainment, RG is in-class Ranking by Grade, and RIQ is in-class ranking by Intelligence Quotient

For ease of interpretation, reverse rankings are used, the smallest number being given the rank of 1, so that the higher the IQ or Grade then higher is the student's rank. Table 1 illustrates calculations of the metric for an artificial data set for a class of 10 students.

Table 1. Data illustrating the calculation of Situated Attainment

Student	Grade%	IQ	RG	-	RIQ	=	SA	
1	40	116	3	-	7	=	-4	Undergraded
2	20	104	1	-	4	=	-3	Undergraded
3	65	108	7	-	5	=	2	Overgraded
4	62	91	4	-	3	=	1	Overgraded
5	83	84	10	-	1	=	9	Overgraded
6	63	125	6	-	10	=	-4	Undergraded
7	68	117	8	-	8	=	0	As Expected
8	30	124	2	-	9	=	-7	Undergraded
9	62	84	4	-	1	=	3	Overgraded
10	69	115	9	-	6	=	3	Overgraded

Key
IQ Intelligence Quotient
RG Rank by Grade
RIQ Rank by IQ
SA Situated Attainment

Although Table 1 illustrates an artificial example, we can see that positive values of SA indicate that the student has been over graded in relation to the prediction expected from their IQ. Similarly, negative values indicate under grading. It is proposed that we can use the SA metric to more sensitively explore variables that may contribute to over and under grading within the classroom, such as age, gender and personality differences.

This study investigated assumptions and uses of Situated Attainment with a sample (n=319) of Jamaican adolescents.

METHOD

Nine Jamaican urban secondary schools were chosen at random for this study. Permissions were obtained for one 9th grade intact class in each of these schools to take part in the study and for the half-year grade percentages of these students to be used in the study. The subjects were 319 Jamaican adolescents, 127 boys and 192 girls, with a median age of 14 years 3 months. The number of students in each class ranged from 30 to 40 with a median of 36. It was considered that students' scores in Mathematics and English would best represent their academic performance across school subjects. Hence, the average of each student's percentage half-year grades in Mathematics and English was used as the Grade measure.

The subjects completed a sub-set of verbal, spatial and logical IQ items chosen from the standardized General Ability Tests 2 (GAT-2) as being culturally appropriate and of fitting difficulty levels for the age of the sample. In addition, subjects were also given instructions to rate, from 0-9, the four self-esteem questions shown in Figure 1.

Figure 1. Instructions and self-esteem questions.

The following statements are about you. Rate each putting the best number from 0 to 9 in the box to show how much you agree that it is true of you.

0 means not true of me   *1-3 means only a little true of me*   *4-5 means mostly true of me*

6-8 means very much true of me   *9 means totally true of me*

Q1 ☐ Today I am very happy

Q2 ☐ I feel I m not achieving as much as my class mates in my schoolwork.

Q3 ☐ I often wish I look like someone else.

The following question is NOT a 0-9 rating. Read the question carefully and answer accurately.

Q4 How many times **last week** did any of your friends avoid you?_____

ANALYSES AND RESULTS

The subjects' IQ scores, together with their half-term grade averages and responses to the self-esteem questions were coded for analysis. In addition, all scores were recorded as in-class ranks with the lowest scores being awarded the rank of 1. The Situated Attainment for each student was calculated by subjecting the student's within-class IQ rank from his or her within-class Grade rank. Calculations with pair-wise or list-wise missing values options gave the following results for the numbers stated.

The normality of the SA metric is illustrated in Figure 2 and shown by the distribution parameters in Table 2 and the following single sample fit statistic: Kolmogorov-Smirnov Z test showed that the SA distribution was close to normal Sig p=0.975 (2-tailed)

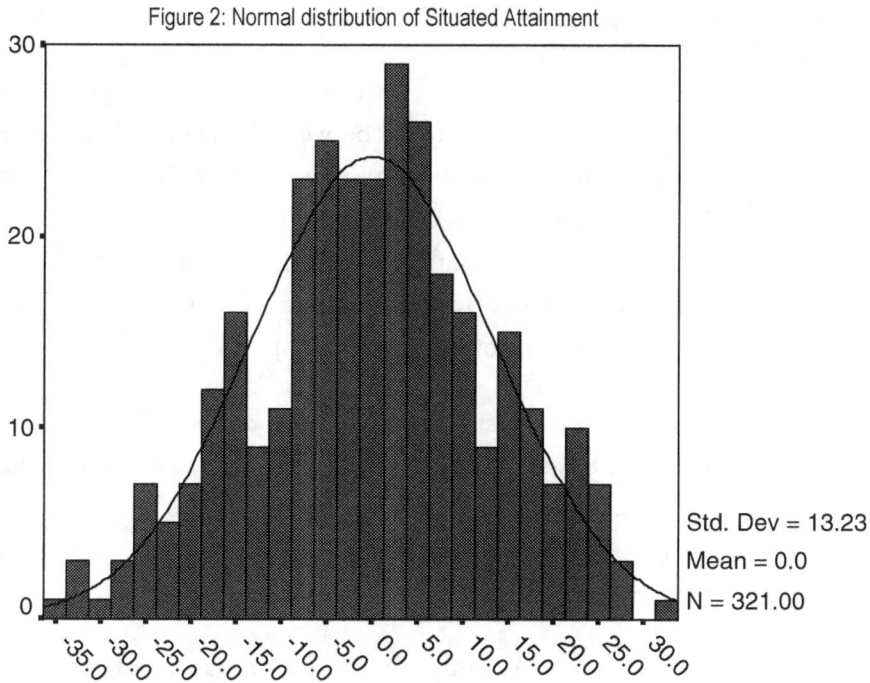

Figure 2: Normal distribution of Situated Attainment

Situated Attainment

Table 2: Distribution parameters of Situated Attainment

SA Distribution Parameters	
N	321.000
Mean	0.000
Median	0.000
Mode	-4.500
Skewness	-0.081
Std. Error of Skewness	0.136
Kurtosis	-0.308
Std. Error of Kurtosis	0.271
Range	67.000
Minimum	-35.500
Maximum	31.500

TESTING THE ASSUMPTIONS OF SITUATED ATTAINMENT

It was postulated that no significant association would be found between Grades and IQs using (a) the individual as the unit of analysis (IUA) or using (b) the school as the unit of analysis (SUA). It was postulated however, that a statistically significant association would be found between Grades and IQs when (c) the class was used as the unit of analysis (CUA).

Assumption (a), that no association would be found using the IUA, was tested using the correlation of IQ with Grade for the whole sample. The correlation of IQ with Grade was not significant at $r=0.077$ ($p=0.169$, $n=321$) as postulated.

Assumption (b), that no association would be found using the SUA, was tested by comparing the mean grades of the schools with the highest and lowest mean IQ scores. First, an ANOVA was used to show that the schools differed significantly in their mean IQ scores. Table 3 shows this ANOVA and Figure 3 shows a plot of the mean IQs of each school.

Table 3 ANOVA showing significantly different mean IQs between the 9 sample schools

IQ

IQ	Sum of Squares	df	Mean Square	F	Sig.
Between Groups	739.006	8	92.376	31.016	.000
Within Groups	929.243	312	2.978		
Total	1668.249	320			

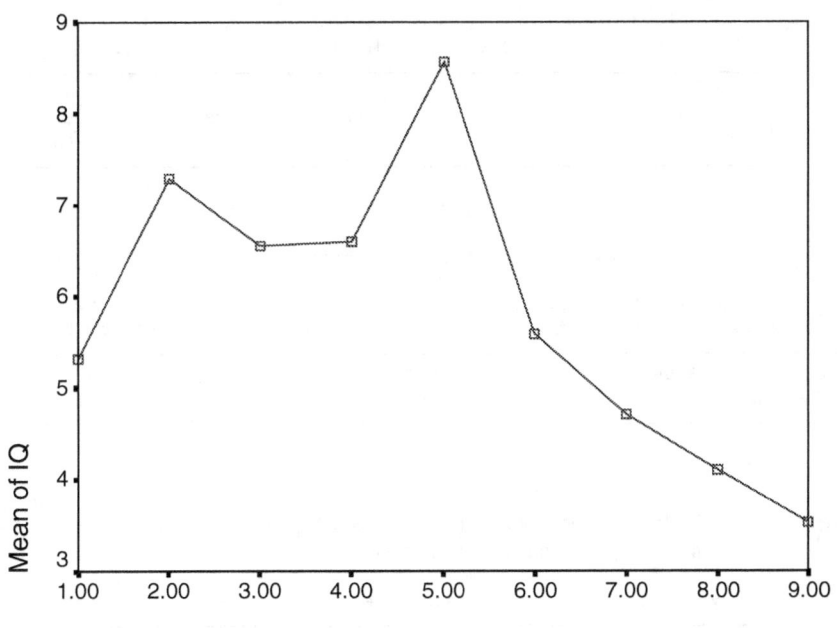

Figure 3: Mean IQ scores of subjects in each school

The four schools with the highest mean IQs were grouped (5, 2, 4, 3) into a 'High IQ' group and the four schools with the lowest mean IQs were grouped (1, 7, 8, 9) into a 'Low IQ' group. A t-test showed that the difference between mean IQs of the two school groups was very large, Table 4. However, Table 5 shows that the mean percentage grades of the two school groups was very close with no significant difference as postulated.

Table 4: Schools' analysis: Large significant differences between mean IQs of two school groups

Variable	Number of Cases	Mean	SD	SE of Mean
IQ				
Low IQ	147	4.4762	1.881	.155
High IQ	142	7.2958	1.953	.164

Mean Difference = -2.8196

Levene's Test for Equality of Variances: F= .014   P= .905

	t-test for Equality of Means				95%
Variances	t-value	df	2-Tail Sig	SE of Diff	CI for Diff
Equal	-12.50	287	.000	.226	(-3.264, -2.376)
Unequal	-12.49	285.52	.000	.226	(-3.264, -2.375)

Table 5: Schools analysis: No significant difference between the mean grade percentages of high and low IQ schools

Variable	Number of Cases	Mean	SD	SE of Mean
GRADE				
Low IQ	147	62.9434	10.113	.834
High IQ	142	63.9544	10.870	.912

Mean Difference = -1.0110

Levene's Test for Equality of Variances: F= 1.022 P= .313

	t-test for Equality of Means				95%
Variances	t-value	df	2-Tail Sig	SE of Diff	CI for Diff
Equal	-.82	287	.413	1.234	(-3.441, 1.419)
Unequal	-.82	283.77	.414	1.236	(-3.444, 1.422)

These results supported assumption (b) that no association between Grades and IQ would be found using the SUA.

Assumption (c), that an association would be shown between Grades and IQ using the CUA, was tested by correlating students' in-class IQ ranks (RIQ) with the in-class ranks of their grades (RG). The correlation of RIQ with RG was statistically significant at r=0.201** (p<0.0005, n=321), which supported the assumption.

USES OF SITUATED ATTAINMENT

GENDER BIAS

We might be interested to know if there are gender differences in how teachers award grades in relation to IQ. Are males, or females systemically under graded or over graded relative to their academic ability? A t-test showed that there was no significant differences between how the groups were graded and the means of both groups was very near to zero (-0.0940 for males and 0.0703 for females) showing that, overall, grading was equal and unbiased for both sexes.

AGE BIAS

We might be interested to know if teachers are influenced by the age spread in their classes when they are grading. The age spread in the whole sample is greater than the age spread in any one class so, as expected, IUA showed IQ increased significantly with Age (r=0.155*, p=0.008, n=290). However, perhaps unexpectedly, IUA also showed that grade levels significantly reduced with Age (r=-0.280**, p<0.0005, n=290), that is, there is a tendency for teachers in the whole sample to award lower grade marks to older students. So do teachers have expectations of older students that are too high? Using the CUA we find that the correlation between rank Age (RA) and RG is significant at r=-0.140* (p=0.17, n=290), indicating that older students are receiving lower grades in-class to a lesser extent than the IUA revealed. However, the correlation between RA and SA was significant at r=-0.143* (p=0.015, n=290). This shows that teachers are grading older students in their classes below the level warranted by their ability.

SOCIAL CONCOMITANTS OF UNDER PERFORMANCE AND UNDER ACHIEVEMENT

Q1 ☐ Today I am very happy

Does a student's serious or flippant attitude affect the grades a teacher awards? Using the Individual as the Unit of Analysis (IUA) there was no significant coloration found between self-reported happiness and Grades (r=-0.035, p=0.552, n=295). However, using the CUA we found happy students had a significantly lower SA, with a significant correlation between ranked scores on question 1 (RQ1) and SA of r=-0.146 (p=0.012, n=295). This means that unhappy students had higher SAs indicating that they were over graded. Why is this? Maybe teachers assumed happy students were more flippant, students who should have tried harder. Maybe teachers interpreted unhappiness as a 'serious' attitude to the work, or maybe teachers wanted to 'cheer up' sad students by over-rewarding them for the work they did.

Q2 ☐ I feel I'm not achieving as much as my class mates in my schoolwork.

The Individual Unit of Analysis (IUA) showed students who get low grades tended to be very dissatisfied with their performance. The correlation between Q2 and Grade was highly significant at $-0.255**$ ($p<0.0005$, $n=320$). As expected, this effect was stronger within the class, because the question is relative to "class mates'. This was shown by the correlation of ranked answers to Q2 (RQ2) with RG of $r= -0.301**$ ($p<0.0005$, $n=320$). However, the significant correlation of RQ2 with SA of $r= -0.243**$ ($p<0.0005$, $n=320$) indicated that many of these students were disappointed in their low grades, not because they had a low potential, but because they had been under graded.

Q3 ☐ I often wish I look like someone else.

Q4 ☐ How many times **last week** did any of your friends avoid you?

There were significant CUA correlations between the in-class ratings of the responses to these questions, RQ3 and RQ4, respectively, with SA. The correlation of RQ3 with SA was $r=-0.157**$ ($p=0.005$, $n=318$) and the correlation of RQ4 with SA was $r= -0.174**$ ($p=0.002$, $n=309$).

The grades used in this study were half-year grades, so that this under grading represented an on-going situation of underachievement for these students. These correlations indicate that this long-term under achievement was accompanied by low self-esteem responses of wishing to look like someone else and by experiences of being avoided by ones friends.

SUMMARY

This study postulated that within-class metrics were more sensitive measures of teacher and student value issues than analyses across schools or comparisons of individuals across varied samples. The reason proposed for this is that teacher and student evaluations are very likely to be normed against their class experiences because of the disproportionate time and involvement teachers and students spend with their class environment. This reason was supported by reviewing studies showing teachers' values influenced grades more than standardized scores. The assumption was empirically supported by showing the lack of association between in-class grades and a standardized measure of intelligence when using the individual and the school a the unit of analyses, compared to significant associations found when analysing IQs and grades ranked within each class.

'Situational attainment' (SA) as a within-class metric, was suggested by a review of literature showing that situational influences, including teachers' values, can enhance or degrade a student's performance as predicted by standardised scores. SA is the difference in a students within-class Grade rank and their IQ ranking. A positive SA indicates over grading or over achievement whereas a negative SA indicates under grading or underachievement. Thus 'underachievement' is achieving less that one's potential and is different from under performance, which is a norm group comparison, such as being below average.

SA analyses on the Jamaican sample showed that teachers were not gender biased in their grading, nor did they over or under grade mails or females. Teachers were, however, highly biased in their grading against older students. SA analysis showed that older students tended to under perform and this under performance was due to Jamaican teachers' higher expectation of older students over and above their ability.

SA analyses also showed that teachers undergrade happy students, perhaps mistaking their happiness for flippancy or interpreting a 'serious' attitude as more fitting academic - or teachers may want to compensate for students unhappiness by over grading their work.

SA analysis showed that students reporting lower grades than their peers were being under graded relative to their potential as indicated by their IQ.

SA analysis also demonstrated the negative effect long-term underachievement has on students' self-esteem.

It should be noted that standardized within-class metrics would probably yield results with greater affect sizes that ranked metrics, because of the greater variance accounted for by standardized measurers. However, SA was defined as a ranked metric to make it more usable to teachers, as teachers can more readily rank their students than norm their scores.

It would appear from the promising results in this study that the SA, and other within-class metrics, may offer more discriminating analyses of the wide value data, such as grades and attitude surveys, obtained from teachers and their students.

REFERENCES

Babad, E. Y. (1993). Pygmalion: Twenty five years after interpersonal expectations in the classroom. In P. D. Blanck (Ed.), *Interpersonal expectations: Theory, research, and applications* (pp. 125-153). Paris: Cambridge University Press.

Baron, R. M., Tom, D. Y. H. & Cooper, H. M. (1985). Social class, race, and teacher expectations. In J. B. Dusek (Ed.), *Teacher expectancies* (pp. 251-270). Hillsdale, NJ: Erlbaum.

Bennett, R., Gottesman, R., Rock, D., & Cerullo, F. (1993). Influence of behavior perceptions and gender on teachers' judgments of students' academic skill. *Journal of Educational Psychology, 85*, 347-356.

Boulon-Diaz, F. (1992, August). *The Effects of Intelligence, Social Class, Early Development and Pre-School Experience on School Achievement of Puerto Rican Children.* Paper presented at the Annual Convention of the American Psychological Association, Washington, DC.

Bridgeman, B., Mccamley-Jenkins, L., & Ervin, N. (2000). *Predictions of Freshman Grade-Point Average from the Revised and Recentered SAT I: Reasoning Test* (College Board Research Report No.2000 - 1/ETS Research Report 00 - 1). New York, NY: ETS.

Brookhart, S. M. (1991). Grading practices and validity. *Educational Measurement: Issues and Practice, 10,* 35-36.

Brophy, J. (1983). Research on the self-fulfilling prophecy and teacher expectations. *Journal of Educational Psychology, 75,* 631-636.

Carvajal, H., & Pauls, K. K. (1995). Relationships among Graduate Record Examination scores, Wechsler Adult Intelligence Scale-Revised IQs, and undergraduate grade point average. *College Student Journal, 29*(4), 414-416.

Clifford, M. M. (1975). Physical attractiveness and academic performance. *Child Study Journal 5,* 201-209.

Cuppens, I. W. (1967). Intelligence, motivation and anxiety as determinants of school achievement in the first class of secondary education: an investigation probing the concept of underachievement. *Anthropology & Medicine. 16*(1), 1-36.

Doherty, J., & Conolly, M. (1985). How accurately can primary school teachers predict the scores of their pupils in standardized tests of attainment? A study of some non-cognitive factors that influence specific judgment. *Educational Studies, 11*, 41-60.

Donovan, M. S., & Cross, C. T. (Eds.) (2002). *Minority Students in Special and Gifted Education*. Committee on Minority Representation in Special Education, Editors, National Research Council. National Academy of Science. Washington, DC: National Academies Press.

Dusek, J. B., & Joseph, G. (1983). The bases of teacher expectancies: A meta-analysis. *Journal of Educational Psychology, 75*, 327-346.

Feldhusen, J., Thurston, J., & Benning, J. (1970). Longitudinal analyses of classroom behavior and school achievement. *Journal of Experimental Education, 38*, 4-10.

Fisher, J. L. (1995). Relationship of Intelligence Quotients to Academic Achievement in the Elementary Grades. ERIC document ERIC Accession No. — ED388428.

Frary, R.B., Cross, L.H., & Weber, L.J. (1993). Testing and grading practices and opinions of secondary teachers of academic subjects: Implications for instruction in measurement. *Educational Measurement: Issues and Practice 12*(3), 23-30.

Goergi, N. J. (1972). The relationship of self-concept in high school Negro students in Muncie, Indiana to intelligence, achievement, and grade point average. (Doctoral dissertation, Ball State University, 1972). *Dissertation Abstracts International, 32*(8-A), 4418.

Hall, V. C., Howe, A., Merkel, S., & Lederman, N. (1986). Behavior, motivation, and achievement in desegregated junior high school science classes. *Journal of Educational Psychology, 7*, 108-115.

Hartley, D. (1982). Ethnicity or sex: Teacher definitions of ability and reading comprehension in an E. P. A. primary school *Research in Education, 28,* 9-24.

Holbrook, J. W. (1982). Pupil temperament characteristics, the teacher's appraisal of their intelligence, and assignment of grades. (Doctoral dissertation, University of Georgia, 1982). *Dissertation Abstracts International,* 43(6-A), 1891

Jussim, L. (1986). Self-fulfilling prophecies: A theoretical and integrative review. *Psychological Review, 93,* 429-445.

Jussim, L. (1989). Teacher expectations: Self-fulfilling prophecies, perceptual biases, and accuracy. Journal of Personality and Social Psychology, 57, 469-490.

Konarzewski, K. (1993). Under what conditions students' intelligence and grades correlate? *Kwartalnik Pedagogiczny, 1,* 111-126.

Krueger, R. L. (1939). Grades and intelligence quotients: A study of the figures for three years in one private school. *School & Society. 50,* 60-64.

Lassiter, K. S. (1995). The Relationship between Young Children's Academic Achievement and Measures of Intelligence. *Psychology in the Schools, 32*(3), 170-77

Malecki, C. (1998). The influence of elementary students' social behaviors on academic achievement. Doctoral Dissertation. University of Wisconsin-Madison.

McCombs, R.C. & Gay, J. (1988). Effects of race, class, and IQ information on judgments of parochial grade school teachers. *Journal-of-Social-Psychology, 128*(5), 647-652

Pedulla, J. J. , Airasian, P. W. & Madaus, G. F. (1980). Do teacher ratings and standardized test results yield the same information? *American Educational Research Journal, 17,* 303-307.

Plake, B. S., & Impara, J. C. (1993). Assessment competencies of teachers: A national survey. *Educational Measurement: Issues and Practice, 12,* 10-25.

Poteat, G. M., Wuensch, K. L. & Gregg, N. B. (1988). An investigation of differential prediction with the WISC—R. *Journal of School Psychology, 26*(1), 59-68.

Rodriguez, V. L., Prewitt D., & Joseph O. (1990). Correlations among GPA and scores on the Spanish version of WISC—R and the Woodcock-Johnson Achievement subtests for 10- to 12-year-old Puerto Rican children. *Psychological Reports, 66*(2), 563-566).

Rosenthal, R., & Jacobson, L. (1968). *Pygmalion in the classroom: Teacher expectations and pupils' intellectual development.* New York: Holt, Rinehart & Wilson.

Ross, M. B. & Salvia, J. (1975). Attractiveness as a biasing factor in teacher judgments. *American Journal of Mental Deficiency, 80*(1), 96-98.

Ross, S. I. & Jackson, J. M. (1991). Teachers' expectations for Black males' and Black females' academic achievement. *Personality and Social Psychology Bulletin, 17,* 78-82.

Schaefer, B. & McDermott P. (1999). Learning behavior and intelligence as explanations for children's scholastic achievement. *Journal of School Psychology, 37,* 299-311.

Sparacino, J., & Hansell, J. (1979). Physical attractiveness and academic performance: Beauty is not always talent. *Journal of Personality, 49*(3), 449-469.

Sternberg, R. J. (1996). What Should We Ask About Intelligence *The American Scholar, 65*(2), 205-217

Weinstein, R. S. (1993). Children's knowledge of differential treatment in school: Implications for motivation. In T. M. Tomlinson (Ed.), *Motivating students to learn: Overcoming barriers to high achievement* (pp. 197-224). Berkeley, CA: McCutchan Publishing.)

Wentzel, K. (1993). Does being good make the grade? Social behavior and academic competence in middle school. *Journal of Educational Psychology, 85*, 357-364.

Yarborough, B. H. & Johnson, R. A. (1980). A six-year study of sex differences in intellectual functioning, reading/language arts, achievement and affective development. *Journal of Psychology, 106*, 55-61.

TONY BASTICK

CHAPTER 5

EL COLECTIVO TONGUAS: THE DEVELOPMENT OF A BILINGUAL, UNIVERSITY-LEVEL CREATIVE WRITING AND PERFORMANCE POETRY EXTRACURRICULAR PROGRAM IN THE PUERTO RICAN CONTEXT

LORETTA COLLINS

ABSTRACT

Monolingual, bilingual, and interlingual creative writing instruction in Puerto Rico is impacted by the politically-charged language debates. The University of Puerto Rico bilingual student creative writing and performance collective, **Tonguas**, has conducted extracurricular activities and initiated changes in the Humanities Faculty English Department creative writing curriculum, in order to motivate students experiencing a myriad of reactions to the language issue and working with varying Spanish/ English competencies. **Tonguas** has staged "slams" and street theater, conducted workshops with Caribbean writers, published a student-edited journal, and organized a performance Ensemble. Creative writing pedagogy should integrate extracurricular activities and formal instruction in an inclusive manner that addresses the range of language choices, artistic influences, and life histories of developing writers in Puerto Rico.

View #1: El Café Pub, El centro estudiantil, Universidad de Puerto Rico, Recinto de Río Piedras, early evening. Students begin to arrive, jockey to play salsa, merengue, pop rock, and reggae songs from the jukebox, and nervously look over their notebooks again before the "slam" begins.

View #2: Mid-week, noon. Estudios Generales building. A small troupe— costumed in khaki, trench coats, El Zorro masks, Ricky Martin pants, or tropical shirts— raises their hands in the air, wrists connected overhead to mime the defiant poses of those arrested protesters in Puerto Rico's small sister island, Vieques, where US military maneuvers practice. As a large curious audience gathers, the street theatre choreopoem *La Bomba Viequense* begins.

View #3: The student editorial board makes its final selections from submissions that show traces of influence from Puerto Rican, Spanish, and Latin American literature, poesía de "spoken word" by Nuyoricans, the Harlem Renaissance and Black Arts Movement of North America, The Last Poets, the Beats, hip-hop, jazz, blues, calypso, slam poetry, and regional writers, such as Kamau Brathwaite, Victor Hernández Cruz, and Edwidge Danticat. Students, a faculty advisor, and a graduate teaching assistant work together on the editing and layout processes of the first issue of *Tonguas,* the University of Puerto Rico's new bilingual "revista de artes literarias y expresión estudiantil."

View #4: Classroom. Three days after spring finals have ended. Forty undergraduates, graduate students, and professors have postponed their summer break. Nuyorican poet Willie Perdomo opens the workshop by reading, with some difficulty, one of his poems translated into Spanish by Puerto Rican writer and critic Mayra Santos-Febres.[1] His poems take us from los barrios of New York to the marketplace of Brixton, London, and Piccadilly Circus, where he romanced a woman whose "Spanish/ was good, too/.... She danced salsa/ better than me/ I called her *mami*/ by mistake/ even though she told me/ that she ain't into that/ *papi* thing/ you know/ that *aye papi si papi/ si papi tuyo papi toito."* Our assigned scenario: Perdomo gives us few hours to live and ten minutes to write missives. In Spanish, English, and mezclas de lenguas, we write and then perform urgent, angry, and loving poems to nuestras familias and el sociedad.

View #5: Although a few creative writing courses have been offered in the General Studies Faculty, the main campus of the island's premier university does not offer a creative writing program in its Humanities Faculty Spanish Department. During the last ten years, no creative writing classes have been taught in Spanish (Santos-Febres, 2002).[2] On the governmental level, the "presencia del inglés en Puerto Rico" continues to provoke a "conflictiva y emotiva" debate regarding "la relación entre inglés y la lengua vernácular de la abrumadora mayoría de los puertorriqueños: el español" (Torres González, 2002, p.1). Modes of cultural and linguistic nationalism play a role in larger clashes of identity, sovereignty, economic development, and partisan politics in a "free associated state" of the United States, Puerto Rico— still a colonial entity decades after decolonization or departmentalization of many other Caribbean islands. The UPR, Río Piedras, Humanities Faculty English Department begins to develop a proposal for an undergraduate creative writing certificate program and broadens the Master's degree program to include a creative thesis option.

View #6: The University of Puerto Rico, Cayey campus, in green mountainous country. Evening. El Museo Río López Martínez divided into gallery spaces of artworks that signify Puerto Rican's postmodern complexity. St. Lucian poet Kendel Hippolyte, invited by Professor David Lizardi for UPR, Cayey's "English Week," creates an intimacy with the audience and enacts his poems of protest and tribute.[3] The Tonguas Ensemble, seven young poets and a musician (ages 15 to 28) from UPR, Río Piedras, who have spent several rehearsals together and an afternoon of reasoning with Hippolyte, move around the gallery spaces, chanting, hip-hopping, and wailing out their social and personal poems and songs that travel a Spanish-English continuum. Their unity and energy as a group draws upon the contradictions that individuals bring with them from their varied reading, performing, intellectual, and life experiences in New York, New Jersey, California, Alabama, Nebraska, Texas, Iowa, Nicaragua, the Dominican Republic, and Puerto Rico.

> We cry our cry of poetry. Our boats are open, and we sail them for everyone (Glissant, 1997, p. 9).

> The driving force has been to rekindle the word and the meaning of words. The effort has been to diversify, to run over mass advertising's dissipation and abuse of language, and to rescue language from the deadening political "isms" that have enveloped it (Algarín, 1994, p. 9).

"Tonguas," a name generated by a screenplay writing student in la Universidad de Puerto Rico, Recinto de Río Piedras,[4] Humanities Faculty English Department, and enthusiastically adopted by a exponentially growing collective of creative writers and performers, signifies the inclusive nature of the group's activities, "idiomas," and aesthetics.[5] As Glissant (1997) defines the poetics of relation, we have sought to devise a "poetics that is latent, open, multilingual in intention, directly in contact with everything possible" (p. 32). Foregrounding the creative continuum of Spanish to English available as resources for expression and experimentation by the young literary artist in Puerto Rico, "Tonguas," of course, combines "tongues" and "lenguas." The Tonguas collective has staged poetry slams and a street theatre choreopoem, launched a student bilingual creative writing journal, and organized the Tonguas Ensemble. For three years, I have served as faculty advisor for Tonguas and its various projects, an instructor of creative writing courses in English, a professor of Anglophone Caribbean literary studies, and a general fan of youth culture. In these capacities, I have attempted to coordinate Tonguas extracurricular activities with formal classroom instruction in order to provide a spectrum of learning and performance settings that most appropriately matches the diverse range of needs, interests, and language choices/dilemmas that young creative writers in Puerto Rico have revealed in our class discussions, rehearsals, and personal interviews. This chapter will document the development of Tonguas and argue in favor of integrating bilingual extracurricular activities and monolingual (Spanish or English) or interlingual classroom instruction for creative writing students in the Puerto Rican context.

ENGLISH/ESPANGLISH CREATIVE WRITING INSTRUCTION IN THE PUERTO RICAN CONTEXT: THE LANGUAGE ISSUE

In Negrón-Mutaner's critique (1997) of the popular and legislative debates regarding language policy and the historical presence of English as a colonial imposition or diluter of the mother tongue,[6] she claimed that Puerto Ricans who "have been raised bilingual in Puerto Rico or the United States" have sometimes been insultingly portrayed as "a race of *tartamudos [stutterers]*, unable to communicate either in English or Spanish (p. 270).[7] In various ways, many Puerto Rican students drawn to creative writing in English or espanglish/Spanglish[8] feel the impact of this kind of discourse. Some students experience what creole linguist Aceto (1998) has called "the specific tugs and pulls of the dynamic, with its own political and educational complexities, between two languages, varieties of American English and Puerto Rican Spanish" (p. 24). The metaphor of the tug-of-war might imply languages placed either in a conflictive binary opposition or an uneasy continuum. Yet, the students have reported varying attitudes and positions in relation to the language issue and the local impact of US cultural/commercial production.

Although they might be acquainted with several island musical forms, few undergraduate students have extensive knowledge of languages, history, or literary arts in the Caribbean region, other than those of Cuba, the Dominican Republic, and Haiti. In this context, a creative writing educator who adheres to the concept of Caribbean language continuum as invaluable expressive medium is challenged to organize extracurricular activities, curriculum, textual materials, and teaching strategies that bring Spanish-dominant, bilingual, and English-dominant students in productive contact, while encouraging regional artistic contact, as well. Tonguas, then, has created multiple extracurricular and academic opportunities for developing writers who choose for varying reasons to write and perform in a collaborative setting with others who compose exclusively or bilingually in registers of Spanish, English, or a combination.[9] The students who participate in Tonguas are neither tongue-tied nor stutterers, but sharp-tongued crafters of language. They attempt to study texts, respond to their own diverse histories, and use as models a variety of poetic and musical traditions from local, regional, and international zones of Spanish, English, (and French) literatures. How does one construct an English Department creative writing program and a bilingual extracurricular organization that accommodate students experiencing a myriad of reactions to the language debate and working with varying competencies in Spanish and English language? Tonguas has served the function of enabling participants to articulate this pedagogical quandary and propose multiple solutions.

The educational challenge is not to de-politicize issues of language, identity, or society, at all, but rather to emphasize the possibilities of deploying fresh, poetic language and forms to suit a literary endeavor. Although Tonguas has been shaped by faculty and students as a liberating forum, it also has provided occasions for students to discuss frankly how the public sphere affects them as developing artists. Tonguas participants have acknowledged in their poems and testimonials the methods by which English has been an imposed and contested colonial language; a language of literature; a "consumed" language of US advertising, shopping mall culture, cable television, films, books, popular music, and "underground" rap or dancehall; a translocalized language carried by migrating Puerto Ricans on "La guagua aérea" (Sánchez; 1985);[10] a language of returning Puerto Ricans raised or educated off-island; a language bilingual Puerto Ricans naturally and pleasurably use during daily conversations with friends; a language that allows writers either a sense of "distance" from their lived experiences, or as a few Tonguas members have noted, a flexibility, or escape from what they perceive as the formality of Spanish literary forms and canons; a Caribbean regional language that enables artistic exchange with neighboring islands; and a language of satire or protest to be turned against US hegemony and militarism.

However, at times, first language Spanish and fluently bilingual creative writing students have an ambivalent or problematic relationship with the mother tongue and Spanish literary models, as well. Students have, reportedly, experienced intimidation by the way that Spanish, Latin American, and Puerto Rican literary canons are introduced. "How is an eleven year old going to relate to Cervantes?" as Tonguas participant Lynette Cintrón remarked during a conversation about her early alienation from the literature of Spain. Tatiana González Pérez has described her fear of writing in Spanish, which she associates with "rules" and literary standards of correctness and form beyond her reach. "If you can't rise up to the excellence of a Federico García Lorca, then that's it." Literature courses in Spanish, at least through high school, "never teach you about what's cooking right now." Some students negotiate the language issues with relative ease. Yet, the creative writing instructor does become aware of the "mined" linguistic and literary terrain that some of the developing writers must traverse.

Tonguas was conceived three years ago out of coursework (an undergraduate course titled "Literature,

Orality, and Performance") and a series of extracurricular "slams." Originally intended as a means to generate enthusiasm for written literature, the spoken word, linguistic virtuosity, and the embodied poem, slams were designed to be as open, non-judgmental, multilingual, and supportive as possible. The slams provided a site where students could freely share works hidden in their notebooks, form a community, and untie their tongues. English-dominant students raised in the US, exchange students, or students from other islands, who might feel less comfortable sharing their works at local events hosted and performed in Spanish, would also have an expressive venue in Tonguas. Although some participants might not fully comprehend the meanings of works performed exclusively in English or Spanish, the Tonguas gatherings have been, for the most part, characterized by a willingness to supportively hear literary efforts presented and work against whatever language barriers exist for those who are not comfortably bilingual.

We began with the premise that "in Caribbean culture the popular is always already embedded in the formal, the oral in the scribal" (Fiet, 1999, p. vii). We embraced forms of orature and music—youth cultural expressions such as hip-hop and graffiti—along with dub or slam poetry and more traditional literary efforts. However, the goal, from the beginning, was also to draw attention to precisely deployed language (Spanish, English, or Espanglish) and lay a foundation for greater critical acumen concerning literary craft. The English department now plans to extend its creative writing offerings at both the undergraduate and graduate level.[11] Although still in the early stages of development (having attracted over three hundred students to its extracurricular experiments), Tonguas may serve as an informal pilot-project for reconceptualizing creative writing curriculum to include bilingual courses conducted in the various modalities of Spanish and English used by developing writers.

In Our Own Voices/ En nuestras proprias voces: Extracurricular Bilingual Activities that Engage Student Creative Writers with the Larger Public Sphere[12]

Prior to the development of Tonguas, University of Puerto Rico students certainly had exposure to poets such as Pedro Pietri, Victor Hernández Cruz, and other Nuyorican writers. Guest writers from other Caribbean islands have visited the University. Cafés and bookstores have offered readings and open microphones. Various theatrical groups have dramatized poetry or utilized it in progressive performance pieces. For instance, the Yerbabruja collective has created sketches based on the poetry of José María Lima, Joserramón "Che" Meléndes, Rafael Acevedo, and Aurelio Lima" (Espada, 1997, p. 26). The English Department's Lowell Fiet directed a student mobile theater troupe that staged poems by Pedro Pietri. The Honors Program also has regularly published an annual collection of poetry, fiction, and essays by honor students. An anthology of poetry, Alma Universitaria (2000), featured student poetry. What sets Tonguas apart as a University of Puerto Rico endeavor is its bilingual directive, its creation of multiple activities suited to students' differing interests and skills, its emphasis on the performance and publishing of original student work, and its connection to coursework for those students who want to study creative writing techniques in English.

How did the collective develop, and what have been its pedagogical imperatives? In spring 2000, I taught the undergraduate course "Literature, Orality, and Performance." In this course, students encountered literature that incorporates elements of oral traditions (secular and religious folk music, dance, story-telling, masquerade), popular music (blues, jazz, rap, dancehall, reggae, salsa), and experimental performance techniques. From US poetry and theatre traditions, we selected movements and artists that had demonstrated the resilience of the English language as a medium of artistic expression and social critique, drawing poems from The Harlem Renaissance, The Last Poets' Jazzoetry, The Black Arts Movement, The Beats, the Chicano El teatro campesino (Luis Váldez), The Nuyorican Poets Cafe, Slam poetry, and Rap. From South Africa, we studied performance poets Mzwakhe Mbuli and Alfred Qabula, and from West Africa, the playwright of ritual theatre, Werewere Liking. From the Caribbean region and its diasporas, we studied texts and recordings of dub poetry and poets influenced by forms of orature or music.[13] The course had four primary goals: to introduce students to a dynamic way of approaching literature and performance texts; to encourage students to "interpret" and perform literature for an audience; to give students the chance to generate original performance pieces inspired by the works we examined and local forms of traditional/ popular expression; and to produce a public performance that would address important social issues in Puerto Rico.

Influenced by the poetry and performance style of the Harlem poetry group The Last Poets, English major Lorilee Cabrera Liberato composed her own performance poem about the protests against the US military practice in Puerto Rico's sister island, Vieques. "When Vieques is Free" was modeled after Abiodun Oyewole's "When the Revolution Comes." By studying The Last Poets, whose shifting members have included African American poets and Puerto Rican Felipe Luciano, students learned not only about earlier collaborations between Puerto Rican performance poets and salsa musicians during the late sixties to early seventies— the era of the Young Lords Party (the Puerto Rican youth movement in New York)—, but also examined links between Puerto Rican and other expressive cultures of the diaspora.[14] Responding to Cabrera Liberato's effort, Mariangie Ramos, a biology student and environmentalist, drafted a performance poem about the ecological destruction of "mogotes," hill-like land structures that serve as natural habitats for many species, in danger of being eliminated by the construction of large shopping malls. Around these two poems, the class built a performance piece that combined original poetry composed by students with dub poems by British-Jamaican Benjamin Zephaniah, the Puerto Rican Christmas season traditional song "Bomba" (in which participants sing a chorus and take turns improvising quatrains)[15], bomba dancing, mime, minimal costuming, and audience interaction (guerrilla street theatre tactics) in order to examine the environmental and societal impact of the US military presence in Vieques and the "cultural imperialism" of shopping malls. They presented the piece La Bomba Viequense as described above (View #2). During the period of preparation, we also staged three slams announced by posted flyers and attended by a small audience of student and community participants (25). Raul "Gorras" Morris, a dynamic bilingual performance poet and director of "lenguas elasticas," Mayra Santos-Febres, and Dannabang Kuwabong, a Ghanian poet and professor, appeared as guests at these slams.[16] Tonguas participants also performed during the Caribbean 2000 symposium organized annually by Professor Lowell Fiet, where they shared the stage with Jamaican poet Lorna Goodison. Contact with these established writers inspired the student collective and gave them an immediate sense of some of the artistic "vectors" connecting Puerto Ricans with African, Caribbean, and Caribbean diaspora writers. From these experiences, Tonguas established the important precedent of taking literature from the classroom to the public setting, where students must become committed to conveying with an appropriate zeal and urgency their creative works. Tonguas activities also promoted students' contact with established regional "living" writers. The student writers were, thereby, given a real public audience and a sense of larger writing communities in which they could take part.

POESÍA PARA EL PUEBLO/ OPEN-MICROPHONE SLAMS: GENERATING STUDENT "AUTHORITY" IN EXTRACURRICULAR ACTIVITIES

Charged by the experience of performing together, the collective continued to plan "slams" during the second year. Participation for each event has grown steadily since the first semester, from 25, to 40 the second year, to around 70 this year (2002). One of the optional texts for the Literature, Orality, and Performance course was June Jordan's Poetry for the People: A Revolutionary Blueprint (1995) which documented poet June Jordan's effort to engage young writers, make connections between university poets and the larger community, and promote social agency and intercultural collaboration in the program of "Poetry for the People" at University of California, Berkeley (early to mid-1990s). Although I was not certain that I was "up to" the daunting effort of organizing the hydra-headed project that Jordan had launched in the California Bay area, or that I was even the right person to be doing so (since I was not part of the Puerto Rican community of writers, I had defected to the camp of scholars rather than that of creative writers during my doctoral work, and my Spanish was— as Tonguas member Raquel Salas-Rivera says of her own Spanish—"in-progress"), I still wanted to create some kind of space that would give back to students, in some limited way, what I had received from extracurricular poetry activities during my undergraduate education. Moreover, I was aware of the dynamic performance poetry collectives of other islands, such as the Jamaica School of Drama's "Poets in Unity." I was encouraged by the moderately successful bilingual "slams," amazed by the seeming lack of formal creative writing instruction in Spanish at the major university of the island, and wishful that students might have a community of established and student writers to socialize with, as I had in the classrooms, art centers, and bars of my Fresno, California bilingual literary beginnings.

Students were beginning to stop me in the halls to ask when we would have the next slam or show me poems drafted in notebooks. At UC Berkeley, Jordan developed a viable solution to her desire to organize a mass poetry movement on-campus without exhausting her own reserves. She trained student teachers who then conducted workshops with other students. Although Tonguas had not developed to that degree yet, I encouraged students to take initiative, which they did by creating an e-mail list, a webpage, and calling for slams. This shifting of responsibility established an important sense of "ownership" for the students. Tonguas participants undergraduate students Lorilee Cabrera Liberato and Nina Dimarie Valedón Santiago penned a description of Tonguas that appears in the preface of the first issue of Tonguas, the student writing journal. They described it as an inclusive association for student creative expression that intends to forge links between what Ramas (1984) has called "la cuidad letrada" and "la cuidad real": "The writers and performers in the Tonguas Collective experiment with mezclas de diferentes lenguas, diferentes pensamientos, diferentes estilos y diferentes géneros artisticos. Tonguas is la nueva generación de creative people that come from los salones, los pasillos, el centro and from cualquier departamento de la UPR, Recinto de Río Piedras. Tonguas is our forum for artistic expression" (2001, p. i). Students, as well as faculty members, became motivated agents responsible for mediating the connection between academic settings and the public realm. A bilingual art, praticed beyond the bounds of the classroom, became a relevant means of intervening culturally and socially in the larger public sphere.

Denouncing the mediocrity of slam poetry and the competitive atmosphere of slams, Medina (2001) has described the "gladiator-like scenarios where they compete for chump change and prestige" (p.xix). Medina preferred the term "Jam" to describe a "democratic orchestration of voices and visions, poets of all ages, ethnicities, and geographic locations coming together to create a dialogue and to jam— not slam" (p. xxi). Tonguas happenings correspond more closely to Medina's concept of jamming, but we have kept the name because of its "cool" factor and its association with the film SLAM, featuring poet and actor Saul Stacey Williams. However, Tonguas slams are never competitive, although a fair amount of cheering and clapping goes on. The event is as non-judgmental as possible. Professors attend, but restrict their participation to cheering and occasionally offering a poem of their own. As graduate student, guitarist, singer, and member of the Tonguas Ensemble Anaïs Alonso told me, she has appreciated the Tonguas slams because they have "given [her] a place to develop confidence in performing in front of an audience." Slams have attracted an eclectic group of poets, musicians, rappers, and balladeers who freely perform either in Spanish, English, or innovative code-switching.

STIMULATING THE CROSS-CULTURAL IMAGINATION[17] : ARTISTIC EXCHANGE BETWEEN PUERTO RICAN STUDENT WRITERS AND ESTABLISHED REGIONAL WRITERS IN A WORKSHOP SETTING

Slams opened up space for interlingual experimentation and student expression in a non-graded, non-threatening milieu; however, except for the informal feedback students received after a slam, these events did not provide students with essential critical appraisal and suggestions for revising their poetry. Desiring to impress students with the trends of local and regional literary production, faculty and students organized three workshops with visiting writers. The intensive workshop setting gave students a chance to receive individualized critique on their writing and performances from Caribbean writers who could serve as role models. Although Tonguas members have attended readings by Sherezada "Chiqui" Vicioso (Dominican Republic), Lorna Goodison (Jamaica), and Pedro Pietri (Puerto Rico-US), three poets— Willie Perdomo (Puerto Rico-US), Kendel Hippolyte (St. Lucia), and Victor Hernández Cruz (Puerto Rico- US), — have conducted workshops with Tonguas. Perdomo gave Tonguas a creative writing workshop (as described above, View # 4), emphasizing the importance of reading poets that serve as models or "mentors," such as his own, Langston Hughes. He turned student attention from the dramatic elements of performance to how their work maintained a poetic integrity on the page. More recently, Hippolyte conducted a workshop with the Tonguas Ensemble. Rather than workshop their written work, he listened to each poet perform and offered suggestions about audience engagement, pacing (allowing the audience time to absorb lines and images), movement, facial composure, vocal timbre and volume, and emotional intensity. The workshop required some translation, which students cooperatively engaged in. Often influenced by the speed of hip-hop or the verbal dexterity and swiftness of slam poetry, they seemed to learn about nuanced performance techniques, enjoying Hippolyte's poetry reading— the cadences, the use of a continuum of language, and the Caribbean contexts of his poems. Hernández Cruz emphasized the importance of reading widely and revising one's poetry painstakingly.

LORETTA COLLINS

THE JOURNAL/ LA REVISTA: THE ACQUISITION OF EDITORIAL SKILLS AND LITERARY STANDARDS THROUGH THE EXTRACURRICULAR PROJECT OF A STUDENT BILINGUAL ARTS JOURNAL

Slams allowed students to hear a sampling of writing produced by their peers and community authors. However, I was concerned about how students might improve without opportunities for structured feedback, workshopping, and attention to literary craft. I also wanted to maintain the pedagogical paradigm of Tonguas as an inclusive bilingual organization, supporting use of the full range of languages available to developing writers in the Puerto Rican/ Caribbean context. The bilingual literary journal, the next step, provided students with a readership. The creation of a student editorial board responsible for selecting publishable works gave students predisposed to critical reading rather than performance an instrumental role to play in determining the aesthetic terrain of Tonguas. Striving for excellence, we also wanted the journal to reflect the energy of the slams and youth "vibes," rather than the formality of other publications that we located both on and off-campus. A sixteen-year old graffitero, "Sir Exor One," provided artwork and cover. Another student volunteered her sister's layout and design skills. A teaching assistant, graduate student Olga M. Auger Vega, added her computer skills and layout expertise. One year later, after more work than we could have anticipated, the 100-page journal was released (d. 2001, released 2002), to a fiesta "launch." Those students who have worked as journal editors, designers, and artists obviously had the opportunity to survey student writing and develop a working set of critical standards in a collaborative bilingual setting. The integration of the extracurricular activities and journal with coursework provided the authors and editors with monolingual/ bilingual /scribal, and academic/ popular contexts in which to draft, revise, perform, and stabilize literary works on the page.

RECONCEPTUALIZATION OF CREATIVE WRITING CURRICULUM: ADDING THE NECESSARY FORMAL DIMENSION OF COURSE WORK IN SPANISH AND ENGLISH TO BILINGUAL EXTRACURRICULAR ACTIVITIES

The faculty and student enthusiasm generated by Tonguas has led to a commitment by the English Department to regularly offer a selection of creative writing courses and develop a certificate program, which will allow students to receive formal recognition for their creative writing coursework after they have completed five courses. Many Tonguas participants have enrolled in the screenplay writing, poetry, and fiction courses offered during the last two years. The expanded selection of creative writing courses adds the needed dimension of instruction in rudimentary technical craft and revision/ editing processes. Courses taught in the English Department and the forthcoming narrative class offered by the Spanish Department will increase students' understanding of the rigors and creative possibilities of literary forms in the respective languages. Moreover, students have taken courses in contemporary poetry,

Caribbean, US Puerto Rican, African American, or American literature, which I recommend to students in the creative writing classes. In these courses, they study a wide range of oral and scribal literatures that may provide (and have provided) contemporary models for their own writing. The Tonguas teaching assistant, on a limited basis, has worked individually with some writers contributing works in Spanish, but we still perceive the obvious need for formal writing instruction for students writing in Spanish. Extracurricular activities and courses need to be developed for students interested in advanced work on collaborative interlingual creative writing and performance projects. The Tonguas Ensemble, the most recent development, was devised to provide an experimental, extracurricular workshop for advanced students interested in such collaboration.

THE TONGUAS ENSEMBLE: AN EXTRACURRICULAR MODEL FOR INTERDISCIPLINARY, INTERLINGUAL WORKSHOPS FOR ADVANCED CREATING WRITING STUDENTS WITH SPECIALIZED INTERESTS

After three years of experimentation and community-building in literary performances and creative writing coursework, Tonguas had, more or less, reached a certain stage of maturity. Likewise, several writers and performers had distinguished themselves significantly enough that it seemed like the right time to gather together a select group of promising writers, performers, and composer-singers into a tightly knit ensemble that could begin working on a coherent collaborative fusion of their various individual works. What I had in mind, as I invited selected poets to participate was Jamaican-Canadian ahdri zhina mandiela's "dub theatre" piece Dark Diaspora in Dub (1991) comprised of twenty-one poems choreographed with a variety of dance vocabularies in traditional, pop, and contemporary modes and incorporating African drumming, the blues, jazz, calypso, soca, steel pan, and reggae dub into the musical mix.[18] Jean "Binta" Breeze's book launch of On the Edge of an Island (1997) in Jamaica served as another possible model, as it combined Breeze's prose monologues and performances of her poems with mime, song, and movement provided by, among others, entertainers Winston Bell and Blacka Ellis. In November of 2001, I had also attended a poetry ensemble performance featuring Kendel Hippolyte, Travis Weekes, and other poets and singers in St. Lucia. Although I was working with young poets, I wanted to use the ensemble work of these established poets from other islands as models for our process and productions. This would, in turn, serve as a means of stressing the Caribbean aesthetics and artistry with which we could beneficially develop a "poetics of relation." At their El Museo Río López Martínez performance with Hippolyte, the Ensemble dynamically performed loosely linked poems in English, Spanish, and mixtures, which addressed Fatherland—Puerto Rico's affinity and shared history with the Dominican Republic, discrimination against Dominicanos in Puerto Rico—, and Motherland— the sexism of the "art of piropos" (flirtatious male banter), social decadence in the urban PR, sexism in billboard advertising, historical myth-making, and domestic relations.

As the following description of the individual artists comprising the Tonguas Ensemble will suggest, the diversity of life experiences, locations of origin and migration, and language competencies/ preferences in just this small selection of creative writers necessitates a very flexible multilingual, inclusive pedagogical approach to creative writing instruction in the Puerto Rican context. The traditional creative writing classroom, conducted in English or Spanish, alone, would not sufficiently serve the advanced development of these writers according to their self-definitions as nascent word-crafters. Lynette Cintrón, 28, has taken English creative writing courses in fiction and poetry in the English Department. Alienated at an early age from the Spanish literary canon, her creative writing language choice is ("and has always been") English. Comparative Literature student from the Spanish Department, Tatiana González Pérez, 19, has taken English creative writing courses in fiction and poetry, as well as Caribbean literature. González Pérez has an inclusive attitude about languages and loves to experiment with combining English and Spanish in stories and poems. She would like to write in Spanish, as well, but she says that the university "doesn't offer [her] the tools." Master's student in History, Luis Ángel Díaz, 26, began performing— exclusively in Spanish— as an MC/poet. He, with another MC and a beat box operator, formed the popular group Conciencia poética. However, he also reads the Russian Futurists and French Symbolists. A student of Psychology, Francisco Stanley Rosario Díaz, 20, believes that his poems should have a social message for his audience. He composes and performs in Spanish. Although he feels his Puerto Rican-ness, Rosario Díaz moved to Puerto Rico twelve years ago from the Dominican Republic. Some of his poems feature social commentary about the prejudicial way that Puerto Ricans, the government, and social agencies regard people from the Dominican Republic. A recent arrival in Puerto Rico, Paola Moreno, 20, was born in Nicaragua, where she lived with her grandparents until joining her mother in Iowa (US) during her early teens. Although she was more recently drawn into poetry composition and performance through hip-hop, MC-style, and slam poetry of Saul Stacey Williams and Sarah Jones, she also attributes her love for poetry and the spoken word to her cultural and familial experiences in Nicaragua. The daughter of Puerto Rican parents, Raquel Salas-Rivera, 15, moved to Puerto Rico two years ago after living in various locations in the United States, California, Nebraska, Alabama, and Texas. Most of her poems are written and performed primarily in English with Puerto Rican inflections. Anaïs Alonso, 24, spent her early years in Jersey City and returned to Puerto Rico to live with her father when she was twelve years old. She composes songs and sings in English.

LORETTA COLLINS

RECENT DEVELOPMENTS IN EL COLECTIVO TONGUAS AND CREATIVE WRITING COURSES: MAKING ANTI-HEGEMONIC SPACES FOR STUDENT WRITING AND CULTURAL WORK ON GENDER AND SEXUALITY ISSUES

In the seven months since the preceding sections of this essay were first drafted, El Colectivo Tonguas has continued to participate in extracurricular and curricular developments at the University of Puerto Rico main campus. However, the collective has undergone transformations that push students and faculty beyond our continuing explorations of the politics of bilingual creative writing pedagogy, as well.[19] As more experimental extracurricular spaces open for bilingual student creative expression, I notice changes both in performance material and in written classroom work. Students now give a higher degree of attention to performance models and Spanish/English language choices. Their own styles are enhanced by "borrowings" from literary and performance modes made available to them in coursework.[20] However, their work is not simply imitative. Student writers and performance artists also confront a wider array of difficult social themes, with greater depth, complexity, and artistic control, than I had seen in Tonguas "slams" previously. This can particularly be seen in works that provocatively challenge hegemonic gender and sexuality formations.

For instance, the Tonguas ensemble that performed with Kendel Hippolyte later imploded during a "gender war" over the issue of the legalization of prostitution. The men in the group continue to perform together, while some of the women plan an independent group "Cultural Guerilla War Babes." Influenced by the text and video of Guillermo Gómez-Peña's Border Brujo— a "postmodern" performance that examines Mexican/ US border relations, bicultural and bilingual identity, stereotypes, and xenophobia—, one of these women, Lynette Cintrón, is beginning to create a bilingual performance piece that blends poetry, ritual ceremony, and feminist-cultural critique of everything from the caricature of the Aunt Jemima-like Mama Inés of Puerto Rican Yaucono coffee advertisement and stereotypical representations of the Latina woman in Hollywood films and television, to the current policies of the Bush administration in the US.[21] Two of the women from the disbanded ensemble enrolled in the Literature, Orality, and Performance course. Two other students in the course had taken several creative writing courses and performed with Tonguas previously. As veterans of the poetry, fiction, and screenplay writing courses— and as women politicized by the debates arising within the ensemble—, the three women of this set served as class leaders and informal tutors, contributing to an atmosphere that encouraged women students to create autobiographical performances and critiques of societal pressure derived from body image and role expectations (bulimia, mothering, and sexualized womanhood) and economics (poverty or prostitution).

The more experienced students, thus, participated in the reconceptualization of the course that originally launched the extracurricular collective three years ago. My awareness of the kind of pieces recently written by these students led me to include in the syllabus a sampling of works that I knew would be enabling for them, works and movements that deploy Spanish-English codes switching and Espanglish— US Puerto Rican poetry, el teatro campesino, and Gómez-Peòa's performance art—, critical essays on Latina feminist performance art, and woman-centered plays by Chicana Cherríe Moraga. Although the reading and critical writing load was intense for the first two-thirds of the semester, the last third functioned as the student-centered "small, flexible, interactive, and interlingual workshop" that I proposed in the section above.

Tonguas extracurricular events and English department creative writing courses have also, increasingly, served as venues for student expression concerning issues of sexual identity. Gay, lesbian, and bisexual students seem to keep a low-profile on campus.[22] In recent months, the Tonguas open-microphones have provided space for two men who perform poems challenging societal constructions of sexuality. Miguel J. Figueroa's poem "I Want" proclaims, "I want to be free in my island/ Walk around and be invisible like the hetero/ Hold my lover's hand and not get bashed/ ….and if they ask, I'll say/ 'Yes, he's my boyfriend.'" As a student in a poetry writing course and a performer at Tonguas slams, David Caleb Acevedo writes poems in celebration of homosexuality and support of HIV-positive lovers, but he also confronts a brother-in-law's "masculinity" sustained through domestic abuse. Marcos Nieves's screenplay, written in the "Reading and Writing the

Screenplay" course, explores the story of a young man who finally commits suicide because his Christian mother rejects his homosexuality.

Tonguas has created a democratic community of writers, divided at times by issues of language, politics, ideology, and personal identity but unified by a sense of common artistic endeavor and social engagement. This sense of diverse community and social responsibility then pervades the classroom, where students feel free enough to explore themes that have their own troubled and troubling place in colonialist and national discourses. El Colectivo Tonguas and student participants have suggested and aided curricular reconceptualization and pedagogical changes in English-language creative writing instruction in the Puerto Rican context, and we—the students, faculty, and institution—are all undergoing creative transformation in the process.

DISCUSSION

The extracurricular work that Tonguas has accomplished could be used as a model for reconceptualizing interdisciplinary studies or team-teaching in the expressive arts and literary studies, so that students such as those described above could study creative writing in multiple settings: in the Spanish Department, the English Department, or Interdisciplinary Studies (in an interlingual setting). Tonguas, the slam series, the intensive workshops, the bilingual student creative writing journal, and ensemble work are all still in exploratory stages, as means to generate University student enthusiasm for and increase expertise in literature and performance in the Spanish and English monolingual, bilingual, and interlingual contexts of Puerto Rico. However, the experiences and student testimonials gleaned from these pedagogical improvisations certainly point to the need for a thoughtful design of creative writing curriculum at the University-level.

As poet Hernández Cruz has commented about the political positioning of Puerto Rico: "Because of our political situation as a territory of the United States, one of the last classic colonial holdings by an empire, we are also a people who live within a great cultural clash, a debate between values. This interlude between Anglo-North American and Hispano-Criollo Caribbean keeps all issues of identity intensive throughout the island and within all the Puerto Rican diaspora communities on the U.S. mainland" (1991, p. 9). Den Tandt (1998) traced the connections between issues of language and political sovereignty, citing Severo Colberg's stance on the language issue: "El español es el secreto, el asiento y el corazón de la puertrriqueñidad, su causa eficiente" (Den Tandt, p. 83).[23] From what has organically developed from Tonguas activities, I think that it would be fair to say that Colectivo Tonguas begins with the premise that the mother tongue, el español, is at the heart of Puerto Rican identity. Roughly sixty to seventy percent of Tonguas activities are conducted in Spanish or Spanish-English code-switching. At the same time, the collective has also held Hernández Cruz's statement to be worthy: "Bilingualism is not a limitation when it is in the hands of the writers" (1991, pp. 9-10). A serious limitation that remains is the lack of formal creative writing instruction in Spanish and infrequent student access to Puerto Rican and Caribbean writers of acclaim. The Tonguas collective has "tried out" several extracurricular activities in the effort to create conducive settings— as open and multilingual as possible— where University literary and performance artists of varying standpoints, starting points, and language preferences may develop. Young writers in Puerto Rico have many dimensions— modalidades nuevas— of (local, regional, colonial, translocal, and global) ideas, history, culture, literary canons, languages, musics, and forms of popular media as potential artistic influences. The extracurricular programs of Tonguas (otros espacios/ other spaces) have supplemented formal instruction and initiated curricular changes that might better facilitate the creative writing students in an inclusive Puerto Rican/ Caribbean context.

ENDNOTES

1 Perdomo's poetry has been featured in anthologies Aloud: Voices from the Nuyorican Cafe and Boricuas: Influential Puerto Rican Writing, as well as his collections Where a Nickel Costs a Dime (issued with CD) and Postcards of el barrio, trans. Santos-Febres and Franco. He has also been featured on the CD compilation Flippin' the Script: Rap Meets Poetry and on television in the PBS special Words in Your Face and The United States of Poetry.

2 In response to student requests, a course in narrative writing was taught during the fall 2002 semester by Mayra Santos-Febres.

3 Playwright and poet Kendel Hippolyte's poetry may be found in his several collections, including Birthright (1991), which he performed from on this occasion and Kwame Dawes' collection of reggae poetry Wheel and Come Again.

4 The main campus in the island's capital city.

5 I wish to thank Dr. María Soledad Rodríguez, Chair of the English Department, Facultad de Humanidades, UPR, Recinto de Río Piedras, for her generous support for Tonguas endeavors. I also must thank Prof. Pedro Pérez Osorio, of the English Department, Facultad de Estudios Generales, UPR, Recinto de Río Piedras, and Dr. Dannabang Kuwabong, of the English Department, Facultad de Humanidades, UPR, Recinto de Río Piedras, both of whom have actively participated in Tonguas slams and now serve as faculty advisors for Tonguas. Thanks are extended, likewise, to UPR political science student Nina Dimarie Valedón Santiago, current President of the Tonguas student organization, for her energetic assistance with organizing and promoting slams.

6 Also see Reyes Benítez (1998). The author defends the 1991 "La Ley del Idioma," which established Spanish as the sole official language (a measure that was repealed by former Governor Pedro Rosselló in 1993, in favor of Spanish and English as dual official languages), by arguing that bilingual education was responsible for "diluyendo y debilitando neustra lengua maternal, que es el español" (147). For the most recent newspaper report on the debate

regarding official language status, see Soledad Calero, (2002, April 12, p. 8).

7 Maldonado Denis (1990, p.28): "La ambiguedad linguística, como bien señala el autro recién citado, podria terminar convirtiéndonos en una sociedad tarada por una terrible tartamudez idiomática, por una especie de gaguera colectiva que terminarse sumiéndose en el triste universo de unas generaciones que no hablan ni ecriben con propriedad y corrección ni una lengua ni la otra, y permanecen engomadas ante la pantalla del televisor, viendo y escuchando, en inglés— gracias a la magica del Cable TV— la última canción que les trae quién sabe cual de los últimos intérpretes del rock norteamericano."[Linguistic ambiguity, as the former author so well indicates, could well end up transforming us into a society incapacitated by a terrible linguistic stutttering, by a form of collective tongue-tiedness, which would end up by confounding itself with the sad universe of generations who neither speak nor write with propriety or accuracy Spanish or English, and instead remain stuck to a TV screen, watching and listening to English— thanks to the magic of cable TV— the last hit song of the latest American rock singer.] Cited and translated by Negrón-Mutaner (1997, p. 270)

8 Although the term "Spanglish" has been used to refer to code-switching and linguistical innovations by speakers of Spanish and English in contact, it has also accrued negative connotations. Perdomo appreciatively reclaimed the term as a resource for creative expression by using the alternative term "espanglish" in his poem "The New Boogaloo" (2002).

9 Discussing the "Spanglish specialist," hip-hop artist, Nuyorican poet, or English-dominant Puerto Rican intellectual, Negrón-Mutaner (1997) argues that "[w]ithin these formulations, 'Spanglish' is not a language or a 'dialect' but a resource, a practice of destabilizing and multiplying meanings, a form of articulating hybrid personal and social experiences." Furthermore, "an engagement with some of the cultural production of the so-called stutterers suggests that far from being unilingual, atrophied, or alienated, forms such as rap and graffiti are extremely sophisticate poetic and musical constructs using and understanding language in precise and politically astute ways" (pp. 272, 271).

10 See Agustín Lao (1997, p. 186). Other authors also acknowledge the importance of Luis Rafael Sánchez's seminal essay "La guagua aérea" (1985), which investigated the impact of the continual transit of Puerto Ricans between the island and the United States.

11 The English Department currently offers introductory courses in poetry, fiction, and screenplay writing, as well as journalism. At the Master's level, a poetry workshop and an independent study in fiction have been offered. A creative thesis option has recently been added to the M. A. Program.

12 For a description of the early efforts and extracurricular activities of Tonguas, see Pérez Osorio (2001, November 3).

13 Performance poetry texts studied included works from Allen, Lillian. (1993). Women do this every day. Toronto: Women's Press; Agard, John. (2000). Weblines. Newcastle Upon Tyne: Bloodaxe Books; Brathwaite, Kamau. (1984). History of

the voice: the development of nation language in Anglophone Caribbean poetry. London and Port of Spain: New Beacon Books; Breeze, Jean "Binta." (2000). The arrival of bright eye and other poems. Newcastle Upon Tyne: Bloodaxe Books; Breeze, Jean "Binta." (1997). On the edge of an island. Newcastle Upon Tyne: Bloodaxe Books; Breeze, Jean "Binta." (1992). Spring cleaning. Reading, Berkshire: Virago Poetry; Breeze, Jean "Binta." (1988). Riddim ravings and other poems. Ed. Mervyn Morris. London: Race Today Publications; Cooper, Afua. (Ed.). (1999) Utterances and incantations: women, poetry and dub. Toronto: Sister Vision; mandiela, ahdri zhina (1985). Speshal rikwes. Toronto: Sister Vision; Habekost, Christian. (Ed.). (1986). Dub poetry: 19 poets from England and Jamaica. Neustadt: Publishers Michael Schwinn; Johnson, Linton Kwesi. (1991). Tings and times. Newcastle Upon Tyne: Bloodaxe Books; Johnson, Linton Kwesi. (1980). Ingan is a bitch. London: Race Today Publications; Mutabaruka. (1987). The first poems. Foreword Christian Habekost. Neustadt: Publishers Michael Schwinn; Sissay, Lemn. (Ed.). (1998). The fire people: A collection of contemporary black British poets. Edinburgh: Payback Press; Pearl Springer, Eintou. (2000). Moving into the light. Kingston, Jamaica: Ian Randle; and Zepaniah, Benjamin. (1992). City psalms and other poems. Newcastle Upon Tyne: Bloodaxe Books.

14 As Luis (1997) notes, Luciano recited his poem "Jíbaro/ My Pretty Nigger" "at Sing Sing Prison in a program with Eddie Palmieri; he later recorded it on Palmieri's salsa record album, Eddie Palmieri Recorded Live at Sing Sing with Harlem River Drive, in 1972" (p. 52).

15 An example of the "bomba" structure: "¡Bomba! Los hombres son unos diablos/ así dicen las murjeres,/ pero siempre andan buscando/ a un diablo que sa las lleve." If a participant cannot quickly make-up the quatrain, the group begins to sing "No sabe na,/ so sabe na,/ no sabe na de bomba,/ no sabe na" (Dúa, 1994, p. 1). Of course, the Tonguas street theater piece played with the double-meaning of "Bomba" and "bombs."
16 Morris, Raul "Gorras." (2000). Caminando entre los muertos. Compact disc. San Juan, P.R.: Poeta Boricua Palabra Dicha; Kuwabong, Dannabing. (1999). Echoes from Dusty Rivers. Hamilton, Ontario: Capricornus Enterprises.
17 "Cross Cultural Imagination" is a term often used by Guyanese writer Wilson Harris.
18 See Collins (2001).
19 In the Humanities Faculty, two new creative writing courses have been approved by the curriculum committee of the English Department; the popularity of the narrative writing course offered for the first time by the Spanish Department has spurred an offering of the course again in the Spring 2003 semester; and the Consejo General de Estudiantes has sponsored an organization of Humanities students in their development of a monthly event that brings together musicians, visual artists, drama students, and creative writers. Members of my fall 2002 semester Literature, Orality, and Performance class led off the first "happening" with "Poetry Circus/ Poesía sin osos polares," a performance of bilingual poetry, dance, singing, "paintcan percussion," and artwork.

20 For the poetry circus, some students adopted vocal techniques influenced by Jamaican-Canadian poet ahdri zhina mandiela, bilingual deconstructionist writing and performing techniques of the "Mexterminator," Guillermo Gómez-Peña, or the persona of Nuyorican poet Miguel Piñero.
21 You may remember from the discussion above that previously Ms. Cintrón wrote creatively exclusively in English.
22 The University occasionally hosts events to promote HIV/AIDS awareness, sponsored by El Centro de Investigación y Educación de VIH/SIDA. This center also conducts research on sexuality. Recent publications include R. L. Ramírez, V. L. Garcia-Toro, and I. Cunningham, eds. (2002). Caribbean Masculinities: Working Papers. San Juan, Puerto Rico: CIEVS. Although gay and lesbian cultural activists are vocal in the public sphere of San Juan, the anti-sodomy law Article 103 of the Puerto Rican Penal Code (Código Penal del ELA, 1974) criminalizes same-sex intercourse. Forms of institutional and popular discrimination against homosexuals persist in the predominantly Roman Catholic island.
23 Roughly trans. as "Spanish is the secret, the foundation [seat or base] and the heart of 'la puertrriqueñidad," its main cause of existence." Severo Colberg Ramírez (1990, Sept. 3, p. 27). As cited by Den Tandt (1998, p. 83).

REFERENCES

Aceto, Michael. (1998). Anglophone and Hispanophone languages in contact: language and identity in English-derived Creole speaking communities in Central America. *Caribe 2000/ Caribbean 2000. Segundo Simposio de Caribe 2000: Hablar, Nombrar, Pertenecer,* 23-36.

Algarín, Miguel. (Intro.). (1994). The sidewalk of high art. *Aloud: voices from the Nuyorican Poets Cafe.* Eds. Miguel Algarín and Bob Holman. New York: Henry Holt and Company, Inc.

Alonso, Anais. (2002, April 4). Personal interview.

Cabrera Liberato, Lorilee and Nina Dimarie Valedón Santiago. (2001, Mayo). Prefacio: El Colectivo Tonguas, who are we? *Tonguas: revista de artes literarias y expresión estudiantil* 1:1: i.

Cintrón, Lynette. (2002, April 9). Personal interview.

Collins, Loretta. (2001). Snow on the canefields/ (the de-icing of a Canadian city): Jamaican-Canadian identity and kinetic language in ahdri zhina mandiela's dub theatre. *Sargasso: Concerning Lorna Goodison:* 39-63.

Den Tandt, Catherine. (1998). Puerto Rico y Québec: dos soledades. *Caribe 2000/ Caribbean 2000. Segundo Simposio de Caribe 2000: Hablar, Nombrar, Pertenecer.* 74-86.

Díaz, Luis Ángel. (2002, April 4). Personal interview.

Dúa, Mohammed. (1994). *La mas nueva coleccion de bombas de Puerto Rico: Apología a la bomba de double sentido en Puerto Rico.* rev. ed. Santurce, P.R.: Mohammed Dúa.

Espada, Margarita. (1997). Colectivo Yerbabruja. *Caribe 2000: Definiciones, identidades y culturas regionales y/o nacionales/ Caribbean 2000: Regional and/ or National Definitions, Identities and Cultures. Primer Simposio de*

Caribe 2000: re-Definiciones: Espacio— global/ nacional/ cultural/ personal— caribeño, 150-154. Reprinted from (1996, 26 Abril-2 Mayo). *Claridad*, p. 26.

Fiet, Lowell. (1999). By way of introduction: performance and text in Caribbean literature and art. *Sargasso, Special Issue*, vii-xiii.

Glissant, Édouard. (1997). *Poetics of relation*. Trans. Betsy Wing. Ann Arbor: The University of Michigan Press.

González Pérez, Tatiana. (2002, April 9). Personal interview.

Hernández Cruz, Victor. (1991). *Red beans*. Minneapolis: Coffee House.

Lao, Augustín. (1997). Islands at the crossroads: Puerto Ricannness traveling between the translocal nation and the global city. *Puerto Rican jam: rethinking colonialism and nationalism, essays on culture and politics*. Eds. Frances Negfrón-Muntaner and Ramón Grosfoguel. Minneapolis and London: University of Minnesota Press.

Luis, William. (1997). *Dance between two cultures: Latino Caribbean literature written in the United States*. Nashville and London: Vanderbuilt University Press.

Maldonado Denis, Manuel. (1990, Aug. 21). Con la lengua española. *El Mundo*, p. 28.

Medina, Tony. (Intro.). (2001). *Bum rush the page: a def poetry jam*. Eds. Tony Medina and Louis Reyes Rivera. New York: Three Rivers Press.

Moreno, Paola. (2002, April 4). Personal interview.

Muller, Laren and the Poetry for the People Collective. (Eds.). (1995). *June Jordan's poetry for the people: a revolutionary blueprint*. New York and London: Routledge.

Negrón-Mutaner, Frances. (1997). English only jamás but Spanish only cuidado: language and nationalism in contemporary Puerto Rico. *Puerto Rican jam: rethinking colonialism and nationalism, essays on culture and politics.* Eds. Frances Negrón-Muntaner and Ramón Grosfoguel. Minneapolis and London: University of Minnesota Press.

Otero Garabís, Juan. (2000). *Nación y ritmo: "descargas" desde el Caribe.* San Juan, P.R.: Ediciones Callejón.

Perdomo, Willie. (2002). *Postcards of el barrio.* (bilingual edition). Eds. Marya Santos-Febres and Rafael Franco. San Juan: Isla Negra.

Pérez Osorio, Pedro. (2001, November 3). From page to stage: the infinite possibilities of slam poetry in the classroom. Unpublished paper delivered at College English Association, Caribbean Chapter, conference in Mayagüez, Puerto Rico.

Rama, Angel. (1984). *La cuidad letrada.* Hanover: Ediciones del Norte.

R. L. Ramírez, V. L. Garcia-Toro, and I. Cunningham, eds. (2002). *Caribbean masculinities: working papers.* San Juan, Puerto Rico: CIEVS.

Reyes Benítez, Iris Yolanda. (1998). El español de Puerto Rico: política lingüistica de 1898 a 1997. *Segundo Simposio de Caribe 2000: Hablar, Nombrar, Pertenecer,* 143-153.

Rosario Díaz, Francisco Stanley. (2002, April 4). Personal interview.

Salas-Rivera, Raquel. (2002, April 4). Personal interview.

Santos-Febres, Mayra. (2002, April 18). Personal conversation.

Soledad Calero, María. (2002, April 12). Senate oks report on bill to declare Spanish as P.R.'s official language. *The San Juan Star,* p. 8.

Torres González, Roamé. (2002). *Idioma, bilingüismo y nacionalidad: la presencia del inglés en Puerto Rico*. San Juan, P.R.: Editorial de la Universidad de Puerto Rico.

Adventures in Womanhood- Chapter 1: Nappy Hair
Curlers and Raices: Rolos and Roots

¡Oye Moreno!
¡Oye Morena!
Let's sing a song,
a children's song,
una inocente canción.

"We're going to Kentucky,
We're going to the fair,
to see the Señorita with curlers
in her hair..."

Curlers and rolos!
Rolos and curlers!
Yes!
Those tubos plásticos
you weekly use
to aplacar las pasitas
that cover your head.

You spend many hours
of your life trying.
Yes!
Only trying

because you still haven't done it.
Trying to cover your roots
with alisados,
curlers,
peines calientes,
even *hot irons,*
and many other *métodos
torturantes*
used to conceal,
to hide,
to transform,
and to deform.

But you know what?
Yes!
¡Tú!

¿Sabes tú qué pasa?
Your **roots,**
your **race,**
your **pasitas,**
and **tu abuela**
are survivors.

Sobrevivientes a través del tiempo,
a través del espacio,
a través de la *historia,*
a través de las *generaciones*
y a través de tus *experimentos:*
experimentos blanqueadores,
experimentos purificadores,
experimentos para adelantar la raza
... *worthless experimentos.*

¿Acaso no sabes?
Doing this tú no sólo atacas tus **pasas.**
You fight against your **nose,**
against your **lips,**
against your **accent,**
against your **hips,**
against your **skin,**
and your **rico sabor.**
Sabor a tambo.
Sabor a ritmo.
Sabor a negro.
Sabor a Caribe.
Sabor a África.
Sabor and **Flavor** a raices.
Raices que no se esconden.
Raices que no se aplacan.
Raices that you should be proud to show in any fair,
Either in Kentucky,
in Illinois,
in any of the other states,
or around the world,
anywhere
and everywhere.

Así que...
¡Oye Moreno!
¡Oye Morena!
Leave the rolos,
Deja los curlers
And show your raices
Y enseña tus roots.

— Lorilee Cabrera Liberato, Tonguas participant

EL COLECTIVO TONGUAS

LORETTA COLLINS

PART 2.

ADAPTING TO SCHOOL AND SOCIETY

CHAPTER 6.

Pages 163 - 214

Identity Development of Caribbean Girls in Canadian Schools.

Beverly-Jean Daniel
University of Toronto, Ontario Canada.

CHAPTER 7.

Pages 215 - 248

Caribbean Student Speakers' Education and Experiences in American Schools: A Constant Struggle with Varied Results

Clarissa N. West-White
Florida Memorial College, USA.

PART 2

CHAPTER 8.

Pages 249 - 284
Racism, Resistance and Resilience: The 3Rs of Educating Caribbean Students in a Canadian Context

Brenda McMahon
Department of Theory and Policy Studies in Education, University of Toronto, Canada

and

Denise Armstrong
and Ontario Institute for Studies in Education, University of Toronto, Canada.

CHAPTER 9.

Pages 285 - 316
Dominican Adolescent Immigrants' Experiences with Schooling

Shana R. Grossman
George Mason University, USA.

CHAPTER 6

IDENTITY DEVELOPMENT OF AFRICAN CARIBBEAN GIRLS IN CANADIAN SCHOOLS

BEVERLY-JEAN DANIEL

INTRODUCTION

> Identity is a complicated matter. Everyone has one but rarely are we aware of how we get one.
>
> *Howard Ramos (2001)*

It is 7:45 a.m. on a cold Monday morning. Riding the subway to an early appointment when my ears are bombarded with the onslaught of profanity emanating from an adolescent female. Necks are straining, eyes are frantically scanning the crowd, searching for the source of the early morning assault on their senses. I hesitate to take a glance over my shoulder in the direction of the sounds, because I can recognize the accent and the intonations. Another Black passenger makes eye contact with me and within that split second we have communicated a world of information and frustration. The sounds are emanating from the mouth of a young Black girl, island of origin unknown, but unimportant. She was one of us, she was young, Black and female. A sigh of relief was perceptible when she and her companion stepped of the train. The Monday morning reverie returned, except for those of who became marked once again by the actions of a few.

Scenes such as this have become all too commonplace in public spheres in Canada. They speak to the struggle that African Caribbean girls are undergoing in their search for an identity and a sense of knowing who they are as Black women. This paper provides a theoretical exploration of the development of racial identity amongst African Caribbean female adolescents in the school system in Canada. Drawing from the existing literature as well as the work I have done with Caribbean students in the Canadian school system, it is evident that the issue of racialized identity development becomes a particularly difficult hurdle that these students are expected to overcome. The narratives that are used in the paper are drawn from my interactions with these students in my role as a school counselor.

First I will discuss the historical background of the situation that has created the unique dynamics for these students. This section will examine the issues of race, representation (including cultural and social markers), immigration and diasporic realities for determining the myriad way in which the identities of Black female students are influenced within the Canadian context.

Secondly, the discussion will examine the role that the school and relationships within the school plays in influencing the students' conception of their raced and gendered selves. This section will highlight the role of the interaction with school staff and peers and examine the manner in which the curriculum is implicated in notions of representation and identity development. Additionally, I will highlight the manner in which these interactions and experiences foreground the Black females' connection to a Caribbean identity. Finally I will discuss the issue of self-esteem and its relation to identity development of Caribbean girls.

BACKGROUND

Caribbean female students within the Canadian school system are positioned within the interlocking systems of race, gender, and diasporic identity locations, all of which speak to the fluidity of identities. Whether they have migrated to Canada as children or are born in Canada to Caribbean parents, their connection to the Caribbean often significantly informs their identity. Located as permanent sojourners, the students are constantly moving back and forth between Black and white worlds, within the borderlands (Anzaldua, 1987). There exists a sense of connection to the Black and Caribbean world while they are continually excluded from fully entering or participating in the white world.

Canada, within historical and contemporary manifestations, is positioned as a white world, given its history of British and French rule and the groups that currently exercise control and power in its public and private institutions. This statement is in no way a dismissal of the Aboriginal roots of Canadian history and development, however, the Aboriginals have also been victimized by colonization and imperial domination by whites who continue to maintain control of those institutions. One can suggest therefore that it is this exclusion from adopting Canadian citizenship that informs the degree to which the identity of Caribbean female adolescents is influenced by their attachment to the Caribbean. According to Amina Mama in her discussion of identity development within the British context, 'It is an attempt to resolve the existential dilemma of being Black in a society that has continuously and irrationally defined itself as white' (1995:114)

Within the school environment, the students continue to be viewed through multiple lenses. The school system and its members continuously view them as belonging in several different and at times competing frames. At one time they are Third World bodies, with the corollary implications of the Third World mythology of poverty. They are also located within Blackness and the multiplicity of living stereotypes that inform notions of what it means to be Black in a white dominated society. Simultaneously these students are positioned within specific island spaces with the inherent implications of what membership within that specific island implies, often through the gaze of the tourist, who 'has been to country X on vacation'. Implicit within those words is the assumed knowledge that the primarily white school staff has regarding Caribbean students.

How do these ideas that frame the reference points of the school staff affect these girls conceptions of themselves? How do these interactions within the school spaces affect the identity of Black Caribbean females? What are the factors that affect their experiences of schooling as well as their academic performance?

Gender is another important lens through which the identity of the Caribbean students must be examined. Given the gender inequalities that are present in Canadian society, the students, beyond, race and geographical displacement, are forced to contend also with this aspect of oppression. Therefore, given the constant onslaught of identities with which they are faced, the Caribbean female student must by necessity invest significant energies and time in the quest for some degree of stability of their identity. I would argue that the very act of their survival in these exclusionary spaces, speaks to the resilience of Black women. Edouard Glissant (1989) speaks of the 'schizophrenic personality' of the Caribbean individual, however, he examines the issue from within an adult space. What of the adolescent student who, while addressing the all too common teenage angst, is also wrapped in the whirlwind of attempting to develop an integrated sense of identity? How do they achieve a sense of integrity, while also dealing with the issues of racism, gender and class biases as well as a sense of alienation that all to often represents their experiences within the Canadian school system?

IMMIGRATION

The migration of Caribbean people to Canada peaked during the 1970's. The vast majority of the migrants were women who came as nannies and maids for white families. Whereas during the earlier periods of immigration, the women were expected to be single with no children, (Agnew1996; Calliste, 1989) the later movement included women who would leave their children in the Caribbean to be cared for by relatives. These children migrated years later to meet their parents. Significant numbers of children have also been born in Canada and are first generation Canadians who were born to West Indian parents.

The children who are born in Canada are citizens and their ancestors have made multiple contributions to the development of Canadian society in general and also to the Caribbean community which has had a strong history here. They have become politicians, doctors, lawyers, and have contributed to the overall development of the society. However, in much the same way that the Blacks who came to Canada through the Underground Railroad in an attempt to escape the inhumane conditions of slavery in the United States and the Aboriginal populations have had their history and presence in Canada all but erased, the contributions of

Caribbean immigrants have suffered a similar fate. This becomes a case of selective historical amnesia.

This amnesia is evident in the school curriculum that recounts the achievements of British and French Canadians, but has erased the history of all other groups. If the histories and accomplishments of non-white groups are included it is often done during Black History Month or as an aspect of the multicultural celebrations. For the Caribbean students their history has been reduced to Jamaican patties, steelband and roti. The students do not see themselves reflected in the school system or society at large.

The media depictions of the non-white immigrants to Canada are consumed with images of violence and chaos. They are regarded as burdens on the economic system (Cheney, 1996) and as people intending to destroy the 'Canadian' way of life. The African Caribbean male is portrayed as being an academic and social failure while the woman is regarded as a tyrannical mother figure that violently disciplines her children. It is against this backdrop that African Caribbean females are attempting to develop a healthy sense of self.

IDENTITY DEVELOPMENT WITHIN DIASPORIC CONTEXTS

This erasure of their history has undermined their sense of citizenship and feelings of belonging. Discussion with the students, both male and female, indicated a sense of reticence towards identifying themselves as being Canadian. For the students who had migrated to Canada, they maintained a connection and identification with the land of their birth. For students who were born in Canada, they identified themselves with the land(s) of origin of their parents, for example being Trinidadian-Canadian or Jamaican-Canadian. Students felt that they had not been accepted as being Canadian and were constantly being asked "Where are you from" (James, 2001; Shadd, 2001) which intensified their sense of detachment from Canada. Always being located as an outsider because of the ways in which questions regarding their identity are framed, these females are forever delineating their identity locations. The exclusionary practices of Canadian society forces them to choose to be Caribbean. The effects of racism was a significant factor in their attributing a greater sense of connection and sense of home to the Caribbean than to Canada.

Students often talked about "Going back home", where many of them felt that they would be more accepted, more welcomed and further to this, not have to deal with the issues of racism, although the implications of skin color gradation becomes a factor in the Caribbean. Within the Canadian context racism is very clearly marked as a Black and white issue wherein which, the darkness of lightness of ones' shade of Black skin is seldom a factor in determining their racialized treatment. Within the Caribbean context, the history of colonialism has clear implications for treatment based on the shade of one's skin. Benefits are accrued based on the closer a person's shade of skin is to whiteness.

George Lamming in the novel, *In the Castle of My Skin,* effectively captures the relationship that Caribbean people have with the shade of a person's skin:

> The saving grace. . . was the color of his skin. He was black too, but not as black as Boy Blue. No one was as black as Boy Blue. Trumper was what we called fair skin, or light skin, or best of all, clear skin. ...No black boy (or girl) wanted to be white, but it was also true that no black boy liked the idea of being black. ...Brown skin was a satisfactory compromise. ... The best looking girls in the village and in the whole island were those whose mothers had consorted with white men. They were brown skin, soft, chocolate creamed with long hair. ...The little girls in the lanes met in the evening to play 'pick up' and they would discuss among themselves the future of their shade (1985, p. 127).

Within the Caribbean context the blackness is positioned on a spectrum with people placed at some point along the continuum. In the Canadian context, within the larger society, the markers of blackness are defined within either/or, polemic categories. However, within the Caribbean community in Canada, the implications of skin shade remain ever-present, the markers of a colonialist history remain firmly implanted in the psyche.

In as much as Canada is the land of their birth or long-term residency, this space lacks a sense of security and comfort; there is no sense of Canada being home. There is this continued sense of being in-between worlds; neither Canadian nor Caribbean, but still very much in need of a sense of security to enable one to develop an integrated sense of identity. The search for home becomes at times a fruitless journey. Some of us have come to regard 'home' as being contained within the body.

Avtar Brah (1996) for example describes 'home' as a site of safety and terror. For African Canadian females, the search for home is evidenced in the ways in which they continually apply symbols from the multiple cultures that mark their history. An example of this is the ways in which their behaviours are continually shifting depending on the space in which their interactions occur. If for example the students are interacting with a white audience, the behaviours are strongly influenced by the media and societal portrayal of Black womanhood. When interacting with members of the community, there is that return to the practices that mark the community interactions. There is this constant slippage between and within worlds that marks their search for self and for home.

> "For Black women there is an inherent contradiction in the very word "home". We can ask ourselves many questions to which there are no easy answers. Where is home for starters? Can you call a country which has systematically colonized your countries of origin, one which refuses through racism in its institutions, media and culture to even recognize your existence and your rights to that existence – can you call this country home" without having your tongue inside your cheek? ...Until we can be both visible and belong, the word "home will remain for us

> ambiguous, ironic and even sarcastic. We will be "Strangers at Home. ...Even this returning, going back, dreaming of a country of origin is beset with problems. Women who have never actually been Home idealize it to such an extent that the "Back Home' fill all the emotional and ideological holes that this 'home' does not. It becomes the ideal place, a true place. It is so romanticized that 'Back Home' itself becomes unreal. A dream (Grewal, et al. 1988. pp. 10-11)

The ideology of home is a problematic one in that many of these students are working from vague recollections of the way things were, while others have developed there concept of home based on the stories they have heard from their parents. They have limited exposure to the realities of life, with its attendant historical, political and cultural strife in the Caribbean society. To some degree, their very survival is wrapped up in imagined sites and spaces (Webster, 1998).

According to Ojo who discusses the issue of identity formation amongst Black girls in the larger social realm, although she herself was 'born and raised in Canada' she did not 'feel Canadian' (1999:1). The author states that:

> Many of us for whom Canada is home, have opted to seek an alternate 'home'. In my case, that home is Trinidad and Tobago. Because Trinidad and Tobago has never actually been my 'home', I create and imagined Trinidad and Tobago that meets my need for belonging. Creating an imagined Trinidad and Tobago is my creative response to the violence of racism and sexism that I face in Canada. Through this imagining, I manage to survive.

It is this need to survive in these diasporic spaces that further reinforces the dynamism of identity development as well as to the ways in which resistance becomes implicated in the process of identity development. For the students who have migrated to Canada, they would have formed their initial conceptions of Black womanhood within a Caribbean context a large part of their identity development is formed within diasporic spaces (Brah, 1996). However, much of what they have learned in the Caribbean, those historical memories that have been indelibly carved on their psyches, can be undermined by the information they receive in Canadian schools and society. Therefore, there exists a degree of cognitive dissonance between the historical and contemporary representation that the students must be able to negotiate. Their placements within diasporic contexts positions them as both Caribbean and Canadian bodies, caught within the ever-shifting sands of identity development within multiple contexts, locations and representations. These are but some of the factors that mark the fluidity of their identities (Raissiguier, 1993).

CULTURAL/SOCIAL MARKERS OF BLACK FEMALE IDENTITY

Much of Canadian popular culture and media is drawn from American television and social influences. The imagery of Black womanhood is filtered into the imagination and psyches of Black adolescents through the media. Parents experience an uphill battle trying to instill in their children the values, morals and beliefs of their particular cultural heritage given the predominance of the media in the lives of these children. The Black female in Canada and within the wider global context, irrespective of her background, is bombarded with historical images of the Black matriarch, the Aunt Jemima character, (Daniel, in press) the insatiable sexual temptress, the mammy and the whore (Bush, 1996). The contemporary images to which they are exposed include the welfare mother, the teenage single mother, the sassy, take-no-nonsense Black woman and the ever-present sexualized image of Black women in movies and music videos. The girls are literally breastfed on these misogynistic images that seldom highlight any positive characteristics of Black womanhood.

These images are present in the interaction of the girls with each other as well as their interactions with their male peers as well as adults. The negative name-calling is prevalent and the bad girl Black female always ready to deliver a swift tongue lashing, is seldom absent. The impact of these images becomes so all-consuming that many females have a difficult time resisting them. It is not uncommon to encounter female students engaged in serious verbal altercations with their peers or teachers. Therefore in much the same way that academic failure becomes associated with Blackness so to has a feisty attitude becomes the marker of Black female identity.

I recall a conversation with a group of adolescent girls in which there was one white student present. This white student proceeded to provide information to the group regarding her interaction with a teacher in which she 'told off' the teacher. At the end of her story, a Black student gleefully commented 'You are so feisty, you should be Black!' The comment caught me off guard but raised an important question in my mind with regard to the manner in which Black females identify themselves. I asked a question of the group if to be feisty meant being Black, and all of them were in agreement that in order to be Black in Canada you had to have 'an attitude' especially when dealing with the white world.

In as much as the females may regard this type of behaviour as a form of empowerment and resistance, to what degree is this example of empowerment simply a replication of the ideologies that have informed their identity development? According to Daniel-Tatum '(t)hey know how to be Black' (1997:60). They have absorbed the stereotypical images of Black youth in the popular culture and are reflecting those images in their self-presentation. And further to this, to what degree are their identities being developed in opposition to whiteness? Many Black females resist the prevailing notions of white womanhood and femininity. The notion of the quiet docile woman, whose life circumstances are determined by external forces, is highly resisted by Black females. There exists a determination to exercise some degree of control over their lives and experiences. Although they are often unaware of it, within those forms of resistance lies the histories of generations of Black women who have resisted the prevailing representation of who they are. However, what is imperative on the part of the females within this Canadian context is the understanding that they need to use their resistance and empowerment in ways that benefit them rather than in ways that allow them to be caught in the stereotyped notion of their abilities and that serve to limit their opportunities.

We also have to remain cognizant of the fact that although these challenging behaviours are attempts on the part of teenagers to define themselves and their identity, the situation becomes more difficult for Black females given the paucity of positive images with whom they can identify. The struggle for self-definition is made even more difficult in that these same negative images cause strain to the relationships between Black girls and older Black females who may be in a position of authority or even teachers. Both in my work and in discussion with other Black female adults who are similarly positioned, we have encountered significant resistance and opposition from Black female students. I believe that the resistance, which is displayed by these females, is being experienced on two levels. First there is the resistance to the social and cultural representation of who they are, and secondly, there is the resistance to what they regard as the 'old ways'.

There are significant numbers of Caribbean women who emigrated during the late seventies and early eighties and we were in large part spared the onslaught of the media portrayals. Many of us still cling to the values with which we were raised and those are the values, behaviours and practices that many adolescent females would now label 'White'. Many of our hard won battles are dismissed and our Blackness erased by the modern-day conception of Black womanhood. Given therefore, that we are not regarded as being Black, the interactions that many of us have had with Black female student are highly problematic. Building relationships with some of these students becomes a test of will power and determination, given the degree of resistance we encounter and the ever-present line that we 'don't know what it means to be Black in Canada'. It is interesting the ways in which these young Black girls' interactions with us are used to further reinforce the negative conceptions of Black womanhood with which they have been breastfed.

Discussions with these students, when you have been able to build a relationship with them, unearth the degree of conflict they undergo in their search for self. The students are fighting to belong to a group while at the same time expressing the fear of being caught up in the labels and stereotypes that define minoritized groups. Oftentimes they have found it easier to be taken along in the tide rather than trying to resist; the fight occurs on so many fronts that they feel overwhelmed. They are trying to fight against the stereotypes when they enter the school, and at the same time their interaction with mainstream society. Another source of conflict is the negative sexual and exploitative interactions with the Black males in the school system (Campbell, 1997; Solomon, 1992; Fuller, 1980).

Added to the above mentioned sources of conflict, there is the fight that goes on with the development of their bodies of which they have no control, but which serves to further inform the manner in which society at large views them. It is not uncommon to hear discussions regarding the precocious physical development of Black girls, a classic case of a child trapped in a woman's body. The term that would be used to describe such an adolescent in Trinidad would be 'forced-ripe'. Onlookers often respond to what they see on the outside failing to consider the age and developmental level of the child developing within.

There are times when their ability to resist the negative labels that are being ascribed to them becomes all consuming and many of them fall within the cracks of the system, falling out or as George Dei (1995) terms it 'being pushed out of schools'. The schools continue to be 'sites of struggle and contestation' (Solomon & Brown, 1998), where the students attempt to develop and define a sense of self and identity that is unique to them. Others continue to struggle, developing a sense of identity after they have left the formal structures of schooling. And still others have been able to straddle the many images and develop it into one that works for them. Developing an understanding of how these females incorporate the multiple images of self with which they are bombarded, to develop a comprehensive sense of self that allows them to survive in Canadian society as well as the demands of the educational system is an important area that is worthy of further research.

The very issue of what it means to be a Black female student within Canada becomes compromised given the dynamics of racism, sexism, colonization and the manner in which these realities inform the very understanding these students have with regard to their identity. Leo-Rhynie (1998) discusses the issue of socialization and gendered identity amongst Caribbean females within the Caribbean context. There are several aspects of socialization that she addresses in her paper, including cultural and belief systems, interactions between parents and their children as well as the influence of role models. Leo-Rhynie defines gender identity as 'a personal recognition and general acknowledgement of oneself as part of a socially defined group – male or female, which may or may not be derived from the basic sex difference from which the group originated' (1998:234). Given the binary determinism of defining gender in terms of male or female, this definition can be challenged on many levels given the contemporary challenges to such deterministic definitions of gender from within gay, lesbian and queer communities. However, this paper will not be examining the issue of sexuality within its scope, and as such the definition is appropriate within the current discussion.

In as much as I endorse Leo-Rhynie's discussion of the application of post-modernist and post-structural conceptions of identity development with the view that identities are fluid and constantly changing, impacted by social circumstances and language, we have to be careful in the positioning race-based issues within post-modernist discourses. Post-modernism and post-structural theories privilege the personal dimensions of experience and therefore interactions tend to be analyzed and judged on an individual basis. This premise becomes dangerous and can provide a loop-hole through which dominant groups can deny the experiences of oppression that are experienced by minoritized groups. The individuation of experiences assumes that the individual issue of oppression is in no way an indication that specific groups are being oppressed. This individual analytical framework also serves to allow racisms and oppressions to be ascribed to the level of the individual psychopathology, rather than examining the systemic and structural factors that reinforce hegemonic, European, male domination thereby limiting the possibility of changing these structures (Hill-Collins, 2000).

There are times when communities should engage in strategic essentialisms to ensure that the experiences to which they are being subjected based on racial, religious, gender or ethnic ascriptions, are not trivialized or completed dismissed. There are material consequences which Black girls experience specifically because of their race that have to be addressed and the racialization of these experiences need to be highlighted rather than being lost within the folds of gendered discussions or notions of individual pathology. Postmodernism, in as much as it allows for the voices of individual experiences to be heard, it focuses too much on the tree and dismisses the interconnectedness and interrelationships of the forest.

Therefore, what also makes the issue of gender more difficult in the Canadian context is the impact that race plays in the development. In as much as the anti-Black sentiment to which Paget Henry (2000) refers is very present in the Caribbean, the degree to which it is present in the Canadian context is an important distinction, which was discussed earlier. The issue of race is ever-present and significantly informs the manner in which social relations develop. In spite of the fact that Canadians present themselves as being liberal and tolerant and compares the situation in Canada to the hot bed of race relation in the United States, the silence of structurally ingrained racisms in Canada becomes extremely dangerous. Many Canadians have lulled themselves into a false sense of racial equality that does not play out in the experiences of minoritized populations existing within its shores.

Gendered discussions tend to focus and centralize the experiences of white women and this is where we have to ensure that the realities of Black females are made visible, highlighted and addressed paying particular attention to the specificities that inform their lives within the Canadian context. In the same way that the experiences of Black women need to be unearthed from the basement of Black male dynamics, the need to be considered in separate and distinct spaces from white women also is important (Daniel, in press).

SCHOOLING AND IDENTITY AMONGST BLACK GIRLS

Schools play an important role in the development of society's members. It is within the walls of schools that students develop ideas about the ways in which society, political and social systems function as well as their role in those systems. The expectations that are set out for Black students by their teachers has implications for the understanding of their roles, as well as the contributions that individuals can make to the betterment of society. It is within these walls unfortunately that students also come to understand the negative conceptions and images that schools have of them and the groups to which they belong.

According to Davidson (1996) teenagers are able to identify a direct connection between schooling, academic engagement and the construction of racial, gender and ethnic categories of identity. Because of this Davidson believes it is important to consider the impact of school-based practices in understanding the process of identity development. Dei et al. (1997) in their analysis of the patterns of dropping out of school on the part of Black youth, questions students regarding the issue of gender and schooling. Based on the interviews that were conducted, the girls felt that Black male students were more negatively targeted than they were. In addition to which the students felt that the stereotypes of Black women were more evidently perpetuated and reinforced by Black males and that most of the harassment they received was also from the same group. These issues have also been reported in other of Black students in Canadian schools (Campbell, 1997; Solomon, 1992).

A corollary issue that appears to be evident within the analysis but is not fully developed by the authors is the issue of the continued invisibility of Black females in the school system. Once again Black women are lost in the shadows of what Gilroy (1998) refers to as the crisis of Black masculinity in which society at large turns its gaze towards the issues experienced by Black males, rendering Black female existence, invisible and in some ways insignificant. In essence the relevance of Black female issues have become invisible to the females themselves. Such is the degree of their erasure from the public sphere.

Therefore, in as much as Black feminist epistemology is not a discourse that focuses on the patriarchal systems of domination and chooses to name issues that are relevant within the Black community as feminist issues, the continued focus on Black male experiences of racism and oppression fails to consider the emotional and psychological consequences of racism and oppression for Black women. bell hooks (1992) regards this situation as highly problematic and believes that Black women need to create spaces wherein which we can begin to address our own issues while examining the manner in which Black male behaviour in our communities can also be taken up as oppressive and violent towards women.

In addition to the collapsing of Black female experiences within Black male discourses, other factors that impact on the experiences of female students in the school system are the almost complete erasure of Black women from the curriculum, the stereotyping evident in curriculum materials and the hidden agendas of the dominant groups (Brah, 1996). According to one student in the Dei (1997) study, although you may occasionally hear about the experiences of Black males, the lives or Black women continue to be missing. This absence affects the identity development of students given that the role models to whom the females are exposed are severely limited.

According to Solomon (1997), positive role models, particularly teachers from minoritized backgrounds, can be a source of inspiration and support for students thereby promoting higher aspirations and challenging the racism in the schools.

But as Crichlow (2001) cautions us however, role modeling is based on the relationship and 'interrelationality' of the parties. If the students are unable to identify with the Black teachers or other teachers of color, the mere presence of these bodies fails to address the issue of lack of representation. For example, if the

Black teachers are regarded as having 'bought into the system', the students a likely to dismiss them as possible role models and the relationships can be strained.

In addition there is the physical and psychological toll that is placed on the teachers of color to assume responsibility for all the minority students in the schools (Solomon, 1997). In my own role in the school, I became marked as the 'professional' who dealt with the minority students, thereby providing the primarily white staff with an escape clause for not addressing the larger systemic issues. My way of addressing that scenario was to ensure that the referring teacher continued to be involved in the entire process and also be involved in devising strategies to meet the needs of the students. The larger issue that needs to be addressed is how do we make all teachers accountable to and for all students in the school irrespective of racial, ethnic or gender affiliation.

Many of the Black female students have a difficult time identifying with white teachers and other white women as role models given that the students have also experienced discrimination at the hands of the same teachers. The pool of role models available to them therefore continues to be severely limited. Therefore while Black male students have the sporting and entertainment figures they can use as role models, albeit a limiting scope, Black females continue to be bombarded with the stereotype of the historical Black figures evidenced as the mammies, the sapphires and the bitches. I believe that is it important for us as educators to examine in greater depth the process of role modeling and its attendant impact on students' academic performance.

POWER AND SCHOOLING AND IDENTITY

The issue of power (Giroux 1983; Foucault, 1972) becomes implicated in this discussion in that the parties with the power to name, give voice and allow voices to be recognized, control the school systems. These choices then determine the ways in which a person's identity development becomes enmeshed in the degree to which they can influence the power dynamics. According to Davidson, 'schools participate in negotiating the meanings students attach to identity, the ways in which teachers and schools handle power and convey ethnically and racially relevant meanings become relevant to the conceptualization of students' behavior' (1996, p. 5).

Knowledge and information are inherently trapped within a capitalist market economy wherein which those who hold the power determine what counts as valid and reliable data. This economic market determines who produces knowledge, whose knowledges are privileged and whose knowledges are either erased or externally developed. Said (1978) speaks to the way in which the knowledges of colonized bodies are exoticized and orientalized, being developed through the minds, unsettling fears and fantasies of white males. Given that colonization is still present albeit in contemporary dimensions, the seat of power still remains in the hands of the colonizers or their modern day representatives. Therefore, in as much as there may have been significant strides in the degree to which Black women have begun to claim their representations, these changes have been slow to penetrate the fortified structures of the schools, its attendant curriculum and practices. The power balance within the school system is still firmly held within the iron-fisted grasp of white males and, to a significant degree, white females.

I include white females here in this discussion given that the vast majority of teachers in Canada continue to be White, middle class females. Their practices, choices and interaction with Black females students have served to reinforce the system of white hegemonic rule. White females' focus on issues of gender inequity and the push to have feminism regarded as a critical interrogative discourse, has served to include and examine issues of gender discrimination and inequality in the curriculum and in teachers' practices. However, white feminist discourses, although flagrantly bandying about the trope of gender, has used the term in essentialist ways that have served to eliminate the issues of race and class from within its folds (Spelman, 2001). At the very best, this form of feminism has tried to include terms such as 'women of color' the result of which has been to absurdly attempt to include the experiences of all minoritized women under one catchall rubric. Therefore issues that are unique to Black women continue to be erased and further marginalized (Collins, 2000; Amos & Parmar, 2001; hooks, 2001; Lorde, 2001). bell hooks in her classic piece 'Ain't I a Woman' (1981) effectively recounts the historical exclusion of Black women from the feminist movement.

Such practices fail to consider the unique intersections of oppressions that result in specific material consequences for differentially positioned females. For example, a Chinese female students who is regarded as being intelligent and academically gifted because of the stereotype of the bright Asian student, the model minority (Asher, 2001), although a female of color, is affected differently from a Black females student who is regarded as academically deficient. In as much as they may both fall within the trope students of color, the expectations and experiences of schooling are different. The expectation that the Asian student 'will' perform well is contrasted with the expectation that the Black student 'will' perform poorly. The ways in which teachers respond to these students will vary dramatically, and the academic, social and career outcomes for each will be significantly different.

A friend of mine, who has also worked in the school system, recounted for me a meeting with her son's teacher at his new school. She was informed during parent teacher interview that because her son's is an immigrant (he is Canadian born), he will not perform as well as the Asian students. And to quote the teacher, "You know how well those Asian students perform!" In that statement lays the reality of the differential treatment that the Black student will receive from the teacher. To further exasperate the efforts of this parent to ensure that her child receives a good education, on an assignment where the student performed above the teacher's expectation, the student was given a lower grade and the teacher commented on the assignment that she was sure the student was given help and the work was not completed entirely by him. This student was not helped on the assignment but had been receiving additional help from a paid tutor. Interactions such as these highlight the degree to which the teachers' perceptions of the students' capabilities influence the ways in which students come to know themselves, to develop their identity within the schools.

The media portrayal and tourism within the Caribbean islands has increased the level of exposure to which white Canadians have had to not only the music but also forms of tourist capital such as foods, dances and costumes. These images often inform the manner in which teachers respond to these girls and to Caribbean students in general. For example, it is not uncommon to have white teachers provide descriptions of life in the Caribbean islands. This information is often prefaced by discussions of the level of poverty that they had seen and the level of sympathy they expressed to the children in those families. Unfortunately those tourist experiences combined with the uncritical media portrayal devoid of a historical or social context, inform the manner in which the teachers respond to the children in their classroom. There is the prevailing ideology that all Caribbean people live in abject poverty and further to this the lack of educational experiences and exposure is an automatic indication of cognitive deficit.

These notions of poverty and deficit are quite evident in their interactions with the students as well as their analysis of difficulties that the students may encounter. Seldom is the behaviour or performance of the student related to experiences the student may be having in the schools in Canada. Further to this, these stereotypes of the educational attainment of Caribbean students all to often result, in them being placed in lower stream classes (Coelho, 1988; Dei, 1997; Solomon, 1998).

Another difficulty with the media influenced tourist gaze is the fact that many of the visitors to the Caribbean islands remain within designated tourist resorts, which in my opinion and experience approximate most closely modern day slave plantations with the attendant slave/master dichotomy. The interaction of the staff with the clients reinforces in the minds of the tourists the image of Black as being in positions of servitude. The careers choices to which Black female students are streamed often reflect these latent and unacknowledged ideas. Females are most often steered into professions such as nursing or child-care provider, wherein which the students can reflect their 'natural predisposition' towards the helping professions; a modern day manifestation of the 'mammy' character. These factors play a strong role in the influencing African-Caribbean female subjectivity and the spaces in which they can envision their futures.

I remember moving to Canada at the age of sixteen with my 'O' level passes, all 'A' and 'B's. At the enrollment interview with the principal, I was asked what was the actual mark out of 100 that an 'A' would represent. I was confused about the meaning of the question and responded that an 'A' would be equivalent to 85% and over and then turned the question back to the principal asking about the meaning in this system. I followed that with a statement regarding the history of British rule and law both in Canada and the Caribbean and that I would assume that such measures would be standard in former British colonies.

This was the first time that my academic abilities were questioned and further to this I was made aware of the 'fact' that I was incapable of getting 'A's and that I should forget about applying to university, something I had dreamed of doing since I was a child. Looking back on those experiences have served to highlight for me that the system is operated in ways that are designed to undermine the students' sense of self and eliminate all aspiration beyond those we are 'told' by the messengers of the system that we are capable of aspiring to. I believe that the recording of such narratives serves to ensure that our voices and our experiences are not silenced. Added to this I believe that it provides examples to younger generations that the struggles continue and at the end of the day, students have to develop a strong sense of self and identity, in spite of the attempts of the school system.

According to Edwards (1991) many West Indian parents assume that the school system in Canada in better than the one they left in their homeland, and that the teachers will take a personal interest in the academic development of their children. These parents unfortunately fail to factor in the issue of racism and the way it impacts on the relationship teachers have with their children. Caribbean parents make the often dangerous assumption that the schools and its personnel will assume the bulk of the responsibility for educating their children. This discussion serves to highlight the fact that the responsibility for appropriately educating African youth irrespective of their 'homeland', must be addressed within the African-Canadian community given the fact that a individual's sense of self influences their academic choices.

Given the prevalence of interchanges such as the ones noted above, it is easy to understand the degree of frustration, anger and sometimes resentment that many of the female students feel towards the school and its representatives. It is also easy to understand their continued longing for 'home' and for the places of safety that they associate with living in the Caribbean. A comment that I have often made is that it is not surprising that so many students fall through the cracks of the system. What is amazing is that in spite of all the obstacles, many students succeed in the system. Many of the African-Caribbean girls have learned how to resist being defeated by the system.

PEERS AND SCHOOLING

The influence of peers is also important in this discussion. All to often when working in the school one is able to see the transformation that many immigrant students undergo, through interaction with their peers. It is not uncommon to have a student who has recently migrated to Canada, address their elders as 'Sir' and "Miss', to be very polite and in some ways quite reticent in their interactions with their peers and the school staff in general. Within months of being in the school, one is able to ascertain very clear changes in their behavior; the attitude begins to take on that of their peers who are engaged varied forms of resistance to the dominant systems or structures of schooling. The student, who was at one time attending classes and being quite respectful to their peers and school staff, becomes challenging and disrespectful. They begin to mold themselves into the stereotyped versions of reality. Often times teachers have expressed dismay at the distinct changes that the students have undergone, puzzled at the transformation.

In addition to the frustration expressed by the teachers, parents also express significant frustration at the changes their children have undergone. The comparison is often made to the 'Nice girl that came up here' and 'now look at the way she behaving'. It is often at this time that parents begin to consider 'Sending them back home'. In as much as this particular choice may have positive effects for the individual child and family, the structural systems that reinforce inadequate access to education for minoritized youth remain unchallenged.

Recently a colleague of mine began having significant difficulties with his adolescent daughter. The daughter, who had been a good student, began having problems in school and with her parents. This colleague made the decision to send his daughter back to Trinidad, given that he felt the system in Canada did not allow parents the latitude necessary to effectively discipline their children. Many immigrant parents are frustrated by the idea that they are unable to use physical discipline in their homes given the right of the children to have their parents arrested and charge. Most importantly, this father felt that being away from the negative influence of her peers would improve her chances for success.

In addition, he felt that with her being in an environment where academic achievement was respected rather than ridiculed, she would have a greater chance at success, both academically and socially. Another important factor was her not having to deal with racism on a constant basis would allow her the space necessary to develop her identity as a proud and competent Black woman, surrounded by many living role models around whom she could pattern her behaviour. Bracks (1998), for example, refers to the ways in which Black women in the Caribbean, because of their closer connection to their African roots have been able to survive racial subjugation. She specifically draws on the life experiences of Mary Prince, a slave woman, who she describes as " a stunning model of Black female strength" (p 4). These are the factors that foreground the interest in and development of Afro-centric schooling and curriculum wherein which the history, knowledge and practices of the students are celebrated rather than pathologized (Kunjufu, 1985; Asante, 1987; Welch & Hodges, 1997; Graham, 2001). The connection between students' attachment to the Caribbean and their level of academic success is an area of research that needs to be explored.

RACE, SCHOOLING AND RESISTANCE.

For many Black students in Canada, schools become a site of resistance to what they perceive as a system that is oppressive to them on many levels. In addition to their erasure from the curriculum, the school staff is seldom representative of the ethnic or racial makeup of the school. Further to this the students become acutely aware of the difference in the ways that punishment and rewards are meted out in the schools and the ways in which race informs those decisions. Therefore, in an attempt to resist the systemic oppression and marginalization, the students begin to engage is behaviors that are designed as forms of resistance (Giroux, 1983; Fordham, 1988; Mirza, 1992; Mac an Ghaill, 1993).

Therefore the markers of success in the school system become markers that the students vehemently oppose and in many cases engage in the exact opposite behaviors. In the case of Black girls however, researchers have clearly stated that in as much as the girls reject schooling, they do not reject the importance of education; they have learned to make that distinction (Fordham, 1988; Fuller, 1988; Mirza, 1992, Mac an Ghaill, 1993). Given that academic excellence is considered important in the system, many students adopt the attitude that to be academically gifted is in some way a betrayal of Blackness. This stance becomes seriously problematic given the reluctance of the students to examine the long-term consequences of these choices.

Students, who make the choice to excel academically, are often ostracized from the bulk of the Black students in the schools and often find themselves involved in more racially and culturally diverse peer groups (Anthony, 1998; Solomon and Allen, 1995). Fordham (1988) employs the concept of racelessness as a strategy that the students adopt to 'achieve vertical mobility (p. 58). According to the author,

> '[M]any Black adolescents are keenly aware of the stigma associated with being successful in school, ...I posit that ambivalence and conflict about academic effort appear to be at the centre of Black students' - especially the high achievers' - responses to school and schooling. Hence they develop complex strategies that enable them to resolve, or, at least cope with, the ambivalence they experience...The strategy that seems to be used frequently by adolescents who succeed in school is the phenomenon that I describe as developing a raceless person (Fordham, 1988, p. 61).

The students experience a great degree of inner conflict and which makes the process of identity development all the more difficult. The community with which you identify informs your concept of self, however these students are positioned in a state of limbo, in between alternate worlds.

There tends to exist significant degrees of animosity between the students who do well and those who don't, this was evident in their interactions in the school at large and amongst the students who were involved in my groups. The animosity extends well beyond the walls of the school and also occurs in the community. The girls who do not perform as well academically often engage in negative acts such as name-calling or spreading rumors about the other students, while the academically strong students limit their contact with members of the Black community (Fordham, 1988). It is not left simply as a case of differing standards, expectations or behaviors. The racial grouping to which the academically gifted student belongs is brought into question and according to Fordham and Ogbu, the 'students have to reassure one another of black loyalty and identity' and refrain from "acting white" (1986, p. 185-186).

'Oreo cookie' is a term that is commonly applied to Black students who are perceived as 'acting white' and these students are often subjected to significant ostracism on the part of the other students. The implication in the name is that students are Black on the outside but really white on the inside. For students who choose to remain with the 'in crowd' of Black student and to do well academically, the student often has to hide their grades or academic accomplishments. In the Fordham and Ogbu (1986) study, several of the academically gifted students either did not perform up to their ability or suppressed their abilities in order to remain a part of their peer group, and to develop a group identity. The result of this type of interaction is that it reinforces in the minds of the predominantly white staff the idea that Black students are not interested in academics. It also reinforces in the minds of Black students that failure is an acceptable option.

Fuller (1980) for example suggests that black girls in a London comprehensive school have been highly strategic in their resistance to the culture of schooling. They are able to effectively resist while continuing to be academically successful. This is evident in the increase in the numbers of Black women attending higher education in comparison to Black males. In as much as I agree with the idea that Black girls are achieving success in the academic realm (Mirza, 1993), we must be wary of being lulled into a false sense of security regarding the young women in the Black women in the community. In addition to which I would like to underscore the notion that individual successes are not an indication that the Black community or Black girls as a group are achieving acceptable levels of success (Fordham, 1988). The numbers of young girls who are failing continues to be significant, while the numbers of teenage parents continues to be quite evident. The image of groups of young Black females pushing strollers is one that is far too familiar. It becomes important therefore to ensure that the structural constraints that affect the lives of Black girls and facilitate the replication of such images, be examined and interrogated.

Solomon and Brown (1998) for example talk of the students' developing a "culture of resistance" that allows them to challenge the existing structures of the school that serves to marginalize them. The new immigrants receive much of their information from their peers and begin to adjust their identity and behaviour patterns to suit the information provided by their peers. I believe that what has to be interrogated is the purpose and goal of engaging in this culture of resistance. Resistance aimed at enacting change or what I shall term success oriented resistance, is a productive outlet and supports the academic success of students. However, terminal resistance, which is at best an oppositional identity, serves to further entrench the marginalization of the students, maintains the status quo, rather than effecting any type of systemic change (McFadden & Walker, 1994). I believe it is important to reiterate that the students engage in resistance to the routine practices of schooling, not to the importance of education (Solomon, 1998; Campbell, 1998) thereby exercising their individual agency.

According to Giroux (2001), resistance has to be understood as conscious acts, wherein which subordinate groups exercise their power to transform existing oppressive structures. He laments the fact that the term resistance is being applied in essentialist and analytically limited ways that serve to reduce the effectiveness of the theoretical concept as well as its transformative nature. The author asserts that 'the concept of resistance highlights the need ...to decipher how the modes of cultural production displayed by subordinate groups can be analyzed to reveal both their limits and their possibilities for enabling critical thinking (Giroux 200, p. 111). It is important that Black females and the wider community consider the ways in which resistance gets taken up and practiced to ensure that it is beneficial rather than destructive to students' educational performance.

IDENTITY AND SELF-ESTEEM

Black female adolescents in Canada as earlier indicated, are enveloped in a multitude of circumstances and situations that influence their self-concepts and their identities. There are several factors that appear to mitigate the negative influences of school, media, racism and peer pressure. The female students develop a strong sense of identification with their cultural and ethnic groups. The attachment they develop to their or their parents' country of origin provides them with alternative images, which they can include in their search for self. According to Rong & Preissle (1998) a high level of ethnic identity as well as a sense of connectedness to their country of origin served to mitigate the effects of discrimination for immigrant students.

The denigration of their racial and ethnic heritage as well as their marginalization (Marshall, 1996), in Canadian society, pushes the females to develop a stronger sense of connection with their Caribbean heritage. In addition to which, the ways in which they are debased because of their gender, becomes challenged through their understanding of gender relations in the Caribbean. This is not to indicate that the issues of patriarchal rule are absent within Caribbean islands, however, the stories that speak to Black women's ability to survive in the face of adversity, are often set in the Caribbean. Stories such as these are all but absent within the public realm of the Canadian context.

According to the Martinez and Duke (1997), Black and Asian females had greater levels of ethnic identity than males which has led them to question whether gender based oppression, combined with racism has led them to be more sensitive to and create a greater affiliation towards their ethnic identity. This increased ethnic affiliation as well as the fact that society fixes its gaze on Black males, could perhaps serve to explain the higher levels of academic achievement than that of Black males. This is an area that is in need of further examination.

Exposure to Caribbean culture also increases the sense of affiliation these females feel to the Caribbean. The females are exposed to the music as well as the celebrations for example in the form of Caribana, which is a replica of the carnival celebrations in the Caribbean.

Another factor that would increase the level of connection that the females feel to the Caribbean culture is the differential degree of freedom that is afforded boys versus girls. The males are afforded a greater degree of freedom that provides them with opportunities to become engaged with other ethnic and racial groups in the society. The girls are more restricted in their movement and are expected to remain closer to home, therefore they are exposed, both directly and indirectly, to more subtle aspects of the Caribbean culture that perhaps the boys may miss out on.

Adolescence is a time that is peppered with push and pull forces. In as much as the adolescent is seeking some degree of closeness to their parents, they are striving to achieve their own sense on independence and individuality. Therefore the connection to the family and other family support systems serves to strengthen their identity development and make the journey in some respects, less tumultuous. This support becomes important not only for the teen who can access other adults to whom they can turn for guidance and nurturance, but for the parents they are provided with additional support systems.

Having these extended support systems provides many of these females with a place wherein which they can explore their identities. Phinney, Cantu and Kurtz (1997), indicate that the students' affiliation with these support systems "leads to an achieved ethnic identity characterized by a strong and secure sense of self as a member of an ethnic group and an accompanying positive self-concept" (p 168).

IMPLICATIONS OF THE RESEARCH AND CONCLUSION

There are several implications that can be identified for this type of research. There are very clear indicators that the school system plays a significant role in the identity development of Black females. As educators, parents and community members we have to ensure that the experiences that Black girls have in the schools are conducive for their optimal development.

As such parents and community members need to be more informed of the structure of schooling and the ways in which the issue of power informs the relationships between teachers and the students. Further to this, the community has to ensure that the school remains accountable to all students thereby ensuring Black girls greater opportunities to succeed. Therefore, issue of the curriculum content, the presence of minority teachers and also ensuring that the schools are free of racial and sexual harassment are important factors that must remain in focus.

At the community level, there need to be a redefinition of Blackness for both males and females. The media, in as much as it exerts strong influence on the information Black children receive, ultimately, the community has to develop ways in which it can continue to resist the domination of those images. Along the same vein, we have to be aware of the ways in which the members of the community reinforce the negative conception of Blackness and continue to challenge and resist them. In the process therefore of understanding the ways in which the identify of Black girls develop, the community can also continue to develop methods of ensuring that the process is strongly grounded in positive notions of Black womanhood.

This paper has provided a preliminary examination into the identity development of African-Caribbean females in the Canadian school system. There are several significant factors that facilitate and constrain the development of positive notions of self. The impact of their experiences of schooling, their interaction with their peers, and the impact of the media portrayal of black womanhood, are all factors that play important roles.

Another significant issue is the sense of being permanent immigrant in the land of their birth or citizenship. The females are forced to draw upon diasporic identities and histories to develop a strong and positive sense of identity. Their sense of connectedness to the Caribbean and its attendant notions of 'home' serve to provide the females with a sense of grounding that is often denied to them within the Canadian context. However, the notion home is at best a tenuous one given the fact that their understandings of a Caribbean home is an imagined space and experience. The African Caribbean female adolescent becomes positioned as a permanent sojourner, seldom settling, often not belonging in either world. In spite of these realities, Black females are adopting strategies of survival that are enabling them to develop integrated personalities in the face of multiple oppressions. They have to some degree parlayed their marginalization into forms of resistance that have enabled them to develop a strong sense of identification. With that said however, there needs to be continued research into the notions of resistance given that resistance can have negative consequences for the girls. Notions of resistance have to be reconfigured so as to provide positive outcomes of the students.

Empirical research that examines the experiences and factors affecting the lives of Black female students in Canada needs to be developed. In as much as there has been research that documents the experiences of Black students in the school system, the dynamics of gender places an added dimension that has to be explored. The factors that have contributed to their success have to be unearthed to provide alternatives for future generations of students in Canada.

The African Caribbean females have maintained and continued to build on their sense of connection to the Caribbean culture and it is this connection that will ensure the survival of those values and beliefs in distant lands. They have drawn on the survival spirit of their ancestors, their own agency and have resisted the negative labels that have marked their lives in Canada.

REFEREENCES

Agnew, V. (1996). *Resisting Discrimination: Women from Asia, Africa and the Caribbean and the women's movement in Canada.* Toronto: University of Toronto Press.

Anthony, S.P. (1998). Black-Eyed Susan: "Blue-Eyed" Schools: Academically-oriented Black girls in Toronto Schools. Doctoral Thesis. Toronto: Department of Theory and Policy Studies: Ontario Institute for Studies in Education of the University of Toronto.

Anzaldua, G. (1987). *Borderlands/La Frontera: The New Mestiza.* San Francisco: Spinsters/Aunt Lute.

Asante, M. (1987). *The Afrocentric idea.* Philadelphia: Temple University Press.

Asher, N. (2001) Checking the box: the label of 'model minority'. In G.M. Hudak, & P. Kihn, (Eds.), *Labeling: Pedagogy and politics* (pp. 75-91). New York: Routledge Falmer.

Bobb-Smith, Y. (1998). "I know who I am. A Caribbean Woman's Identity in Canada: Agency and Resistance in Community Organizing." Doctoral Thesis. Toronto: Department of Adult Education, Community Development and Counseling Psychology: Ontario Institute for Studies in Education of the University of Toronto.

Bracks, L.L. (1998). *Writings of Black Women of the Diaspora: History, Language and Ethnicity.* New York and London: Garland Publishing Inc.

Brah, Avtar (1996). *Cartographies of Diaspora: Contesting Identities.* London and New York: Routledge.

Bush, B. (1996). History, Memory or Myth? Reconstructing the History (or Histories) of Black Women in the African Diaspora. In Stephanie Newell (Ed), *Images of African and Caribbean Women: Migration, Displacement, Diaspora* (pp. 3-28). University of Sterling: Centre for Commonwealth Studies.

Calliste, A. (1989). Canada's Immigration Policy and the Domestics from the Caribbean: The Second Domestic Scheme. In, *Race, Class, Gender: Bonds and Barriers.* Socialist Studies: A Canadian Annual, 5:133-165: Between the Lines.

Campbell, A. (1997). Black Talk: Perceptions of African-Canadian Working-Class Girls and their Social Relations in an Urban Middle School. M.Ed. Research Project: York University.

Cheney, D. (1996). Those who the immigration law has kept apart - let no one join together: a view on immigration incantation. In, McCauley, D. (Ed.), *Reconstructing womanhood, Reconstructing feminism: Writings on Black women* (pp. 58-84). New York: Routledge.

Coelho, E. (1988). *Caribbean students in Canadian schools.* Toronto: CARIB-CAN Publishers.

Crichlow, W. (2001). Labeling heroes: role models in higher education. In, G. M. Hudak, & P. Kihn, P. (Eds.), *Labeling: Pedagogy and politics* (p. 147-160). New York: Routledge Falmer.

Daniel, B.J. (In Press) Researching African Canadian Women: Indigenous Knowledges and the Politics of Representation.

Daniel-Tatum, B. (1997). *"Why are all the Black Kids Sitting Together in the Cafeteria?" and other conversations about race.* New York: Basic Books.

Davidson, A. 1996. Making and Molding Identity in Schools: Student Narratives on Race, Gender and Academic engagement.

Dei, G.J.S. (1995). Drop Out or Push Out? The Dynamics of Black Student Disengagement from School. A report prepared for the Ontario Ministry of education and Training. Toronto: Ontario Institute for Studies in Education.

Dei, G.J.S., Mazzuca, J., McIsaac, E., Zine, J. (1997). *Reconstructing Dropout: A critical ethnography of the Dynamics of Black student' disengagement from school.* Toronto: University of Toronto Press.

Edwards, H.G. (1992). *The Immigrant Family: Framework for Adaptation and Excellence.* Canada: Miracle Press.

Fordham, S. & Ogbu, J. (1986). Black student's school success: Coping with the burden of "acting white". *The Urban Review,* 18(3), 176-206.

Fordham, S. (1988). Racelessness as a factor in Black students' school success: Pragmatic strategy or Pyrrhic victory? *Harvard Educational Review,* 58(1), 54-84.

Foucault, M. (1972). *The Archeology of Knowledge.* Translated by A.S. London. New York: Pantheon.

Fuller, M. (1980). Black girls in a London comprehensive school. In R. Deem, (Ed.), *Schooling for women's work* (pp. 52-65). London: Routledge & Kegan Paul.

Gilroy, P. (1993b). *Small Acts: thoughts on the Politics of Black Culture.* London: Serpents Tail.

Giroux, H. (1983). *Theory and resistance in education: A pedagogy for the opposition.* South Hadley, Mass., Bergin and Garvey.

Giroux, H. (2001). *Theory and resistance in education: Towards a pedagogy for the opposition.* Connecticut: Bergin and Garvey

Glissant, E. (1989). *Caribbean Discourses.* Translated by Michael J. Dash. Lexington, VA: University of Virginia Press.

Graham, M. (2001). The 'miseducation' of Black children in the British educational system - towards an African-centered orientation to knowledge. In R. Majors, (Ed.), *Educating our Black Children: New directions and radical approaches* (pp. 61-79). London: Routledge Falmer.

Grewal, S., Kay, J., Landor, L., Lewis, G., Parmar, P. (1988)*Charting the Journeys: Writings by Black and third world women.* London: Sheba.

Henry, P. (2000). *Caliban's reason: Introducing Afro-Caribbean Philosophy.* New York and London: Routledge.

Hill-Collins, P. (2000). "What's going on: Black feminist Thought and the Politics of Postmodernism." In E. A. St. Pierre & W.S. Pillow (Eds.), *Working the ruins: Feminist Poststructural Theory and Methods in Education* (pp. 41-73). New York and London: Routledge.

Hill-Collins, P. (2000). *Black feminist thought: Knowledge, consciousness and pedagogy.* New York: Routledge.

hooks, bell (1981). *Ain't I a woman. Black women and feminism.* Boston: South End Press.

hooks, bell. (1992). *Black Looks: race and Representation.* Boston, MA: South End Press.

hooks, bell (2001). Black women shaping feminist theory. In K. Bhavnani, (Ed.), *Feminism and race* (pp. 33- 39). Oxford: Oxford University Press.

James, C. (2001). Encounters in Race, Ethnicity and Language. In C. James and A. Shadd (Eds), *Talking About Identity: Encounters in Race, Ethnicity and Language* (p 1-8). Toronto: Between the Lines.

Lamming, G. (1985). *In the castle of my skin.* Essex: Longman Group Ltd.

Leo-Rhynie, E.A., (1998). Socialization and the Development of Gender Identity: Theoretical Formulations and Caribbean Research. In C. Barrow (Ed.) *Caribbean Portraits: Essay on Gender Ideologies and Identities.* Kingston: Ian Randle Publishers.

Lorde, A. (2001). The master's tool will never dismantle the master's house. In, K. Bhavnani, K. (Ed.), *Feminism and race* (pp. 89-92). Oxford: Oxford University Press.

Mama, A. (1995). *Beyond the Masks: Race, Gender and Subjectivity.* London and New York: Routledge.

McFadden, & Walker, J.C. (1994). Resistance theory. In Husen & Postlethwaite (Eds.), *International Encyclopedia,* 9, 5056-5060.

Marshall, A. (1996). From Sexual denigration to Self-respect: Resisting images of Black female sexuality. In D. Jarrett-Macauley, (Ed.) *Reconstruction Womanhood, Reconstructing Feminism: Writings on Black Women.* London: Routledge.

Mirza, H. S. (1992). *Young, female and Black.* London: Routledge.

Ogbu, J. (1978). *Minority education and caste: The American system in cross-cultural perspective.* New York: Academic Press.

Ojo, K. (1999). Finding a place in the sun: young Black women negotiating their identities in oppositional spaces. Masters thesis, Department of Sociology and Equity Studies in Education at Ontario Institute for Studies in Education at the University of Toronto.

Phinney, J.S., Cantu, C.L., & Kurtz, D.A. (1997). Ethnic and American Identity as Predictors of Self-Esteem Among African American, Latino and White Adolescents. *Journal of Youth and Adolescence,* 26(2), 165-185.

Raissiguier, C. (1993). Negotiating work, identity and desire: The adolescent dilemmas of working-class girls of French and Algerian descent in a vocational high school. In C. McCarthy, & W. Crichlow, (Eds.), *Race, identity and representation in education* (pp. 140-156). New York: Routledge.

Rong, X.L. & Peissle, J. (1998). *Educating immigrant students: What we need to know to meet the challenges.* California: Corwin Press Inc.

Said, E. (1978). *Orientalism.* London: Routledge and Kegan Paul.

Shadd, A. (2001) "Where are you Really From?" Notes of an "Immigrant" from North Buxton, Ontario. In James, C. and Shadd, A. (Eds.), *Talking About Identity: Encounters in Race, Ethnicity and Language* (pp. 10-16). Toronto: Between the Lines.

Solomon, R.P. (1992). *Black resistance in high school: Forging a separatist culture.* Albany: SUNY.

Solomon, R. P. & Allen, A.M. (1995). The Success and Failure of Black Students in the Greater Toronto Area Schools: Contributing Factors. Unpublished report: York University.

Solomon, R.P. (1997). Race, role-modeling and representation in teacher education and teaching. *Canadian Journal of Education,* 22(4) 395-410.

Solomon, R.P. & Brown, D.A. (1998). From badness to sickness: pathological conception of Black students culture and behaviour. In V.R. D'Oyley & C.E. James, (Eds.), *Re/Visioning Canadian Perspectives on the education of Africans in the late 20th Century.* Toronto: CAPTUS Press.

Spelman, E. (2001). Gender and race: The ampersand problem in feminist thought. In, Bhavnani, K. (Ed.), *Feminism and race* (pp. 74-89). Oxford: Oxford University Press.

Webster, W. (1998). *Imagining Home: Gender, 'race' and national identity, 1954-64.* London: University College London Press.

Welch, O.M. & Hodges, C.R. (1997). *Standing Outside on the Inside. Black adolescents and the construction of academic identity.* Albany: SUNY.

BEVERLY-JEAN DANIEL

CHAPTER 7

CARIBBEAN STUDENT SPEAKERS' EDUCATION & EXPERIENCES IN AMERICAN SCHOOLS: A CONSTANT STRUGGLE WITH VARIED RESULTS

CLARISSA WEST-WHITE

INTRODUCTION

Teaching at a small, private historically Black college in the southeastern region of the United States has its advantages. Due to our location we are fortunate to have a diverse student body, with students representing over 39 countries and territories. A large portion of the students hail from the Caribbean Islands, with large concentrations of students from the Bahamas, Jamaica, Haiti and the United States Virgin Islands. With nearly 80 percent of the new immigrants arriving to the United States from Latin America, Asia and the Caribbean being "people of color" (Henry, 2001; Loeb & Friedman, 1993), more schools public and private, rural and urban, large and small, will face providing English instruction to these newly arrived immigrants. Many such schools will place students who arrive and speak "nontraditional" languages at a disadvantage. For example, at a rural high school in the northern region of the state, a Haitian student, speaking only French Creole enrolled and was immediately sent to the French teacher's classroom where she remained for nearly two months. When she was finally mainstreamed into a basic proficiency English class she simply doodled, stared blankly at the teacher or out the window. When the first grading period ended, she was given the customary "D" since teachers were often told that failing an ESL student would require too much documentation. Teachers associated her inability to speak English with ignorance and inferiority, and arrogantly concluded that *all* Haitians and non-English speaking "foreigners" were thus lost causes.

However, contrary to popular belief, the majority of immigrants who arrived between 1980 and 1990 have high-school educations, do not rob citizens of jobs but either expand employment niches or take jobs few Americans want, do not rely on welfare, immigrants took home salaries comparable to those of nonimmigrant Americans, and do not demonstrate significant differences in political opinions (Loeb & Friedman, 1993, p. 48). "How immigrant children fare in our schools will in many cases forecast their contributions as members of our society," and their presence which fuels the "surge in new immigrant populations" in rural, urban and suburban schools "are taking school districts by surprise and are generating new challenges to which districts must respond" (Henry, 2001, pp. 579-580).

This chapter attempts to assist educators in ensuring that their states, districts, and schools are adequately prepared to meet these "new challenges" head on. Thusly, educators and practitioners at all levels – primary to post-secondary and beyond – must equip themselves with as much knowledge regarding the educational, political and social systems from which their Caribbean students hail. They must also observe how Caribbean students learn in their classes, focus on proven and sound teaching strategies and be adequately trained and versed in "accomplished practices" that will assist students. Teachers should integrate technology into their English classes as often as possible, so that Caribbean students are made aware of how technological advances when accompanied by structured guidelines can assist in improving their writing skills and proficiency. Educators must also be aware that many of their Caribbean students' frustrations, unfortunately, will be located in the socio-economic and political contexts of America, which often places restrictions on students according to their social class and color. Therefore, many of the solutions that address their problems are solutions that are useful to all students of color who, according to recent national test results, continue to lag behind their white counterparts. Finally, teacher training program supervisors, administrators, and teachers/practitioners must evaluate substantive information in terms of their respective positions and ask – what does this mean to me?

TESTING & TEACHING IN THE CARIBBEAN: OVERVIEW, VIEWPOINTS, AND SUCCESS

Students from Caribbean countries often reminisce about the numerous exams they were required to pass in order to progress from primary to middle to secondary school, as does the aforementioned student from the Bahamas:

> At the end of my high school life I was faced with the biggest obstacle ever. This was to achieve a position in the graduating class. This was a serious task because there were so many requirements to be met. There were many exams to be completed and passed, including the SAT, Pitman exam, and external as well as internal school examinations. After this, one would be able to graduate.

The CXC (Caribbean Examinations Council) provides examinations and certification at the secondary and post-secondary levels. The Caribbean Examinations Council was established in 1972 under agreement by the participating governments in the area to conduct such examinations as it may think appropriate and award certificates and diplomas on the results of any such examinations so conducted. The Council is empowered to regulate the conduct of any such examinations and prescribe the qualification requirements of candidates and the fees payable by them (www.cxc.org).

In recent years, Caribbean examinations have come under close scrutiny. Following revelation that it has been plagued by fraud and that it causes stress to children, the controversial Comment Entrance

Examination (CEE) which screens children under 12-year old for high school places will 'definitely' be phased out by 1999 (William, 1996). The CEE, originally introduced in the late 1950s, provides a significant number of children from poor families to attend high school, but the one-day exam is no longer an effective measure of a child's ability (The Voice, Schools face shakeup, p. 16). Similar to complaints made by American English teachers, Caribbean teachers complain that children come to them ill prepared, with very poor English language delivery and comprehension skills, and the complaints do not stop there. Lectures at the University of West Indies claim that students are unable to write good English and have thus introduced a requirement that some students complete an English proficiency test before beginning a degree program ("Schools face shake-up," 1994).

Because students are required to pass a number of exams in order to receive their diploma from Caribbean schools, those who migrate to the United States are quite familiar with high-stakes assessment. Students in my classes continue to compare their education in their home country to that in America. "I think we get a better education in the Bahamas. The teachers don't put up with what children get away with here in America," said Barbara a 21-year old students who received her education on the Grand Bahamas Island and is in her second year of college. "The things I see others learning here [college] in America, we had in high school," says Aliaia, a graduate of schools in the US Virgin Islands, with a heavy Caribbean accent that I have now grown accustomed. "We move at a faster pace and are more respectful of teachers and eager to learn. That's not the case in America. Even though I was educated in the *United States'* Virgin Islands I would have to say that my education there was more strict and challenging than the education I see here [US]." Students in New York City echoed similar sentiments, not only did they prefer their Caribbean education, but felt that they were given more individual instruction, especially in math, even though teacher pupil ratios in most public schools in their home countries were equal or higher than in the United States. They also provided a frank description of American classrooms regarding safety and class management issues; they possess "much fear for their own safety within an educational system that continues to be plagued with violent incidents involving some students" (deCoteau, 1995, p. 20).

Likewise, according to a Boston professor in a keynote address at the 1994 graduation ceremony of the University of West Indies, Caribbean schools outclass US schools and America would do well to take a leaf out of the Caribbean's education system (The Weekly Journal, 7). Ironic since teachers in Jamaica continue to complain that students are not being given the same caliber of education they once received, and went on strike six months later. "The strike by teachers who, even with university degrees are said to earn below J$8,000 per month after taxation and other deductions, comes on top of recent allegations of widespread cheating in the nation's CXC exams" (Roberts, 6).

Recent research by Rong and Brown (2001) using data from the 1990 US census, support in part some of the theories surrounding Afro-Caribbean success. They report that US born children of both Caribbean Black and European White immigrants outperform their peers who were born abroad or who are the children of US born parents. Black immigrant children are more likely to be ahead of other children in their grade levels. They tend to go to school at an early age, stay in school, and make satisfactory academic progress. They also found that a much larger proportion of Caribbean youth are immigrants, and possess the largest percentage of second generation immigrants in the United States. Caribbeans have the highest grammar school completion rate, but a slightly lower four-year college completion rate than that of Europeans, but more astonishing is their finding that prolonged residence in the United States is not associated with more years of schooling for any group. Caribbeans, do, however, attain higher educational levels than Africans in the second generation, and researchers attribute this finding to the large communities and strong ethnic networks Jamaicans and Haitians often generate.

THE CARIBBEAN STUDENT IN AMERICAN ENGLISH CLASSES

Due to the various forms of Patois and Creole languages, speaking and writing patterns, and word order and choice, teaching students who have not always been thought of as bi-lingual, has proven a delightful challenge since my previous teaching stints were in the atypical – Black/White – school setting. Diversity and multiculturalism were often measured by the number of migrant workers, mostly Mexicans, who attended the school. Instantaneously noticeable among Caribbean students is that they possess a number of distinguishing characteristics and traits that make them such pleasures to teach: hard-work, diligence, the ability to remain focused, high levels of self-esteem, ambition, and well defined goals. They tend to reveal less negative talk and do not offer excuses for not being able to complete assignments.

However, one detrimental weakness students possess is their inability to adequately assess their writing skills. Others include, their tendency to produce subject-verb errors, as well as problems with parallelism, and punctuation. Many problems related to their use of verbs can be accounted for since the verb is the most central syntactic feature to Caribbean Creole English (CCE) speakers, whereas adjectives function as a subcategory of verbs (Nero, 2000). Nero also found that the four Caribbean participants in his study who were placed in basic writing classes upon entrance into college produced "academic interlanguage" which he defines as "a written form of English that reflects some Creole English influence along with instances of overgeneralization of standard English rules, inconsistent application of the rules of prescriptive grammar, or both" (p. 500). To a small degree these "overgeneralizations" appear in the writings of nearly every student, even those who use African-American Vernacular English (AAVE).

It should be noted that Caribbean Creoles are sociohistorical products of more than two languages converging out of the conditions of slavery. When Europeans invaded Africa, they shipped its inhabitants to plantations in the Americas. Slave traders grouped speakers of dissimilar languages together, fearful of revolt. Thus, as part of their strategies for survival in these strange new lands, Africans creatively developed new and common tongues. English Caribbean Creoles (e.g., Jamaican Creole) have substratum grammars and other grammatical features (such as tones) originating from West African and Bantu languages (Henry, 2001; Nero, 2000).

Although Caribbean students may speak "proper English" rather well, code-switching only when appropriate or when their switching is germane to their story or point of view, for many Caribbean students their writing tells a different story. It is evident that interlanguage indeed plays a role in ethnic students writing and perception of their writing abilities. Mira, a forty something woman from Haiti, who was educated in Haiti prior to coming to America at age seven states why learning to write well is one of her main priorities:

> At work, my supervisor always corrects my writing. When I look over my original memorandum and compare it to hers, I am left asking what's the difference? Didn't I say that? She changes words around that's all, like if I say "around" she'll cross through that and write "circumvent." I always thought I wrote well, until her constant corrections left me doubting my writing ability and skill.

Undeniably, Mira's writing shows promise and she has set herself apart from many students. Mira wrote in her research paper on the mistreatment of women in Kabul:

> During a sporting event held in a stadium located in Kabul, Afghanistan, "thousands of people watched as a woman, cowering beneath a pale blue all-enveloping burqa *(veil)*, was shot and killed today in the first public execution of a woman in Kabul since the Taliban (the fundamentalist group ruling most of Afghanistan) religious armies took control three years ago. The woman was the mother of seven children all of whom were present in the stadium and were crying out loudly for her." This incident is not a rare scene in Afghanistan because that country does not have or believe in women's rights and although not public women are executed, stoned, and burned to death for may reasons.

There exist only a few errors in Mira's opening paragraph. First, as exhibited by many students regardless of educational levels or language proficiency, Mira failed to cite the sources of her information, although it has been shown that plagiarism is a major obstacle in higher education to bilingual students, especially those not taught using Western philosophies of teaching (Thompson, 1995; Wilson 1999). Secondly, due probably to a typo, Mira says *for may reasons* when she clearly meant *many*. Finally, she omitted a number of commas; one should be placed between the words *public* and *women* to assist the reader in capturing her point. It could be argued that Mira could have edited the first part of the last sentence-*This incident is not a rare scene in*

Afghanistan because that country does not have or believe in women's rights-so that it reflects the skill level of a college student's vocabulary and word choice, unless, of course, it is the original text provided by her unidentified source.

Recalling prior teaching experiences of African-, Mexican-, and Southern White-American students, I cringe at the numerous essays and writing assignments filled with code-switching and "bad-grammar". Providing instruction on avoiding code-switching in their academic writing when inappropriate proved to be a rather fascinating task once students realized that their languages, these codes, were valid systems of communication. Unlike the previously mentioned assortment of American students, Caribbean students tended to separate their writing styles from their speech patterns, but not with the same effect. Caribbean students would often speak better than they wrote. Even though research cited by Nero (2000) shows that the academic writing of AAVE speakers exhibits many of the same features as that of CCE, this twist often landed Caribbean students in remedial, basic writing or ESL classes when schools elicited writing samples in order to determine their placement upon entering secondary and post-secondary schools.

Even those who found themselves at the top of their classes in their home country or in their high school's graduating classes in the US, now find themselves placed in lower level, skill and drill intensive courses that focus on: improving vocabulary skills, identifying stated and implied main ideas and major and minor details, determining relationships within and between sentences, recognizing fact vs. opinion, drawing inferences, interpreting purpose and tone, detecting bias and propaganda techniques, evaluating arguments, applying and demonstrating reading skills through writing and oral presentations. Many students will spend a year, or more, taking such classes that will not count toward graduation, but are required for the student to pass in order to begin taking the more traditional freshman and sophomore college writing classes. A student from Guyana recalls that even though her English educators in Guyana "emphasized grammatical correctness in her writing and would correct her "bad" (Creole) pronunciation whenever she read aloud in class," she experienced difficulty with some writing assignments in her Honors English class in New York City because her teachers pushed for more analysis and elaboration (Nero, 2000, p. 495). This student was victim to *cosmetic English* – if it is pronounced correctly or sounds correct, grammatically speaking, then it must be - the listener presumes that the speaker is proficient in English, which may or may not be true. This cosmetic glossing of English will eventually hinder the Caribbean student in the long run since much of the new global market is written.

THE NEED TO FIT IN AND ITS TOLL ON CARIBBEAN STUDENTS' WRITING & COHABITATION

Students also display problems with proper word placement and word choice, which seriously affect the meaning they are attempting to convey. Many of the students' speech patterns have been influenced by their environment and *slang* that's prevalent among their peers and communities, much of which works its way into students' writings. "To fit in socially with their peer group, children of immigrants may adopt the values and behavior of their mainstream American peers" (Rong & Brown, 2001, p. 540). Even those who write well, by most "Western" and "American" standards, have trouble with present and past tenses, subject and verb agreement and word order. Many also have problems expressing their thoughts in terms of "American" ideals, or finding the "American" way to say common expressions and colloquialisms. One teacher "working with young women caught in the mix and borrowing from both cultures," discovers that these young women wanted to become "Americans" but spoke a language devalued in American classrooms. Speaking of Caribbean student speakers in American schools, Henry (2001) says, "They were insecure expressing themselves orally and in writing, unacquainted with the kinds of "liberal" inquiry-based teaching/learning situations advocated in American schools. Living in the fold of old wounds also evoked a linguistic history that had negative educational consequences" (p. 188). For example, Barbara a Haitian student, who received her education in the United States and grew up in a predominate Haitian neighborhood wrote in a research paper about Florence Nightingale the following:

> Yuck! Working with blood, diseases and pregnancies is some of the many things that a nurse (practitioner) and a midwife are qualified to do. These occupations take a lot out of people who are in that field. It takes many wonders and dedication to be able to progress in those fields. In the past it did not take much to become a midwife or a nurse. One, manly because it was natural for a woman to have a midwife present. Another, is because any woman that was capable of aiding someone was qualified to be a nurse. Now days, things has changed. To become a nurse takes a good amount of time in college. And this is the same for midwifery.

The above student has demonstrated vast improvement since submitting the above research paper, and not by sheer coincidence. According to Rong & Brown (2001), they discover that youngsters who identify themselves as Caribbean Blacks are more likely to live in an ethnic community where subcultures are built on ethnic ethos, self-defined identity, and social networks. These youngsters and their parents tend to see more opportunities and rewards for their efforts and initiative; they tend to study more and watch less television. Therefore, it is not surprising that these parameters, coupled with diligence and practice account for marked strides Caribbean students make once their weaknesses have been identified. Another student, a male who completed his primary and secondary education in the Bahamas, demonstrates sentence construction, word order and word choice issues in his autobiographical sketch:

> It was on the island of Nassau, Bahamas I was born and grew up.... My primary education continued for six years and at each level I would not only advance in my academics but also in sports. One of the biggest obstacles however, was maintaining a balance between both. Nevertheless, I strived and endured each moment of it, although this was difficult. It did, however, result in great success. The most extreme obstacle to cross at this time, which would result in the greatest achievement, was graduation. After six years of primary school I graduated from the sixth grade, therefore enabling me to enter the seventh and begin my high school life.

Due to poor time management and tumultuous financial crises, which many Caribbean students at the college face, the above writer's writing skills never fully matured. Many of the problems he exhibited in his earlier writings continued to be present throughout the course, which he subsequently failed since he did not complete a number of assignments.

Since Caribbean students are genuinely concerned about their appearance and speech when in the company of an authoritative figure, such as their teacher, older peers, officials, etc. many make exhaustive attempts to form a positive impression. Therefore, they are very careful not speak "ghetto" or use dialectic expressions that would label them "foreign". Nero (2000) states that all of the participants in his study often "felt the need to be formal...by trying to speak... "straight

English"" in the presence of those who they perceive as authorities (p. 493). Henry (2001) offers as an explanation of this duality the assertion that Caribbean students are "grappling with living a double life-being bicultural/ bidialectal, required to code-switch between American and Caribbean linguistic, cultural, and social modes" (p. 185).

This "grappling" explains why many Caribbean students who switch between their cultural identities report feeling isolated and reviled by their African-American classmates. One key element that is often missing from class discussions that would assist Caribbean students is *tact*. For example, a male student from The Bahamas stated during a discussion of Alice Dark's *In the Gloaming,* "We don't have faggots in the Bahamas. They aren't tolerated. That's what he gets for doing something so bad." Unfortunately, the student did not take into consideration the feelings of others; he assumed that everyone shared his worldview. He also did not know that in that particular class was a 40-something Columbian woman who was HIV infected, nor that there was a 20 year old male student whose mother was recently diagnosed with AIDS.

The Caribbean students I have encountered frequently say what is on their minds, which in itself is not an atrocity; however, they are habitually unaware of the multiple meanings words carry in Standard American English. For instance, a former co-worker remarked that he had to adjourn his literature class early because tempers flared when a Caribbean student inadvertently misused the word "fool". A mishap occurred in my class recently, when discussing a local political issue, many Caribbean students attempted to play both sides against the middle. On one hand, they would exhibit an attitude of "we Jamaicans would never do that," or "that's what separates people from the islands from you all [American Blacks]." Then, a few minutes later, when the conversation took a turn to discuss reparations they said, "We are all in this together; the only thing that separates us is our accents. We want to be treated equally." During this same discussion, the class was asked whether or not they had registered to vote. Many Caribbean students said they had not and had no intentions of doing so, yet stated that they felt ignored by local politicians. I also noticed this phenomenon when I taught high school English classes, in the more diverse area of the state, in which Cubans and students from South American and Latin countries would commonly identify themselves as Caucasian. At least until they were faced with blatant racism and would then make statements such as "we minorities must stick together and take a stand."

ACCOMPLISHED PRACTICES

In researching this topic, there amongst the theory of assimilation, acculturation, language learning, language xenophobia, and language acquisition, were many suggestions for practices that teachers can adapt, adopt and instill in their daily classroom instruction. One idea comes in the form of an online response to the National Institute for Literacy by Howard Herrnstadt (2002). After presenting the basic idea for the course in English, he launches into Spanish as an example of the ability to function adequately in different language systems. This causes an uproar since no one is able to understand what is said, but it serves as an effective example of bilingualism. Herrnstadt then teaches his Caribbean patois speaking students Standard English as a second means of communication by adapting the material in a Caribbean freshman English college text. Additionally, he uses several small groups and continuously informs students that their various forms of patois are wonderful means of communication in their homes and communities but that they need to be bilingual with Standard English to function in academics and business in North America. He further goes to great lengths to explain that he is not out to erase their lovely accents, but to help make their grammar correct when they speak or write standard English and their speech clear enough for North Americans to understand them.

In her experiences with eight Caribbean middle-school girls placed in an English-as-a-Second Language class in a reading/writing/discussion group between 1995 and 1999, Henry (2001) deduces that these students do not come to the US "tabula rasa" but are "already reading." That is, they come "as readers and writers with a particular set of sociocultural understandings about the world" (p. 185). Her primary aim is to facilitate the girls' confident participation in American society as bicultural/bilingual individuals. She does this by having students present their ideas through drawing, discuss engaging and relevant topics, and read each others' writing as well as read to each other (p. 188).

Suarez-Orozco (2001), suggests providing role models and mentors, and fostering climates of cooperative learning and high expectations for all students. Other practices teachers should integrate into their teaching methods are to foster supportive relationships among students from a range of ethnic and socioeconomic backgrounds, use role models to provide internship experiences and help transform the professional goal from an abstract ideal to the attainable reality, engage in supportive relationships with their students, concurrently maintain high expectations of them, recognize that the expectations for children at different age levels vary significantly from one cultural context to another, and distinguish between the experiences of different immigrant generations (p. 580).

Nero (2000) also suggests that students read, write, and share stories in their home language and standard English; read literature by community members who write both in the home language and standard English; encourage dialogue writing and role playing using both the home dialect and standard English as a way of teaching language variation in different social contexts; have students do research projects on the community language; use the discourse patters found in students' writings to discuss their appropriateness for various genres and audiences and to compare and contrast the rhetorical styles used in the home and school cultures (p. 503).

Brokop (1999) provides a number of teaching strategies derived from tutor-training to assist in teaching ESL students. Teachers may choose to: restructure dictated sentences to reflect English grammar rules; offer suggestions of appropriate vocabulary if a student cannot use the "right" word they wish to use; include pronunciation along with word identification follow-up activities; and provide key words as a bridge between talking about the topic and dictating the language-experience story. Brokop further suggests that in addition to modifying reading and writing strategies for ESL students, teachers must be aware of how cultural differences can affect reading and writing instruction. For example, descriptive and narrative writing come easier for students whose language tradition is oral; however, comparison and argumentative writing may be extremely difficult and considered rude in cultures which value a harmonious sense of order.

USING TECHNOLOGY TO ASSIST CARIBBEAN STUDENTS

Teachers are faced with integrating as much technology into classes as possible in an effort to prepare students for the multiple tasks many new-market-jobs require. Attempting to create a paperless classroom created challenges for students. Students are required to forward their completed papers as attachments. Once received, these documents are then downloaded, edited using the Track Changes and Comment features of Microsoft Word and then are attached to an email, with grade in tow, back to the student. Students initially had a hard time coping with the idea of not receiving a colorfully marked paper *handed* back to them. However, many have become accustomed to the ritual and state that the immediate response and ability to see their mistakes *along with* suggestions for corrections really aid them in the writing process.

It was also beneficial for students to use the Highlight feature in Word to emphasize parts of the paper that were effective and then use a different color to highlight an area that needed work. Students were then able to locate their own errors quicker the next time as well as pinpoint their own weaknesses and errors. When given a questionnaire to complete during the first class meeting, less than half of the students stated that writing was their problem area when given the choice between speaking, writing, and reading. As this finding suggests, what Afro-Caribbean students, whether born and educated in America or in the schools of their respective countries, suffer is the overwhelming belief that their writing is good as is and is certainly better than those from other countries where English is not their official language. One participant "with the lowest level of proficiency in standard oral or writing English" even with ineffective schooling in overcrowded and under-resourced facilities in Guyana and New York, the student "did not perceive any problems with his writing precisely because he had had so little practice with the process" (Nero, 2000, pp. 494-495).

Students were asked to critique an essay written by a former Cuban high school honor student that was filled with structural and grammatical errors (the original essay appears below). The essay had been emailed to them prior to the start of class. The high school student was given a writing prompt that asked them to propose a holiday for their local school board to consider adding to the existing school calendar.

A Holiday I would pick to ad would be September 11th, why you ask because a terrible thing happened the World Trade Center, Pentagon, and part of Pennsylvania got hit against terroists in Airplanes. Thousands of people died this day for no reason. We should remember this day forever to know that in our time of need we still stand strong and will not put this down for we are Americans and as being Americans we will find Justice. we should have a holiday to take the hurt away and remember the good times we had before what happened to these innocent people. This is my way of saying we're sorry for what has happened and by doing this I think many people will feel better not just kids for off school but for everyone that needs time to cope This is basically my opinion for you to make September 11th a holiday to remember what has happened to the World Trade Center and all the innocent people. This is why ask you to make a holiday.

Many of the Caribbean students felt that they could easily produce a much better writing sample and that their overall writing was much better, even though they could not identify the many problems, other than spelling, present in the essay. They simply knew that something was wrong, but had no idea what or how to begin correcting them. When then given the task of writing an essay using the same prompt, many of the errors found in the sample essay above were visible in their completed essays.

SOCIETAL ISSUES: ARE SOLUTIONS POSSIBLE?

What may also help students from the Caribbean in the United States, some believe, are increased opportunities for students to be taught by teachers from their homelands. For example, in New York City, which boasts one of the largest concentrations of Jamaican and West Indian peoples, the public school system undertook a major recruiting drive. In response, nearly 700 applicants turned out at the University of the West Indies Mona campus in Kingston to fill out applications for a two-year teaching stint (English, 2001). Much of what these new teachers will ultimately require, is further faculty development, mentoring, and intensive cultural awareness of their new surroundings and old issues such as linguistic racism and segregation. Although skeptics may argue that the lure of making up to eight times more a year and recent layoffs in Jamaica may be the overriding impetus for the interest in teaching in

America, most teachers state that "they wanted to help immigrant Caribbean students who score low and are blamed for discipline problems in New York City public schools" (English, 2001). Predictably, this is usually the standard reply given by most teachers when asked why they entered the profession – *we want to help.*

Clearly, Caribbean students, no matter where they receive their education often experience displacement within systems that pledge to help, yet hinder students' acquisition of necessary skills and knowledge needed in order to survive and effectively compete within the construct of a new society. Some years ago Caribbean-American educators, elected leaders and community activists sought the establishment of a Caribbean school district in Brooklyn (Hinds, 1994, p. 6); however, more recently, California and Arizona, and perhaps New York and Massachusetts, are now thinking of dismantling bilingual education (Suarez-Orozco, 2001). Caribbean and other ethnic and linguistic minorities suffer while states and politicians ponder what to do to solve education's numerous and varied "problems". Likewise, it will be interesting to see how rural and underfunded school districts will respond to President Bush's *No Child Left Behind* educational reformation policy signed into law in 2002. In a 1999 workshop sponsored by the International Federation for the Teaching of English lead by Don Wilson and Lawrence Carrington, titled *Creole speakers and language education in schools,* the participants noted that current politics of education in the United Kingdom does not favor the identification of Caribbean students as a group requiring special support.

A study cited in Nero (2000) "showed that linguistic difficulties and (mis)placement in ESL classes were two factors...responsible for the academic underachievement of anglophone Caribbean students in Canadian schools" (p. 489). Sewell (1996) suggests that Britain needs a Black university similar to Howard and Morehouse. British students of Caribbean origins have a poorer chance of getting into "old" universities as a result of direct or indirect discriminating practices against black candidates (Kausar, 1994, p. 3). Rasekoala reports (1997) that only 6% of African-Caribbean men entered British colleges or universities at age 18, nearly 40% of entrants were over 25, however, about 30% of African-Caribbean women were over 25 on entry. British born Afro-Caribbean students are over-represented in higher and further education, but this is not the case in jobs in science and technology. A European report warns against 'channeling lower-achieving students in educational ghettos" instead of creating "high quality options." Also according to Rasekoala, Black pupils know of their White teachers' low expectations and are thus forced to attend schools in Africa and the Caribbean in order to acquire the necessary skills they need in order to return to the UK. Moreover, African-Caribbean students are five times less likely to get into medical school compared with white students with the same or lower grades, stated articles in the British Medical Journal (Joseph-Achikeobi, 1995, 3).

Not surprisingly, Caribbean students who find themselves in American primary, secondary, and post secondary institutions frequently and surprisingly find themselves in special education or ESL classes. "Having no other language than their English to lay claim to, many of these students are genuinely surprised at the perception of their language by outsiders, especially educators, as not quite English" (Nero, 2000, p. 484). Caribbean immigrant parents in New York City say, after learning that Caribbean students' grade levels in reading and math fall below the city's average of 50.6%, that their children who speak only Patois are sometimes evaluated and placed in special education classes (deCoteau, 1995). The lack of an established orientation program, which addresses these issues as well as linguistic, socio-emotional, psychological and educational needs of these children, is a concern in the Caribbean community (p. 17).

Caribbean parents and the educational system across several continents are faced with the dilemma of either maintaining or erasing patois in Caribbean children. This is supported by findings of Brokop (1999) who reports that the majority of students participating in basic level literacy programs are students for whom English is a second language. Such mislabeling occurs when teachers in the host country, the USA, UK or Canada, view these students' English as substandard or nonnative, since their speaking forms do not fit the conventional model of native speaker, subsequently, students are misplaced into ESL classes (Nero, 2000). English (2001) cites these concerns as one of the major reasons for the push to bring Caribbean teachers to New York; there is a "need to bridge a language gap that is often viewed as a roadblock to the scholastic achievement of many immigrant Caribbean students."

In an effort to combat this "roadblock" New York State intends to create bilingual education classes for students from English-speaking nations in the Caribbean such as Barbados, the Bahamas and Jamaica: call it Caribonics (Ravitch, 1997, p. 138). According to the plan, students who speak or understand a Creole language will take an English test; if they score in the bottom 40% and if they are in school with 19 others who speak the same Creole, they will be placed in a bilingual program where the language of instruction will be the Creole of their native land." When discussing this plan with a number of Creole and Patios speaking Caribbean students in my English classes, a number of them were outraged. "This is stupid! Why do this when these same kids are going to have to write letters explaining why they want to go to college? Do they think the admissions boards are going to employ the same number of Creole speaking recruiters?" asked Barbara. Mira echoed similar sentiments, "Are they going to be able to write in all their other classes using this "Caribonics"? What happens when they take the SAT, GRE, or CLAST (now known as the test of General Knowledge), tests that have a writing component?" Aliaia questioned further still, "This makes it seem as if we can't learn English. Weren't most of the Caribbean Islands owned by the British? And what is it that they speak? Is it not English?"

Considering the state of New York identifies nearly two dozen distinct Creole languages, what's often lost in many articles about Caribbean education in America, is that many of these English-language Caribbean countries and their inhabitants are given instruction in school in English, not in the local Creole (Ravitch, 1997). Many in fact prescribe to the same methods of English instruction as do teachers in the US, secondary schools in Barbados, Guyana, Jamaica, and the Bahamas, to name a few, use rote grammar exercises, rigid writing drills, intensive mathematical problem-solving, enforce strict discipline, give heavy loads of homework and expect strong parental support and hold high parental expectations (Ravitch, 1997; Nero, 2000; deCoteau, 1995; Suarez-Orozco, 2001).

WHAT CAN THEY DO?

So the question teacher training programs, administrators and teachers find themselves asking, "Is what can they do to offset such injustices and misplacement of Caribbean students?" According to deCoteau (1995), students need prompt attention, special orientation prior to placement, provision of accurate information to aid academic and career choices, comprehensive information regarding the structure, policies and goals of the particular school, active involvement of parents in the schools, reduction in number of Caribbean students being placed in Special Education classes, need for democratic voice in student body, culturally sensitive teachers, administrators, peers and curricula, multi-cultural education and language skills development (p. 21-22). When these essentials are not met, unsurprisingly, English (2001) says school districts with high percentages of Caribbean students perform poorly.

TEACHER TRAINING PROGRAMS

Teacher training programs must prepare teachers to address immigrant students' distinctive needs, include courses in sociolinguistics, and along with school districts develop curriculum and professional development programs that recognize the needs of culturally and linguistically diverse immigrant students and the challenges teachers confront in instructing these diverse students (Suarez-Orozco, 2001; Nero, 2000). Also, in order to reflect the populations being served and enhance their learning experiences, recruitment efforts should focus on diversifying the teaching force; special efforts must be made to adequately, fairly, and systematically assess the specific learning strengths and challenges of individual incoming immigrant student (Suarez-Orozco, 2001).

ADMINISTRATORS

Administrators must make certain their schools, serving immigrant students, provide engaging curriculum while children are in the process of acquiring English language skills and ensure that information is provided multimodally in order to scaffold the available linguistic and cultural resources (Suarez-Orozco, 2001). Nero's (2000) research shows that schools must also find the appropriate placement and literacy instruction for bidialectal speakers, especially for Creole Caribbean English speakers since they are more likely to be (mis)placed in ESL classes because their nonstandard language is coupled with the immigrant status; schools must also develop a specialized curriculum that focuses and incorporates the linguistic features of CCE speakers while presenting culturally relevant content (pp. 489, 502). Administrators should make certain that their schools mediate the tensions between cultural values and school practices, schools make cultural concessions to their students, and reconceptualize their notions of what constitutes parent involvement. (Suarez-Orozco, 2001)

TEACHERS AND PRACTITIONERS

The bulk of correcting the problem seems to fall upon the already weighted shoulders of teachers. According to Caribbean students in New York, they felt a sense of rejection based on the "host country's" negative perception of the immigrant students' cultural and linguistic background (deCoteau, 1995). They feel that the public school system is lacking in staff members who are culturally sensitive to their social, psychological and educational needs. The persistent failure on the part of the Board of Education to give recognition to the prior learning of "new immigrants students" contributes negatively towards these students' social and emotional well-being" (p. 20). Teachers must combat such feelings of alienation and awkwardness. Teachers must have a greater understanding of the students' language and culture and resist internal temptations to view students who speak CCE as being deficient and assigning them inappropriately to learning-disabled, special education, or ESL classes (Henry, 2001; Nero, 2000; Suarez-Orozco, 2001). They must strive to move away from large, impersonal, competitive institutions to smaller learning communities in which immigrant students are fully engaged in learning (p. 580). Teachers need to also be more informed about language and linguistic terminology if they are to grasp some of the critical characteristics of Caribbean Creoles, and teachers can exploit variation in West Indian speech behavior and the number of different Creoles...as a resource for their classroom activities (Wilson & Carrington, 1999).

It becomes crucial for practitioners to learn as much about the student's culture, values and language(s) in order to teach reading and writing in English. Literacy instruction of ESL students will need to include increased emphasis on the development of oral skills, using resources which are appropriate for adult students and which relate to the ESL student's interests and experiences, since many ESL students may lack English language skills in content areas they are very familiar with (Brokop, 1999). However, Anglophone Caribbean students are not always well served in ESL classes ...because they perceive themselves as speakers of English, they are less motivated to frame themselves as learners of English under the conditions of traditional ESL classes....Anglophone Caribbean students' receptive knowledge of standard oral and written English far exceeds that of many speakers of languages other than English because of the constant interaction between Creole and standard English along the Creole continuum" (Nero, 2000, 504).

REFERENCES

Brokop, F. (1999). Literacy and ESL learners. *Literacy partners of Manitoba* [On-line], Available: http://www.mb.literacy.ca/Newslet/nwriteon/dec99/page13.htm

Caribbean schools outclass US: Top Boston professor John Silber says America would do well to take a leaf out of the Caribbean education system. (1994, December 1). *The Weekly Journal,* 135, 7.

CXC's Examinations.[On-line], Available: http://www.cxc.org

deCoteau, H. (1995, February 28). Caribbean immigrant students in the New York Public School System. *Everybody's: The Caribbean-American Magazine,* 19, 17.

English, M. (2001, May 29). Teachers Board of Ed goes to the Caribbean to seek recruits. *New York Newsday* [On-line], Available: http://www.onenation.org/0105/052901a.htm.

Henry, A. (2001). The politics of unpredictability in a reading/writing/discussion group with girls from the Caribbean. *Theory into Practice, 40,* 184+.

Herrnstadt, H. (2002, January 8). Tom Sticht's Democracy. *National Institute for Literacy* [On-line], Available: http://www.nifl.gov/nifl-esl/2002/0019.html

Hinds, L. (1994, October 22). Caribbean school district a new wrinkle in the wash. *New York Amsterdam News,* 85, p. 6.

Joseph-Achikeobi, E. (1995, March 2). Med school shame: Black students are not getting the places at medical school their grades deserve because of dubious recruitment methods. *The Weekly Journal,* 147, p. C.

Kausar, B. (1994, September 8). Undergrads face 'unfair' selection. *The Weekly Journal,* 123, p. 3.

Loeb, P., & Friedman, D. (1993, October 4). To make a nation. *US News & World Report,* 115, I 13, pp. 47-52.

Meditz, S. W., & Hanratty, D. M. (1987). Caribbean Islands, social and economic developments, 1800-1960. Library of Congress [On-line], Available: http://memory.loc.gov/frd/cs/cxtoc.html

Nero, S. J. (2000). The changing faces of English: A Caribbean perspective. *TESOL Quarterly, v. 34,* pp. 483-510.

Rasekoala, E. (1997, March 31). Lost in lab land: Why are Black students falling behind in science and technology? *The Voice,* 748, p. 32.

Ravitch, D. (1997, September 22). Shi Taiad. *Forbes, 160,* p. 138.

Wilson, D., & Carrington, L. (1999). Report of the workshop: Creole speakers and language education in schools. The International Federation for the Teaching of English [On-line], Available: http://www.nyu.edu/education/teachlearn/ifte/creole.htm

Roberts, I. (1995, June 15). Teachers step up protests. *The Weekly Journal,* 163, p. 6.

Rong, X.L. & Brown, F. (2001). The effects of immigrant generation and ethnicity on educational attainment among young African and Caribbean Blacks in the United States. *Harvard Educational Review, 71,* pp.536-565.

Schools face shake-up: The Caribbean education system is undergoing a major over haul. But will it be enough to take the islands into the next millennium? (1998, March 16). *The Voice*, 797, p. 16.

Sewell, T. (1996, May 28) Live & kicking: Learning the American way. *The Voice*, 704. p. 11.

Suarez-Orozco, C. (2001). Afterword: Understanding and serving the children of immigrants. *Harvard Educational Review, 71,* p. 579+.

Thompson, L. C. (1995). But I changed three words! Plagiarism in the ESL classroom. *The Clearing House*, 69, 27-29.

William, H. (1996, June 4). 'Stressful and corrupt' school system slammed: JA leads way in education reform by scrapping high school exam. *The Voice,* 705, p. 15.

Wilson, K. (1999). Note-taking in the Academic Process of Non-native Speaker Students: Is It Important as a Process or a Product? *Journal of College Reading and Learning, 29,* 166.

CHAPTER 8

RACISM, RESISTANCE AND RESILIENCE: THE 3RS OF EDUCATING CARIBBEAN STUDENTS IN A CANADIAN CONTEXT

BRENDA MCMAHON &
DENISE ARMSTRONG

INTRODUCTION

The education of Black Caribbean students[1] in Canada has been an issue of concern for community members since the early 1970s, and continues to be a contested area for students, parents and educators. Over the past three decades, the recurring themes of system racism and student resistance have framed the discourse on schooling, as successive generations of researchers have provided evidence of high levels of academic failure (Brathwaite & James, 1996; Dei, 1997; Solomon, 1992). The triumvirate of high levels of alienation, disproportionate numbers of Black students in vocational streams and increasing drop-out rates are indicators of a system in a state of crisis, which has failed, and continues to fail to meet the needs of minority students in general and Black students in particular (Brathwaite & James, 1996; Coelho, 1988; Dei, 1997; Solomon, 1992). These assertions are encapsulated in the following comment by Spence (1999): "The present, well documented crisis in Canadian education is personified for Black students. This crisis is revealed in part by statistical parameters including low test scores, suspensions and dropout rates" (p.15).

Many of the difficulties Black Caribbean youth encounter result from racism and discrimination based on racial and cultural differences (Brathwaite & James, 1996; Dei, 1996). The existence of ingrained racism in the sociocultural fabric of our society and our daily interactions in schools is documented by authors such as Coelho (1988), who contends that "the fact of racial discrimination in Canada has been asserted and demonstrated very clearly in many research reports and official commissions" (p.54). Schools mirror the economic, political and ideological stratifications of the society in which they exist and act as forces that maintain, reproduce and perpetuate existing social inequities (Boyd, 1996; Giroux, 1983; Solomon, 1992). Through dominant Eurocentric notions of what is valid and invalid knowledge, schools replicate racial, cultural and class inequities (Dei & Karumanchery, 2001). Students are sorted, taught and streamed according to their projected socioeconomic status and as a result, students from racial minority groups and low socioeconomic status are more likely to be in the lowest academic streams (Oakes, Wells, Jones & Datnow, 1997).

Within the education system, racism operates as a complex dynamic in overt and covert ways. Powell's (1997) image of a racism as a knot made of black and white threads is a powerful analogy of the symbiotic interdependence of whiteness and blackness in schools. White systemic, individual and group privilege and power are inseparable from minority disadvantage and marginalization. Throughout this knot, the black or white threads are made visible or invisible depending on the issue, the intent or perspective of the individual or group. The white threads are strengthened by hegemonic structures which are reinforced by rules and regulations, administrative discretionary powers and exclusionary curriculum. The pervasive nature of racism makes the black threads problematic, while ignoring the stranglehold of the white ones. Blackness tends to be highlighted when the emphasis is on deviance, academic failure and lack of adjustment to the system. In order to loosen or unravel this discourse, it is important to focus on the role that Whiteness plays in sustaining, tightening or disentangling the strands. Integral to this process is the ability to generate possibilities for the white threads to interact with the black ones to weave an inclusive tapestry.

This paper extends the dialogue on Black student achievement by focusing specifically on the education of Caribbean students within metropolitan Toronto. The voices of Black Caribbean students and teachers enrich our understanding of their perceptions of education systems within multicultural contexts, their definitions of success and the factors that enhance and impede its attainment. Their individual and collective stories are testimony to the impact of institutional racism and system and student resistance on the lives of students. Using their experiences as a base, we examine the dynamic tensions inherent in institutional and student interactions and establish connections between the phenomena of racism, resistance and student resilience. Our discussion is premised on an axis of possibilities, scaffolded by the institutionalization of systematic anti-racist approaches. These are founded on the following key principles: educators' respect for students' strengths and agency; acceptance of the system's and individual educator's responsibility for student success; and enactment of articulated policies and values related to inclusive antiracist education.

METHODOLOGY

This study was conducted in the east end of Metropolitan Toronto, a large multicultural and multiethnic city. Within the metro region, this area is home to the largest concentration of Black families. Using statistics from the 1996 census, the Toronto Youth Profile showed that 37% of Toronto youth were born outside of Canada. Eleven percent of these young people, age 15 to 24 were born in the Caribbean. The census also identified 23% of the youth population as Black, many of whom are of Caribbean descent (Community and Neighbourhood Services Dept., 2000).

We conducted semi-structured interviews with ten Black educators of Caribbean origin who are employed by a large metropolitan school board. The participants were selected through referrals from their colleagues based on their experience with and knowledge of Caribbean and Canadian systems, and their success in working with Caribbean-Canadian students. They were also selected because they were parents of children who were either enrolled in or had completed their secondary school education in Ontario. Five interviewees were from Barbados, three from Jamaica, one from Antigua, and one from Trinidad. Six interviewees were female and four were male. They taught a variety of subjects and had an average of 25 years of teaching experience in Canada, Guyana, Barbados, and Jamaica. Of these respondents, nine were educated in both the Canadian and Caribbean systems, and one was educated in Canada. Their teaching experience in Canada was with highly diverse multicultural multiethnic populations in a variety of educational settings at the secondary level.

We also led focus groups with sixteen Black secondary school students of Caribbean origin, six of whom were female and ten were male.[2] Student participants were in the senior grades and attended large urban multicultural secondary schools. All of their schools had racially and culturally diverse student populations with predominately White, middle class teaching populations and administrative teams. Teachers involved in a tutorial program, who were not participants in the study, identified student respondents to represent varying levels of academic achievement, socioeconomic background and country of origin. In terms of their heritage, eight students were from Jamaica, four from Barbados, three from Trinidad, and one from St. Vincent.[3]

FINDINGS AND DISCUSSION

The literature, individual interviews and focus group discussions speak to the complexity of the tensions inherent in the education of Caribbean students. The student and teacher participants reflect on the conflicted nature of doing school in a multicultural society and sometimes are overwhelmed by the magnitude of their challenges. While at the same time acknowledging students' and parents' responsibility for student success, they express disappointment, frustration and anger at the system's entrenched racism and its lack of respect and responsiveness to their needs. They consider possibilities for success and cite individual instances of resilience. As they struggle to understand the paradoxes of schooling in Canada, the educators are torn by their contradictory status as both employee insiders and immigrant outsiders of the system.

COMING TO TERMS WITH RACISM

Students' and teachers' descriptions of their experiences support the call by theorists (Brathwaite & James, 1996; Dei, 1997; Solomon, 1992; Spence, 1999) to address racism at individual, institutional and cultural levels. Brathwaite and James (1996) and Solomon (1992) report that school districts' stated intent through their policies and procedures is to provide equitable learning opportunities for all students. However, their refusal to acknowledge systemic and individual racism combined with a lack of commitment to antiracist education has contributed to failure to launch these initiatives. Furthermore, researchers indicate that Black students in White dominant schools have not benefited from Canada's policy of multiculturalism (Coehlo, 1988; Ellis, 1999; Harper, 1997; Solomon, 1992; Spence, 1999). For example, Eurocentric approaches to pedagogy dominate schools, in spite of the national policy that was designed to encourage and reflect Canada's racial and cultural diversity (Solomon, 1992). Token gestures to multicultural celebrations with their focus on the 3Fs of foods, festivals and folklore, enable school systems to abdicate their responsibility, and mask the need for authentic structural changes that create opportunities for inclusion (Harper, 1997).

Individual, institutional and cultural racism are manifest in the education system through "deficit thinking" (Pearl, 1997) and discriminatory treatment by teachers, counselors and administrators (Dei, 1997; Soloman, 1992; Spence, 1999). Teacher and student responses provide clear instances of systemic and individual racism and identify them as a fact of life in Canada. A student describes her experiences with individual stereotyping and the conflicting emotions that accompany these acts. "They look at you as if to say, 'Where are you from?' Or they make jokes about your accent and try to mock you. Sometimes it can be fun and other times it can be annoying." The following comment by an educator reflects the endemic nature of Canadian racism and the difficulty in naming and consequently changing it.

> I don't want to say racism because I am not sure if that's what it is. I think sometimes it is a mindset, a stereotype about kids. Sometimes people just feel if kids come from a certain place, then they just don't know.

This supports Wright's (2000) contention that one of the impediments to rectifying the inequitable treatment of students in schools resides in our reluctance to acknowledge structural and individual forms of racism, which contradict our image as fair people. "It [racism] is an extremely uncomfortable word. It does not fit with Canadians' sense of themselves. Racism does not happen here! It describes events that happen elsewhere" (p.72).

Hixson and Tinzmann (1990) and Pearl (1997) point to the pervasive nature of institutional racism in the form of deficit thinking in schools. Racism is actualized in part through *"differential encouragements* maintained by statute, enacted by policy and informally practiced by classroom teachers and administrators" (Pearl, 1997, p.213). Denial of encouragement, exclusion from involvement in the life of the school, and perpetuation of curriculum that is elitist and reinforces beliefs in deficits are critical threads in the knot of underachievement. A teacher articulates concerns about their impact on students' ability to succeed in school.

"Having expectations, no expectations or low expectations are critical in what happens with Black kids and how they get streamed and steered away from more academic programs." The preservation of inequitable treatment and opportunities is made possible by a belief that students who come to school with social cues and experiences which differ from those of the dominant class are deficient. A teacher participant connects this insensitivity to educators' ignorance of other cultures. "I think many teachers don't try to understand other cultures. I notice that most teachers think that students from the West Indies are all stupid. That they are lacking something."

Educator and student participants' stories depict this lack of value for student strengths as a pervasive obstacle to success, and express frustration and anger at racism in the form of low expectations for Black students. In their research on deficit thinking, Peart and Campbell (1999) highlight how attributes related to race shape teachers attitudes to students and their practice. "Teachers who expect less may subtly communicate a sense of inadequacy to students, especially if these expectations are differential, depending on race. Whereas numerous factors may influence teacher expectations, race is one of the more significant" (p.271).

The following observation by a teacher demonstrates how these divergent expectations lead to inequitable treatment by race.

In this school if you are Asian and you're quiet, your mark goes up by ten percent because teachers assume you know the answers. If you are Black or Brown, and quiet, your mark goes down by ten percent because they assume you don't know the answers.

In his study of racism and stereotyping in a Toronto school, Ryan (1998) documents how similar patterns of differential expectations by race are covertly communicated.

Although teachers do not come out and explicitly say that African students as a group are less able academically than other groups, this belief is implied in much of their talk. For example, they never allude to them when citing gifted groups, but may single out individuals as if they are an exception to the rule... On the other hand, both teachers and students believe that Asian and Chinese students are the most gifted intellectually (p.294).

This juxtaposition of low expectations for Black students with positive evaluations of other racial groups compounds the damage to the personal and cultural self-worth of Caribbean students. Barr and Parrett (2001) report that students live up or down to the beliefs of their teachers, and it is almost impossible for students to overcome these negative perceptions. This accompanying sense of hopelessness is a mitigating factor in student disengagement and failure. They begin to internalize negative self-concepts that compromise their self-esteem, and feel that the demands of schooling are beyond their capabilities. In their work with Black Caribbean/Canadian males, Boehm-Hill (1993), Solomon (1992) and Spence (1996) observe that many become cognizant of educational, employment and economic barriers and as a result do not envision education as a key to increased opportunity. Student participants are honest in acknowledging that they play a role in this dynamic. "A lot of times, we procrastinate. We go home the night before a test and then we begin to study for it." Dei's (1997) work illustrates the role of systemic racial bias in marginalizing students who eventually drop out or are pushed out of schools.

Students and teacher respondents identify role models and mentors as important to the development of a positive cultural identity and personal self-esteem. At times, they attributed Caribbean students' lack of success to the paucity of teachers, guidance counsellors, and administrators with whom they can identify. This supports Dei's (1997) contention that the power and privilege of White society is reinforced by the lack of representation of others and is also related to the sense of invisibility many Black students experience. A student describes the cultural and emotional void created by this omission for students and holds it up as another indication of systemic inequities.

> The Chinese kids have Chinese teachers and the White people, even though their population in the school is very low, they can turn left, right and center and they can find somebody who they can talk to, or somebody willing to mentor them. There are not a lot of positive influences around us who we can look up to.

Ellis (1999) points to the insidious nature of systemic biases which exist to the extent that "students who are not middle class and politically White can find it challenging to develop a coherent, positive social identity and do well in school" (p.189). Respondents express a sense of estrangement from mainstream culture. The feeling of being an outsider is independent of the length of time in Canada. An educator describes the void which causes students' feelings of alienation. "Somehow we have missed a piece. It's like a puzzle and a chunk is missing. I don't think there is anything happening in the school to help that piece." Adolescent developmental identity issues, coupled with the feeling of being a minority perhaps for the first time, further exacerbate the ramifications of marginalization from mainstream culture. A teacher further describes the resulting cross-cultural dissonance.

> The kids see their 'Caribbeanness' being assaulted by their 'Canadianness' and they can't put the two of them together. They have a solid set of cultural norms and they come into a school that clashes with their norms and they cannot handle it.

The absence of significant role models within the education system, the presence of stereotypical racial images throughout society, and the lack of forums to discuss and share cultural aspects lead to erroneous beliefs by Blacks and Whites alike. Teachers describe the existence of an essentialist and hierarchical view of individuals as defined solely by race and political-geographic location. In schools, this engenders the creation of a master narrative which is directly linked to the tendency to use popular media stereotypes of American Blacks as reference points. An educator describes this phenomenon as multi-faceted.

> I think Americanism has been detrimental to Caribbean people. Caribbean-Canadian students are buying the nonsense. I think that too many children are growing up with false personas. They're growing up with an interpretation of their reality that they get through television, records or movies and in fact, it is not their reality.

Within the education system this trend is also reflected in approaches to teacher professional development. For example, one of the teachers comments,

> I don't know how many race-relations conferences I've been to and they bring somebody in at large sums of money from America. I'm thinking always when I'm hearing these people, 'You're foreign to me.' So why aren't you bringing somebody from one of the Caribbean countries? We don't do that. We're not passing on to the teachers anything about the Caribbean people. We're passing on a model that doesn't fit.

The majority of the student respondents see schools, teachers, and the system as unresponsive to inclusionary practices and to groups who do not fit the White middleclass stereotype. Brathwaite and James (1996) and Solomon (1992) indicate that the curriculum may be a source of cultural dissonance for students and may not reflect their presence, experiences or values. Students' responses mirror the patterns of student narratives in Dei's (1997) study which show that racial issues and Eurocentric curricula play significant roles in discouraging Black students. Students express feelings of frustration about not receiving school support in forming a Caribbean club and perceive this as discriminatory. "In the school we even have a Tamil club. How come we do not have one for us?" This comment supports Pearl's (1997) claims that elitist curriculum exists through inclusion and exclusion. "Aspects of the 'hidden curriculum' such as the images and events that are celebrated in the school, also give strong messages about the relevance or importance of the different racial and cultural groups in the school" (Coelho, 1998, p.37). Exclusion extends beyond the classroom to experiences within the larger school culture. In an interview with Miner (1995) Enid Lee further elaborates on the systemic nature of elitist curriculum and demonstrates how it excludes students of Caribbean origin by negating their experience.

> When teachers choose literature that they say will deal with a universal theme of story, like childhood, all the people in the stories are of European origin; it's basically White culture and civilization. That culture is different from others, but it doesn't get named as different. It gets named as normal (p.10).

This lack of inclusion of multiple ways of being combined with the normalization of Whiteness is seen as inhibiting success for students of Caribbean origin (Brathwaite & James, 1996; Dei, 1997; Ellis, 1999; and Miner, 1995).

LOCATING RESISTANCE

Much of the discourse on resistance equates it with deviance and connects it directly to students' attitudes and behaviours. Giroux (1983) contradicts this hegemonic notion and claims that resistance is often located in "moral and political indignation" (p.107). The following student illustrates her position. "Some teachers think that because they tell us something and we don't challenge it that we have to take it." When we reframe Giroux's (1983) notions within Powell's (1997) metaphor of the knot, we locate resistance within the white and black threads. In resistant interactions, the knot tightens and individual white or black threads can be seen as changing relationships to the others. Resistance in schools is present in the iterations that emerge as a result of the interactive processes between teachers and students, and the diverging patterns that evolve. Within school communities the white threads, by virtue of their relative location in the hierarchy are stronger, thicker and more powerful. Consequently, in instances of escalating oppositional resistance, the black threads are more easily frayed, broken or strangled by the tightening of the knot.

Bellous (2001) comments on the ambiguity of resistance, as enacted in conciliatory and/or adversarial ways in order to gain control of curricular and co-curricular activities, physical space, identity and image. Solomon's (1992) ethnography of Black male students in a Toronto high school demonstrates how these power struggles generate a negative spiral that contributes to

Black separation and alienation from mainstream culture and its apparent futility against the system. "While this may be instantly gratifying and potentially emancipatory, a misguided oppositional culture is at risk to unsympathetic institutional structures" (p. 113). This is consistent with respondents' depictions of resistance as rooted in the exercise of power and played out through strategic moves and countermoves by school authorities and students. They identify escalating staff and institutional resistance as impediments to success for Black Caribbean students.

Legally embedded power differentials within school rules and structures are often used to support system resistance by keeping students in their place and silencing them, as exemplified by the following student comment. "You need staff support to do anything in the school. I don't know one staff member in this school who actually helps me because they want to. Most of them don't help me at all." Staff resistance is often combined with patronizing attitudes, as another student comment illustrates. "They get at you with their smart comments and try to put you down with their intelligent ways. That is the most annoying thing in the world." Conflictual relationships resulting from a lack of respect by school personnel for cultural differences, demonstrated through students' attempts to assert themselves, lead to attributions of student deviance. Students who do not conform to the status quo are labeled as 'trouble-makers', "a stereotype which is particularly difficult to negate once it is attached to a race" (Dei, 1997, p.87).

Within coercive systems, students may use forms of resistance in self-defeating ways (Bellous, 2001). This contention is supported by portrayals of the ambiguities and complexities inherent in Black Caribbean resistance in Toronto (Dei, 1997; James & Brathwaite, 1996; Solomon, 1992; Spence, 1996). Their studies show that high drop out rates among Blacks persist in spite of importance parents, students and community place on education. Although the stated goals of the students and the system are similar, they are sometimes enacted in parallel, perpendicular and oppositional ways. Student and teacher narratives illustrate aspects of the dynamic push and pull of Black Caribbean resistance within high schools.

> We are struggling and they keep bringing us down. When they bring you down, it's kind of like stomping on your self-esteem and self-confidence because like I'm pushing myself this much to get this done and you're going to bring me down. It only takes that one second and one thought to kill everything.

The dissonance between the structure of the education system and the culture of the students, and the system's and the students' articulated goals and actions mitigate against respondents' abilities to envision possibilities for student empowerment. Educators and students indicate that some students choose the "path of least resistance" and fail, thus reinforcing their teachers' negative stereotypes. Some students react in this manner because they see achieving academic success as an insurmountable task. "You always feel you have to prove something. When it gets difficult the easiest way out is what's looked at as the dumbest thing to do – to give up." Students espouse high educational goals "while falling back on their own subordinate oppositional culture to resist the structure. This paradox of high educational aspirations and low effort investment packaged with oppositional cultural forms is a significant feature of resistance mediated by race" (Solomon, 1992, p.104). It is compounded by students' ambivalence, which is expressed through challenges to authority and disengagement from the academic process.

System resistance leads to student frustration, alienation and feelings of disempowerment. In response to being marginalized, students say they feel compelled to assert their 'blackness' in response to the 'whiteness' of the system and to maintain their sense of racial, cultural and personal identity. Studies of Black and Caribbean youth conducted by Dei (1997) and Solomon (1992) show that students use resistant responses to protect their identity and to gain power when the system refuses to value their strengths. They come to see schools and other social institutions as "barriers to their development and actively resist their regularities, forms of knowledge and social practices" (Solomon, 1992). A student comment supports the existence of this dynamic "You're always ready to rebel in school." As participants in spirals of resistance, students' conscious and unconscious responses are exhibited through passive, passive-aggressive, and/or defiant behaviours and attitudes. In attempts to gain a sense of control, they report that they intentionally employ tactics to "toy with teachers' brains"; "use slang purposely just to get them mad"; "claim specific territories in schools as Black areas" and "push limits of school rules such as dress codes."

An educator speaks to the role that a form of student resistance plays in escalating teacher reactions. "Their hostile responses to racism and accusations turn off teachers." Students and teachers become locked into behaviours which are counterproductive to their goal of achieving academic success. Solomon's (1992) research in a multiracial educational context supports the finding that Black students' attempts to assert themselves and establish their identities are met with strong disapproval and fear from teachers. "In a conflict-ridden environment, student-teacher interactions mediated by fear will be exploited by oppositional students who are constantly exploring ways to undermine, antagonize, and manipulate authority structures they perceive as not serving their interest" (p.115). This is consistent with Ryan's (1998) findings that, "most teachers will go out of their way to avoid students of African heritage, particularly in the halls of the school, because many of them are intimidated by these young people" (p. 293). The resulting psychological and social costs for students are apparent in their responses. "We can't get anywhere when we always have something negative to think about. It completely depletes your self-esteem. You feel like garbage. You think, 'To hell with everybody.'"

Attempts by students to hold teachers accountable for their actions are met with failure, leading to further frustration and distrust of the system. According to a student,

> I was raised to say don't let anybody walk over you so if I prove a teacher wrong on a question, then the teacher's going to get defensive and stuff and start to yell. Then it's only natural to rebel against them.

A lack of trust in teachers and the school system is realized through self-protective attitudes and feelings of the need to be constantly vigilant. "I get very defensive. I always have to be standing on guard ready for something to be thrown at us because we're being dealt with differently." Interpreted as noncompliance, student resistance is met with a lack of understanding and increased regimentation by the school in the form of suspensions and exclusions. This spiral of behaviour escalates as school personnel attempt to control the students with harsher consequences and the students refuse to comply. School authorities become entrenched in their positions and impose stricter rules (Solomon, 1992). The following student narrative is illustrative of a sequence in the cycle of escalating conflict.

> Teachers go and lie and say how this student threatened to kill them and stuff like that. You end up getting suspended and your marks go down because they are just abusing the power. They were telling me in the office, when I came back that I shouldn't rebel against them. 'Don't take it to heart. What they say does not really mean anything!'

Respondents point to the involvement of external sources of authority by administrators, as exemplified by the high level of police involvement within schools. They express concern about the large number of arrests related to incidents that occur within schools. Criticizing this practice, an educator says, "When kids go wrong we lock them up. And in fact, sometimes they really haven't gone wrong and we lock them up."

FOSTERING RESILIENCE

Contemporaneous with challenges and barriers which limit Black Caribbean students in Canadian schools, are instances of possibilities within which students of Caribbean origin are experiencing academic success. They can be understood by extending Powell's (1997) metaphor of the knot. Through various interactions within school systems some of the black threads become stronger and more elastic in response to the pressures exerted by the white ones. At the same time some of the white threads interweave with the black ones instead of in opposition to them, loosening and reconfiguring the knot. The tensile strengths inherent within the threads and in the relationships among them can be seen as analogous to "protective factors" or "protective processes" identified by theorists as integral to student resilience (Benard, 1995; Johnson, 1997; McMillan & Reed, 1994; Smokowski, Reynolds & Beruczko, 1999; Westfall & Pisapia, 1994). Protective factors are located within students and consequently dependent on student agency for their realization. A teacher comments on students' perseverance and determination.

> My, they are so resilient! This is especially true for students who emigrate here from the Caribbean. They come to school and see people with their funny ways and their funny talk. And they keep coming back day after day.

Unlike some of their less academically successful peers, resilient Black Caribbean students respond to systemic racism by refusing to let it hinder the achievement of their goals. An educator speaks of inner strength and connects resilience to students having the ability "to develop a thickness of skin." "I think there is a real strength in character because I believe that those kinds of frustrations and adversities that they deal with on a day to day basis make them stronger."

Students' definitions of success include but are not limited to academic achievement. Their depictions of it as dependent on individual goals is consistent with the protective factors of an internal locus of control, a strong sense of purpose and hope for the future identified in literature on resilience in education (Benard, 1995; Westfall & Pisapia, 1994). According to a female student, success is "an inner peace kind of thing. Trying to find what you like doing." Student respondents demonstrate an orientation which, while grounded in the present is focused towards future goals. A female respondent identifies the importance of making a commitment to the future as she offers the following advice to other participants in her focus group.

> Make the best out of whatever time you have in high school. Get the grades and you won't have the problems. You will be in college or university for the next five years or three years depending on what you want to do. After that is your chance to go and make your money and do whatever. I understand that it is hard because I have to be working hard.

Sanders (1997) asserts that in order to counteract negative stereotypes, successful Black students make a strong commitment to academic achievement. The students comment that although they perceive themselves as hardworking, teachers and the society at large identify Black as 'lazy' or 'criminal'. "They don't see us as somebody who works hard. When we work hard, we work damn hard for what we get." Students' behaviours, which demonstrate their refusals to succumb to systemic depictions, combined with beliefs that they have to "work twice as hard to succeed" are indicative of their persistence. Brathwaite and James (1996) report that successful students "believed that individual effort, qualification and ability would ultimately help them to realize their goals in society. They tended to be determined that neither discrimination or colour would be a barrier for them" (p.20). According to a student,

> What you put in is what you get out. If you get a poor mark you have to approach the teacher and ask, 'How come I got this mark? I don't understand. Will you give me another chance to make this up?'

In addition, students report that an understanding of their minority status combined with encouragement from parents and self-determination leads to the realization that they can overcome the impediments of systemic and individual racism. A student describes a strategy she uses, "You have to get used to the racism on the street. You have to get used to people putting you down." They also demonstrate an attitude of self-reliance and independence. For many students self-sufficiency is correlated to economic achievement. One of the male students speaks of his need for financial independence. "When I am older, I won't be asking anybody for money." Another respondent indicates the importance of academic achievement and connects his success to a sense of commitment and the importance of taking initiative.

> Nobody comes and says do you want to sign up for a club? I signed up for a science challenge. I went because it is something I am interested in. On a Saturday morning at 7:00 a.m., I went to the university and sat in a three-hour lecture to find out about it.

An educator, emphasizing the significance of protective factors of perseverance and maintaining a sense of humour, recalls attempts to organize inter-school cricket matches for students.

> It was one thing after another. First, we were told to speak to the head of the physical education department. When we approached him about forming a cricket team, he said there was no money for equipment. Once we got over that obstacle, we were told there was no space for practice. Then when they finally agreed that we could play cricket, they put it in the rainy season.

Student participants who demonstrate resilience are cognizant that the protective factors, which they identify as important to their academic achievement were absent from the actions of some of the other Black Caribbean students. Respondents made comments such as, "You need to get your priorities straight. That's one thing that I don't think a lot of Black students do;" and, "A lot of us don't ask...how come?" These are indicators of their belief that self-sufficiency can enable them to achieve success as they define it. They may be also indicative of a tendency to rely on master narratives that achievement and success reside within individuals rather than in the relationships and the institutions within which they are constructed.

Contrary to this approach which demands that the oppressed assume responsibility for their own oppression, Hixson and Tinzmann (1990), Johnson (1994), and Norman (2000) identify protective processes which are located within relationships between students, significant others and institutions as essential for resilience. Teachers' responses support Datnow and Cooper's (1996) emphasis on the importance of external psychological and social support systems that value academic achievement. Teachers identify a need for social interactions that contribute to resilience such as a need for "teachers who understand the human condition and students' socialization process and are able to help them translate the social cues and teach them in a Canadian context." Smokowski, Reynolds & Beruczko (1999) state that "relational bonds" between teachers and adolescents are important in buffering risks and facilitating adaptive development. For resilient students, these relationships are with "teachers that had positive expectations and that push the students while remaining very supportive and understanding" (Westfall & Pisapia, 1994, p.3). Respondents emphasize the importance of offering culturally specific group support and the need to connect with outside Caribbean agencies. A teacher expresses it as a "need to get these kids together within schools and talk about issues that relate to them, how they are going to deal with these issues and help them to strategize, cope and set expectations." Suggestions also include providing opportunities for student groups to come together to discuss experiences, enrich system literacy, develop problem-solving strategies, and create cultural celebrations within Caribbean Canadian groups assist in bridging cultural gaps.

RECOMMENDATIONS AND CONCLUSION

The preceding discussion highlights the need for educators to address issues of cultural, systemic and individual racism and their impact on resistance and resilience within schools. In order to transform school culture into arenas of resilience, sustainable changes are required in the implicit and explicit curricula structures. Schools need to adopt antiracist approaches which enhance protective factors and processes, and challenge belief systems and policies which support ingrained inequities. McLaren (1995) speaks of antiracist pedagogy as "transforming the social, cultural, and institutional relations in which meanings are generated" (p.42). It creates environments within which "students from diverse racial, ethnic, and social-class groups will experience educational equality and a sense of empowerment" (Banks, 1993, p.27). It affirms diversity within a politics of cultural criticism and a commitment to social justice and is important in developing resilience. Such practices and approaches will teach Caribbean students how to read social and political situations, familiarize themselves with power interests, and connect ethical values with political actions in order to bring about change.

The participants' experiences speak to issues related specifically to curriculum. Antiracist pedagogy addresses their concerns as it crosses all disciplines "and addresses the histories and experiences of people who have been left out of the curriculum" (Miner, 1995, p.9). One method of achieving these goals is to include significant contributions of a wide variety of racial, ethnic, and cultural groups in curriculum content (Gay, 1995, p.167). Curriculum that integrates aspects of geographical, social and cultural lives contributes to engaging students of Caribbean origin. An example of meaningful curriculum, which connects to Caribbean students lived experiences involves including diverse perspectives and voices. Within the English curriculum, this includes the addition of authors such as Cecil Foster, Olive Senior, and Louise Bennett, Jamaica Kincaid, and Paul Keens-Douglas, reflecting the diverse heritages of Caribbean students. Inclusive learning communities can enhance success for students of Caribbean origin, create opportunities for engagement, and provide models of positive resistance and resilience.

A commitment to a climate that cultivates resilience involves providing meaningful opportunities for student participation and leadership, inside and outside of the classroom. Having high expectations for Caribbean students, providing them with challenging curriculum and supporting them academically, socially and emotionally engender possibilities for equitable outcomes. Pedagogical strategies that encourage questioning, integrate and value students' experience and knowledge base, and foster positive expressions of resistance and resilience can be facilitated through open dialogue with students. Such staff-student exchanges encourage understanding of the diversity and richness of the students' backgrounds and an appreciation of their strengths. They allow for greater understanding of the impact of the role of culture and privilege, as well as the ways in which racist ideology affects classroom practice. They also enable teachers to reduce their fear, recognize the roots of conflict, take responsibility for their own resistance, and deescalate the spiral of negative resistance.

The students and educators identify the need for cultural and emotional identity and academic support for Caribbean students. Beyond the classroom, student involvement in clubs, extra curricular activities, and leadership opportunities are important for building self-esteem and fostering student engagement and academic achievement. Tutorial and mentoring programs and practices should be based on individual and group needs of students and established in conjunction with parents, community organizations and Caribbean agencies. Schools have a responsibility to work proactively, creating respectful, welcoming environments which encourage parents to be equal partners in their children's education. When implementing strategies, policies and procedures, it is important that school personnel initiate honest communication with students, parents, community members and agencies. In addressing the hidden curriculum, schools and boards need to ensure that their recruitment, hiring and promotion practices generate staff that is representative of their student populations. At the same time, all teachers have a responsibility to act as role models for all students by being understanding, caring, and informed (Coelho, 1988; Nieto, 2000). Boards have an obligation to support existing staff by providing professional development in antiracist sensitization, conflict resolution and fostering resilience. In order to avoid the pitfalls of essentialism, training needs to be specifically related to the education of students of Caribbean origin.

Education is a promise that the Canadian school system has held out to the Caribbean community and which they have tenaciously believed, in spite of the structural inequities which characterize the system. It is clear that schools have a moral responsibility to fulfill this obligation and it is imperative that they take steps to ensure equitable outcomes for all students. A system-wide process of self-examination needs to bring to consciousness, the beliefs, values and practices educators employ in their daily interactions with Black children. Taking responsibility for their role in student failure and making a commitment to disentangling the knots of racism and underachievement is a necessary step. The onus is on educators and the school system to move existing equity policies from articulation to implementation. Enacting anti-racist policies and practices which are integrative rather than additive would close the existing implementation gap, and contribute to the establishment of a culture of excellence. Through sustainable dialogue students and teachers can work together to challenge the structural, social economic and political forces that restrict their lives. In applying this pedagogy of possibilities to Powell's (1997) metaphor, we can reconfigure the black and white threads as a rich tapestry, forming positive patterns and strengthened by the mutual interlacing of all threads.

ENDNOTES

[1] In this study we focus on the experiences of Black students of Caribbean origin as opposed to all Black students or all students of Caribbean origin. We are cognizant of the fact that Caribbean students belong to multiple racial groups and that there is no singular Black experience.

[2] Although there is concern about the disparity in academic performance between males and females, levels of

achievement between male and female participants were not substantively different. While globally significant, issues of gender as related to academic success are outside of the scope of this study.

[3] Socioeconomic status could be seen to have an effect on students' responsibilities outside of school, but it did not appear to significantly impact on their experiences with racism within the schools themselves.

REFERENCES

Banks, J. (1993). Multicultural education: Development, dimensions, and challenges. *Phi Delta Kappan*, Sept. 22-28.

Barr, R. and Parrett, W. (2001). *Hope fulfilled for at-risk and violent youth: K-12 programs that work* (2nd ed.). Boston: Allyn and Bacon.

Bellous, J. (2001). Should we teach students to resist? In W. Hare & J.P. Portelli (Eds.), *Philosophy of education: Introductory readings* (3rd ed.). (pp. 131-143). Calgary: Detselig.

Benard, B. (1991). *Fostering resilience in kids: Protective factors in the family, school, and community*. San Francisco: Far West Laboratory for Educational Research and Development.

Boehm-Hill, C. (1993). Empowering an endangered species: The African-Caribbean/Canadian male. *Education Canada*, Summer, 31-35.

Boyd, D. (1996). Dominance concealed through diversity: Implications of inadequate perspectives on cultural pluralism. *Harvard Educational Review,* 66(3), 609-630.

Brathwaite, K. S. & James, C. E. (Eds) (1996). *Educating African Canadians*. Toronto: James Lorimer & Co.

Coelho, E. (1988). *Caribbean students in Canadian schools Book 1.* Toronto: Carib-Can.

Coelho, E. (1998). *Teaching and learning in multicultural schools.* Toronto: Multilingual Matters

Community and Neighbourhood Services Department. (1999). *Toronto youth profile: Volumne 1.* Toronto: City of Toronto.

Datnow, A. & Cooper, R. (1996). Peer networks of African American students in independent schools: Affirming academic success and racial identity. *Journal of Negro Education,* 65, 56-72.

Dei, G. (1996). Listening to voices: Developing a pedagogy of change from the narratives of African- Canadian students and their parents. In K. Brathwaite & C. James (Eds.), *Educating African Canadians* (pp. 32-57). Toronto: James Lorimer.

Dei, G. (1997). *Drop out or push out? The dynamics of Black students' disengagement from school.* Toronto: OISE.

Dei, G. and Karunmanchery, L. (2001). School reforms in Ontario: The marketization of Education" and the resulting silence on equity. In J. P. Portelli & P. Solomon (Eds.), *The Erosion of Democracy in Education.* Calgary: Detselig Enterprises.

Ellis, J. (1999). Children and place: Stories we have, stories we need. *Interchange,* 30(2), 171-190.

Gay, G. (1995) Mirror images on common issues: Parallels between multicultural education and critical pedagogy. In C. Sleeter & P. McLaren (Eds.). *Multicultural education, critical pedagogy, and the politics of difference.* Albany: SUNY.

Giroux, H. (1983). *Theory and resistance in education: A pedagogy for the opposition.* Boston: Bergin & Garvey.

Harper, H. (1997). Difference and diversity in Ontario schooling. *Canadian Journal of Education,* 22(2), 192-206.

Hixson, J. and Tinzmann, M.B. (1990). *Who are the "at-risk" students of the 1990s?* Portland: North Central Regional Educational Laboratory.

Johnson, G. (1994). An ecological framework for conceptualizing educational risk. *Urban Education,* 29(1), 34-49.

Johnson, G. (1997). Resilient at-risk students in the inner-city. *McGill Journal of Education,* 32(1), 35-49.

McLaren, P. (1995). White terror and oppositional agency: Towards a critical multiculturalism. In C. Sleeter & P. McLaren (Eds.). *Multicultural education, critical pedagogy, and the politics of difference* (pp. 30-70). Albany: SUNY.

McMillan, J. and Reed, D. (1994). At-risk students and resiliency: Factors contributing to academic success. *Clearing House,* 67 (3),137-140.

Miner, B. (1995). Taking multicultural, anti-racist education seriously: an interview with Enid Lee. In D. Levine et al. *Rethinking schools* (pp. 9-15). New York: The New Press.

Nieto, S. (2000). Affirming diversity: implications for teachers, schools, and families. In *Affirming Diversity: The sociopolitical context of multicultural education* (pp. 323-348). New York: Longman.

Norman, E. (2000). The strengths perspective and resiliency enhancement - a natural partnership. In E. Norman (Ed.) *Resiliency Enhancement: Putting the strengths perspective into Social Work practice* (pp. 1-16). New York: Columbia University Press.

Oakes, J., Wells, A., Jones, M., and Datnow, A. (1997). Detracking: The social construction of ability, cultural politics, and resistance to reform. *Teachers College Record,* 98(3), 483-510.

Pearl, A. (1997). Democratic education as an alternative to deficit thinking. In R. Valencia (Ed.) *The evolution of deficit thinking: Educational thought and practice* (pp. 211-241). Bristol, PA: Falmer.

Peart, N. and Campbell, F. (1999). At-risk students' perceptions of teacher effectiveness. *Journal for a Just and Caring Education,* 5(3), 269-284.

Powell, L. (1997). The achievement (k)not:Whiteness and "Black under achievement". In M. Fine, L. Weis, L. Powell & L. Mun Wong. *Off White: Readings in race, power and society* (pp. 3-12). New York: Routlege

Ryan, J. (1998). Understanding racial/ethnic stereotyping in schools: From image to discourse. *Alberta Journal of Educational Research,* XLIV(3), 284-301.

Sanders, M. G. (1997). Overcoming Obstacles: Academic achievement as a response to racism and discrimination. *Journal of Negro Education,* 66, 83-93.

Smokowski, P., Reynolds, A. and Bezruczko, N. (2000). Resilience and protective factors in adolescence: An autobiographical perspective from disadvantaged youth. *Journal of School Psychology,* 37(4), 425-448.

Solomon, R. P. (1992). *Black resistance in high school: Forging a separatist culture.* Albany: SUNY.

Spence, C. (1999). *The skin I'm in: Racism, sports and education.* Halifax: Fernwood.

Westfall, A. and Pisapia, J. (1994). *Students who defy the odds: A study of resilient at-risks students.* Richmond: Metropolitan Educational Research Consortium.

Wright, O. (2000). Multicultural and anti-racist education. In T. Goldstein & D. Selby (Ed.). *Weaving connections: Educating for peace, social and environmental justice* (pp.57-98). Toronto: Sumach.

BRENDA MCMAHON AND DENISE ARMSTRONG

CHAPTER 9

ADAPTING TO SCHOOL AND SOCIETY IN THE UNITED STATES: EXPERIENCES OF IMMIGRANT ADOLESCENTS FROM THE DOMINICAN REPUBLIC

SHANA GROSSMAN

ABSTRACT

This chapter summarizes the findings of a qualitative, single-case study of adolescent immigrants from the Dominican Republic to the United States. The purpose of this study was to identify key factors that participants perceive as borders, boundaries or bridges between their home, school and peer worlds. This chapter focuses on the findings related to the Dominican educational system, and highlights what the adolescents reported as the major contrasts between the Dominican and U.S. educational systems. Many of the factors that Dominican students perceive as borders may apply to other Caribbean students who immigrate to the U.S. as well.

SHANA R. GROSSMAN

INTRODUCTION

As a newEnglish to Speakers of Other Languages' (ESOL) U.S. public high school teacher, I was first given a class called ESOL Literacy. This class was designed for students who had interrupted education and whose first language literacy, academic skills and/or behavior were considered too low for the regular introductory ESOL class. My first student was Roamer, a Dominican boy appropriately named because of his inability to sit still for any extended period of time. Over the next five years, Roamer became an integral part of my teaching life: the first two years in my U.S. History and ESOL Literacy classes, then in my Government class, and later coming for help after school with his night school class and other more advanced ESOL classes. We had our ups and downs, times when he went running out of the school building with me chasing after him but after five years, he finally graduated. Why was graduating from high school so difficult for this bright, outgoing, albeit mischievous, boy?

As I continued to teach, I noticed that students from the Dominican Republic were always represented in my literacy class. I noted that, of the recent immigrant groups I worked with, the Dominican students often seemed to have the hardest time adjusting to the U.S. school culture. Their ebullient personalities often did not fit with the passive behavior expected in most classrooms. It was not unusual to hear a teacher explaining that a class was especially difficult to manage because it had a large number of Dominican students.

Racial stereotyping and prejudice of teachers and other students, particularly other Latinos, seems to have a strong impact on the self-concept and performance of Dominicans. As a recent article in The Washington Post pointed out, "to assimilate, or even to fit in, the Black Latinos must adapt not only to white America and black America but to Latino America" (Escobar, 1999, p. A3). Also, because many Dominican families move back and forth between countries, Dominican adolescents, like other youth from transnational ethnicities, may have a harder time feeling fully accepted in either society.

As my interest in this population grew, I began a pilot study in which I interviewed six Dominican students whose school records documented interruptions in their education (not necessarily related to immigration), many of whom had been in my literacy class (Grossman, S., 1998). Later, I decided to explore the Dominican immigrant adolescent's worlds further in a larger study. In this article, I will briefly summarize the major findings of this study and then focus in on the differences between the U.S. and Dominican educational systems that the participants cited as having the greatest impact on their adjustment to school in the U.S.

DEFINITION OF TERMS AND THEORETICAL FRAMEWORK THE STUDENTS' MULTIPLE WORLDS MODEL

The terms "borders," "boundaries," and "bridges" were central to this study. As described by

Erickson (1993), boundaries exist when cultural differences are perceived as neutral and are transcended without much difficulty; however, borders are created when one type of cultural knowledge, skills, and behavior is given greater value than other types. These borders become obstacles to learning in the academic realm. Phelan, Davidson, and Yu (1994, 1998) expanded upon these concepts as they developed the Students' Multiple Worlds Model, which serves as the organizational framework for this study as well. The term "world" is used to mean the "cultural knowledge and behavior found within the boundaries of students' particular families, peer groups, and schools" (Phelan, et al., 1998, p. 7). For these researchers, borders and boundaries are not limited to cultural aspects but can exist due to socioeconomic, psychosocial, linguistic, gender, heterosexist, and structural or bureaucratic factors as well. According to Phelan, et al. (1998, p. 10), where borders exist, transitions between the students' family, self, peer, and school worlds are negotiated with much difficulty and high costs; whereas, where boundaries exist transitions between worlds are negotiated with minor discomfort. Of course, borders and boundaries vary within cultural groups as well, depending on socio-economic status and other within-group variability factors.The term "bridges" as defined by Phelan, et al. (1998, p. 13) refers to features within the students' school world that link students with services, opportunities, and resources that may be beneficial for them; for the purpose of my study, the concept of "bridges" was expanded to refer to any factor that facilitates transitions between students' multiple worlds. As the research progressed it became clear that in some cases a factor that functions as a border for one student can function as a boundary for another and as a bridge for yet another student.

The Students Multiple Worlds Model and the concepts of borders, boundaries, and bridges (Erickson, 1993; Phelan, et al., 1998) formed the basis for my conceptual and organizational framework. Other theories from the fields of immigration history and sociology were incorporated as well. Also utilized throughout the study were concepts from the field of second language acquisition research. School context research and research on effective schools for language minority students enriched my theoretical framework and contributed to the formulation of practical implications.

RESEARCH DESIGN AND DATA COLLECTION

The study had a qualitative, single-case study design that employed holistic, ethnographic methods. The site for this study was a multi-ethnic, semi-urban community in a mid-Atlantic state on the East Coast of the U.S. While much of the fieldwork was conducted in the high school of the community, I looked at the surrounding community as well, including one of the middle schools, community centers, popular Dominican restaurants, and the neighborhood in which most of the Dominican students reside. All names used in the study are pseudonyms used to preserve the anonymity of the participants and the research site.

The sampling was criterion-based and purposeful, beginning with the convenience of using students I knew and snowballing, using their references. The criteria for the sample was adolescents or young adults between the ages of 13 and 22 who immigrated from the Dominican Republic within the last ten years and who reside in the community being studied. Some slightly older participants, including several graduates and several participants who did not complete high school, were used to gain "temporal triangulation;" a term used to describe the ability to more coherently reflect on experiences that are already in the past (Phelan, et al., 1998, p. 5). In selecting the students to be interviewed extensively I tried for a representative sample ranging across genders, grade point averages, academic placement, length of time in the U.S., and grade level from 9th to 12th.

Data collection included conducting 10 student focus groups, 6 pilot study interviews, 11 individual in-depth student interviews, and 2 days of U.S. classroom observations. In addition, I visited 5 schools in the Dominican Republic. Over 34 U.S. educators and 17 community members or service providers were interviewed. One parent focus group was conducted as well as three in-depth parent interviews. Interviews were conducted in the language preferred by the participants.

DATA ANALYSIS

The analytic strategies employed in the project fit with the overall goal of identifying borders, boundaries, and bridges between the Dominican student's multiple worlds. Analysis was ongoing throughout the data collection process through researcher comments in my field notes and analytic memos and/or concept maps after each formal interview. The analysis was traditional qualitative thematic analysis, done via coding and bracketing the interview transcripts, using the qualitative software program Ethnograph Version 5.06.

I started by coding with descriptive categories, including the seven borders from the Adolescent's Worlds study (Phelan, et al. 1998), but as the research continued I looked for themes across the student interviews, as well as patterns in the data and metaphors that could be applied to the data. Many of the codes from my pilot study were used initially to categorize the data; however, emic codes, generated by the participants, were added wherever possible. Although narrative analysis was not the primary data analysis strategy, student interviews were examined for narratives that conveyed crucial turning points or revelations in the students' educational experiences that would aid in the identification of the key factors. Finally, I employed abductive reasoning, relating the data to broader concepts in the Dominican context, my theoretical framework, and in the literature in general.

As a tool to organize the major themes for writing, I first coded the educator interviews according to the seven borders from the Adolescent's Worlds study (Phelan, et al., 1998). After transcribing and re-reading the student interviews and other data, however, I realized that the emerging themes did not always fit neatly into the seven border categories, but that some of them were factors that were applicable to several different types of borders. I then decided to become more emic, coding the remainder of the data and re-coding the educator interviews via the key factors mentioned by the participants, while continuing to keep the borders in mind as appropriate. Although each key factor was sub-coded under either "home," "self/peer," or "school" worlds, as the analysis progressed it became apparent that some factors were more relevant to a different world and thus were re-categorized as needed.

As discussed above, the interpretation of the research findings were qualitative and interpretivist. Beginning with a firm base in the literature, the interpretation strategies were ongoing and generative. Since the emphasis was on student meanings, emic interpretations that were grounded in the data were sought for throughout the project. As discussed earlier, observations that may be generalizable to other populations beyond the study are presented as well.

MAJOR FINDINGS

The primary research question of the study was: What are the key factors influencing Dominican adolescents' transitions between their home, self, peer, and school worlds? A secondary aim of the study was to investigate the context of the students' learning experiences. It is beyond the scope of this chapter to expand upon all the findings of the study, but I will summarize the major findings below. For greater detail, the reader may refer to the complete study (Grossman, 2001). The findings were organized according to each of the students multiple worlds. What follows is a listing of the major findings, with more extensive description provided below:

1. Students' home world
    1. Lack of a strong community
    2. Isolation indoors
    3. Extended vs. nuclear family-orientations
    4. Separations and reunification issues
    5. Gender issues and parent-child interaction issues
    6. Work habitus
2. Students' self/peer world
    1. Peer pressure vs. peer support
        1. drug/gang activity
        2. non-academic attitudes and work
        3. lack of extra-curricular involvement
        4. Structural rationale of clearly defined future goals
        5. U.S. educator's misperceptions

2. Binational or transnational identity
3. Racial and cultural prejudices encountered
4. Linguistic factors as entry point into social circles
5. Segmented assimilation as the "1.5" generation
6. Strong ethnic identity as "dominicanos/as"
3. Students' school world
   1. Differences in "cultural capital" – miscommunication between home and school
   2. Structural differences in school systems
      1. academic segregation
      2. rigid extracurricular activity participation policy
      3. Curricular mismatches
      4. School climate perceived as alienating
      5. Institutional bridges link students with resources
      6. Teacher attitudes and pedagogical styles

In terms of the students' home world, participants reported that the lack of a large, active Dominican community in the local area functioned as a sociocultural border, as did the U.S. cultural orientation toward indoor versus outdoor spaces: participants described feeling isolated indoors in their new community. The more fluid, extended and/or fictive Dominican family structure, in contrast to the U.S. nuclear family-oriented society, acts as a sociocultural or a structural border in some ways but as a psychosocial bridge in other ways for the adolescents. Extended separations from biological parents and relationships with their fathers are often psychosocial borders for the students; however, for a few of them these were neutral boundaries or even positive bridges to their new home world. Reunification is in many cases a greater psychosocial border than the separation itself. Gender borders and issues related to parent-child interaction, including discipline, communication with parents, and family time or lack thereof play a part in the adolescents' developing identities. Emulating their parents' work ethic, Dominican adolescents incorporate working into their habitus (Bourdieu & Passeron, 1977) and it sometimes becomes both a socioeconomic and a sociocultural border between their home and school worlds.

As regards their self and peer worlds, Dominicans often come across more peer pressures than peer support as they attempt to transition from their home to peer to school worlds. For most, drug and gang activity is a boundary to be avoided, but for some it is a border that terminates their school careers and distances them from their family world as well. Peer pressure to adopt a non-academic attitude is strong, the pull to quit school and work instead distracts quite a few Dominican males from academics, and their lack of involvement in extra-curricular activities is another border that keeps them from feeling a part of the high school experience. Having clearly defined goals for the future appears to be a psychosocial bridge between the students' self and school world, providing those students who have them with a structural rationale (D'Amato, 1993) for completing high school. U.S. educators' misperceptions of the students' goals functions as a sociocultural border between those two worlds which lowers educators' expectations of Dominican students, perpetuates stereotypes and leads the Dominican student to be more likely to give up on academic pursuits.

Within their self and peer world, there are a number of factors influencing the Dominican adolescent's developing identity. The study found that Dominicans are a "binational" or "transnational" immigrant group, since they have strong economic, political, and family ties in both countries and since they often "shuttle" back and forth between countries (Ogbu, 1995a, 1995b; Ogbu & Simons, 1998; Suarez-Orozco & Suarez-Orozco, 2001). Being binational immigrants can act as a border or a bridge, depending on the individual and the context. While Dominican adolescent immigrants struggle to maintain their strong ethnic identity, they encounter the sociocultural border of racism from all sides. Linguistic factors act as borders in some cases but also serve as an entry point into a variety of social circles: the honor student in the study speaks Spanish at home, comes to school and socializes primarily with African Americans, and attends classes in which she adopts the academic language of the primarily European American middle class. Being members of the "1.5" or "halfway" generation (Eldering, 1997; Rumbuat, 1994) Dominicans follow similar segmented assimilation patterns to other second generation Caribbean immigrants (Fernandez-Kelly & Schauffler, 1994; Gibson, 1997; Portes & Rumbaut, 1996; Rumbaut, 1994; Waters, 1994), but with the difference that they tend to maintain their strong ethnic and binational identity while simultaneously pragmatically adapting from the U.S. Hispanic and African American sub-cultures. Their strong ethnic identity – "soy dominicano!" – functions as a bridge that holds them above the racial categories they encounter in the U.S. and allows them to form friendships with a variety of diverse peers.

In terms of their school world, Dominican adolescents face psychosocial, linguistic and sociocultural borders or boundaries based on their prior education and literacy skills. Differences in cultural capital (Bourdieu & Passeron, 1977) also sometimes become a border between the home and school worlds, leading to a lack of communication and misperceptions among both parents and educators. There are a multitude of structural or system-based factors that impact on Dominican adolescents' transition to their school world, many of which will be detailed in the following section which compares the U.S. and Dominican educational systems. Within the U.S. system, school-imposed segregation and a misguided extracurricular activity eligibility policy deprive many Dominican students of interaction with native English speaking peers, a factor second language acquisition researcher believe is crucial to attaining proficiency in the new language (Ellis, 1985). Curricular mismatches also deprive Dominican students of comprehensible input, curriculum that is meaningful and relevant to the students' current realities and needs (Krashen, 1988). When the overall school climate is perceived as alienating rather than welcoming, as is the case with several of the participants in the study, it is more likely that the adolescent will drop out of school (Lucas, 1993, 1997; Minicucci & Olson, 1992; Ortiz, 1996; Phelan, et al., 1998; Valdez-Pierce, 1991; Valverde, 1987). Institutional bridges – parent specialists, counselors, mentors, teachers, and programs that actively recruit Dominican students — on the other hand, link students with services or resources and have the potential for helping students overcome the structural barriers they encounter in their school world. Those bridges that take a personal, welcoming approach are the most effective in gaining the trust of Dominican adolescents and their families. Finally, teacher attitudes and pedagogical styles can be a crucial socio-affective bridge or border for Dominican students.

THE DOMINICAN EDUCATIONAL CONTEXT

As mentioned above, differences between the Dominican and U.S. educational systems have an impact on the students in a variety of ways, creating a multitude of structural and sociocultural borders for students when they adjust to U.S. schools. This section illustrates in detail the major differences emphasized by the students and/or noted by the researcher during school visits in the Dominican Republic, and explains how these differences may affect the students as they adjust to U.S. schools.

The most striking difference is in school schedules. The norm across public, private, and parochial schools in the Dominican Republic is half-day schooling, a morning shift from 8 a.m. to 12 or 1 p.m. and then an afternoon shift for a different age group of students from 2 p.m. to 5 or 6 p.m. There are also evening high schools for working students from 7 to 10 p.m. As the Dominican American school administrator interviewed for this study explained, this schedule permits a more efficient use of space, eliminates the expense of having to feed students, and focuses the curriculum on core subjects, eliminating electives (personal communication, July 20, 1999). Students interviewed for this study believe that the Dominican system therefore teaches more efficiently, as Oscar, one of the students, describes, "I would be getting off earlier, but I would still get the same education." Nonetheless, students arriving to the U.S. face a difficult adjustment to a longer school day.

In terms of content, in the primary schools I visited, there appeared to be five core subjects: Spanish language, science, religion, mathematics, and history. The high schools also offered English, French, and computers. Technical high schools offer other courses as well, but Dominican students may not be familiar with "electives" classes when they enter U.S. schools.

In the Dominican Republic the line between public, private, and religious schools is much less clear than it is in the U.S. The student who had attended the first elementary school I visited in the Dominican Republic described it to me as a private school, but the eighth grade teacher I observed at the school informed me that the school is government-funded and the students do not pay tuition. Although funded by the government, nuns ran this "private" school. The public elementary school, on the other hand, had daily religion lessons, as well as more crowded classes.

Private and public high schools overlap as well: the private Catholic, all-boys high school I visited had an evening session for the general public that was partly government-subsidized. One of the public high schools I saw was attempting to become a quasi-technical school, by offering computers and electronics training, similar to the popular private technical high schools.

One reason for the blurred line between school types in the Dominican Republic may be due to the bad reputation of the public schools. A U.S. parent specialist who is Dominican reports: "One thing I can tell you is the public schools aren't good there. Not one of my nieces or nephews goes to public schools. My relatives chuckle when I say my kids go to good public schools!" Students interviewed for this study had similar comments, explaining that "it was like you have to be really really poor to go to a public school cause there usually is private schools over there," and that "see, a public school is just the worst you could think about...You know mostly every child tries to go to a private school because you don't really get an education when you're in public school."

Private schools are reported to sometimes have slightly longer hours than public schools, or offer extra study sessions after school hours. Public schools, in contrast, are reported to close often due to strikes, sometimes for weeks or months at a time. Several students expressed their preferences for private schools because they explain that there is a lot of "tigeraje" {delinquency} in the public schools; whereas in private schools students get expelled for such behavior. Several of the boys explained that they avoided public schools because they are notoriously violent, with students fighting each other and teachers using corporal punishment on a regular basis. As one boy, Joaquin, reports, "Ud. sabe que la escuela pública ellos no, no le dan mente a eso y wow, se lo echan a pelear y todo eso." {You know that in the public school they [students] don't care about that and wow, they start fighting and all that.}

On the other hand, some students mentioned that because of the money involved, corruption is sometimes rampant in private schools. Maria reports "Porqué, cuando estudian para allá, si tú pagas a la escuela, te dan el diploma rápido." {Because, when you study over there, if you pay the school, they'll give you the diploma quickly.} Melissa, a recent immigrant, contrasts the corruption in private schools with that of public ones:

> En el colegio, cuando pagan más cuando se queda en una materia o si no, no estás entendiendo, y le pagas a un profesor y ya hasta el examen te pasa, en algunos colegios. Pero en la escuela pública no. En la escuela pública, esto, tienes que pasar obligatoriamente, tú no tienes que pagarle a nadie, es tu cabeza.
>
> {In the private school, when they paid more when they were retained in a subject or if not, if you're not understanding, and you pay the teacher they'll pass you right through the exam, in some private schools. But not in public school. In public school, um, you have to pass mandatorily; you can't pay anyone, it's your head.}

This large variation in school types and quality, not to mention the difference between urban and rural schools, accounts for the large variety of academic background in students who emigrate from the Dominican Republic as well. Teaching and classroom conditions in the Dominican Republic do not seem to vary quite as much as the school types. In most of the schools I visited, the class sizes were larger than the norm in U.S. schools. Both of the public high schools were overcrowded, each being the only high school for its part of the city. One Dominican history class I observed had 62 students on the roster; most classes I saw had between 40 and 50 students in them. While the public high schools had one air-conditioned computer lab each, none of the other classes I saw had air conditioning. The lack of air conditioning made the classrooms much louder than what I was accustomed to in the United States, since it was necessary to keep doors and windows open and noise from the halls and courtyards invaded the classrooms. The teachers had to speak at the top of their voices to be heard across the room, and students in the back could not hear students in the front. Many Dominican students complain of being reprimanded by U.S. teachers and other students for being too loud in classes when they come to the U.S.; this tendency may be partly due to the necessity of speaking loudly in Dominican schools.

A lack of basic equipment and school supplies leads from a physical difference to a pedagogical difference as well. The eighth grade teacher complained that the lack of books in the primary grades meant that the teachers tend to focus on seatwork rather than reading. The Dominican history teacher concluded his lesson by explaining that he has one resource, the map, and that his teaching comes more from his throat than from the map. Other than the computer labs in the two high schools, there were no computers, televisions, VCRs, or audiocassette players in any classroom visited. None of the teachers had overhead projectors, and it appeared that there were no photocopies being made in any of the schools either. The lack of copies, as well as the fact that not all the students had the textbook, meant that much of the class time was spent on dictation and/or copying items from the board.

Teachers in the Dominican Republic do not earn enough to live on so most teachers, as well as principals, work at more than one school. Almost all the Dominican teachers interviewed taught at more than one school, and were not paid for any planning or grading time. In all of the classes I observed, it appeared that the students were responsible for checking their own notebooks and would be evaluated by the teacher only on the exam.

As in any educational system, Dominican teachers observed for this study range from extremely dynamic to utterly ineffectual. Regardless of the individual teacher's talent, all the teachers I saw shared the same teaching style: teacher-directed. The currently popular U.S. idea of "teacher as facilitator" was nowhere to be found in the schools I visited. In each class, the teacher was primarily in the front of the room and the students sat in rows facing him or her as he or she led the class through lecture, seatwork, call and response, or some whole class discussion.

A Dominican student faced with a student-centered teaching style in the United States may therefore assume that the teacher is not doing his or her job in a professional manner. In fact, many of the students interviewed for this study expressed the belief that Dominican schools are "harder," more rigorous and demanding, than U.S. schools. Students may perceive that Dominican schools are harder because students there have to take a greater role in their own instruction, as seen above, in terms of checking their own work and copying or listening to dictations rather than being handed a pre-printed worksheet. Rote learning and memorization is viewed as more rigorous instruction than cooperative learning or group activities:

> Danilo (student): You have to do more work, study more, memorize a lot of pages for the next day. Here, you don't have to memorize anything on the exam. You have to memorize a page and say it to the teacher the next day. And I think that's better because you learn faster.

The students interviewed for this study also expressed their belief that the Dominican curriculum is more advanced that the U.S. one. As one focus group participant reports, "Allá en el quinto grado ya están dando la biología. Lo que le dan aquí en el diez, décimo grado, se lo dan allá en el quinto." {There in the fifth grade they're already offering biology. What they offer here in ten, tenth grade, they give you there in the fifth.}

One reason for the students' perception that Dominican schools are more rigorous is because of the Dominican national curriculum that includes grade level exams (Lopez, 1996). In 8th grade and 12th grade – and until recently in 4th grade as well – students are given a battery of tests called the "Pruebas Nacionales," or National Exams. Students reported that if they failed any single subject's grade level exam, they would have to repeat the entire grade the following year, not just the one subject. The Dominican eighth grade teacher interviewed for this study confirmed this; however, the director of one of the public high schools reported that under a new national curriculum written in 1995, the grade level exams are now supposed to only count for 30% of the total grade for the year, instead of 100%.

Either way, there is a definite trend toward grade repetition in the Dominican Republic that leads to confusion and clashes in perceptions for students entering U.S. schools. In the Dominican Republic, only 7% of students who enter first grade complete eighth grade in eight years (Luna, Gonzalez, & Wolfe, 1990, p. 363). Among the participants in this study, grade retention was described as very common in the Dominican Republic:

> Danilo (student): If you fail a test twice for any one class, you have to repeat the whole year. You get two chances to take the test. It never happened to me, but I knew a lot of people it happened to.

> Focus group student: The other thing is, we don't get a lot of chances like here. So everyone is like pushing themselves to pass, because if you fail [one course] you fail the whole year.

Repeating a grade is termed "quemarse," literally "to burn oneself," and is described as a traumatic event. Nevertheless, on the whole Dominican students view the grade retention policy of their country as more positive evidence that the Dominican system is "harder" than the U.S. one:

> Oscar (student): Uh huh, it's better, 'cause like you don't get no second chance, like here, like summer school, like none of that. So the kids like try real hard to like pass their classes, because they fail one class they fail the whole year and you gotta stay back.

Dominican students describe being bumped up a number of grades to be with same-age peers upon arrival in the U.S. as disruptive also, as Roamer explains:

> Entonces, algo malo tienen en este país que - por ej - si - si un alumno en Santo Domingo viene, con 13 años, ya lo ponen en el seis grado, y está mal, porque entonces, si llegué nuevo a la escuela, llega como, como un desierto. No sabe donde está nada, ni sabe lo que tiene que hacer, y entonces, tiene que ser bien inteligente para catar todo rapido.
>
> {So, something bad about this country is – for ex – if – if a student from Santo Domingo comes, 13 years old, they already put him in sixth grade, and this is bad, because then, if he arrives new to school, he comes like, like a desert. He doesn't know where anything is, he doesn't know what he has to do, and so, one has to be very intelligent to take in everything quickly.}

Another transition issue is that Dominican students who immigrate to the U.S. are going from a society with an almost completely homogeneous student body to a society with students from a spectrum of ethnic, religious, racial, and economic backgrounds. The Dominican school policy of uniforms makes the student body seem even more homogeneous, particularly obscuring socioeconomic differences, a feature that appeals to many Dominican students, as Oscar expresses: "People don't be like showing off. Over there you have to wear uniforms so they won't be showing off, like I got better clothes than you." Students describe this policy as another example of how the Dominican educational system is more rigorous than the U.S. one, explaining that schools send students home if they cannot afford a uniform, if their uniform is not clean, their nails are not trimmed, and their hair is not short or pulled back:

> Emma: And there's a uniform. You know those girls try to look nice even in their uniforms. You can't dye your hair. You can't let your hair out. Your skirt has to be down to here, ok? And your shirt, you can't roll it up. It has to be down to there. You have to be, you have to have, you know "grasa" like for your hair, grease? You better put some or they won't let you in!

Other institutional differences impact on Dominican adolescent immigrants' adjustment to U.S. schools as well. In the Dominican Republic, students do not change classrooms but rather remain in the same room with their grade level peers for the full day, with teachers changing rooms for each subject. This gives the students a primary peer group with which to bond intensively throughout the year, and the focus of peer group interactions tend to be inside rather than outside the classroom. All of this changes when students enter U.S. schools, where they do not remain together throughout the school day and where peer group interactions tend to be outside the classrooms, in the hallways, bathrooms, cafeterias, etc. (Lopez, 1996). Thus, school in the U.S. may become associated with socializing outside of class, leading to tardiness and attendance problems.

Although schooling in the Dominican Republic is mandatory until junior high school (Lopez,

1996), according to the informants in this study, attendance is not rigidly enforced. On the contrary, students are sent home from school in many cases if they do not have clean uniforms, books, or school supplies. This is a relevant point since many of the Dominican students at the U.S. high school of this study lose course credit when they have too many unexcused tardies, and don't seem to understand the high school's strict attendance policy.

This difference in attendance policy is part of a larger difference in the cultural perception of "classroom management." At the primary school level, and especially in the public schools, students report that teachers commonly use corporal punishment to discipline the students:

> Alejandro: aquí el maestro no tienen el derecho de pegarte, pero también en aquel país los maestros tienen el derecho de pegarte, si hiciste algo mal. {here the teacher doesn't have the right to beat you, but in that country the teachers have the right to beat you, if you do something bad.}

> Maria: Allá las profesoras te jalan la oreja. Te dan con una regla. Eso es diferente. Aquí no, aquí a lo mejor te ponen la mano, te puedes meterle en problemas muy grandes. {Over there the teachers pull your ears. They give it to you with a ruler. This is different. Here no, here if they touch you, you can get them in very big problems.}

Although students explain that this type of discipline is utilized primarily for smaller children and appears to be going out of fashion, even Emma, one of the youngest students in the study, cautions, "you need to respect the teachers because they will pull out a belt on you." For students accustomed to this type of punishment, the milder forms of discipline employed by U.S. educators may initially seem ineffectual and a sign of weakness or lack of control.

At the Dominican high school level, in contrast, education is viewed as a privilege and those who make it to this level are rather serious students. There is no such thing as "class rules" posted on the wall in a Dominican high school, as they are in U.S. classrooms; teachers do not waste their time reprimanding students for chewing gum or talking, but rather ignore disruptions and continue to teach over them, raising their own voices if necessary, from what was observed. In turn, the students were overall very serious and on-task. Teachers are respected as the clear authority figure in the room. This respect goes both ways, as teachers are very respectful of the students as well, and assume that the students are responsible for their own attendance, punctuality, homework, and attention to class discussion or face the built-in consequence of failing the grade-level exam. For students who immigrate from such an environment, the close monitoring of attendance and homework by U.S. teachers may be interpreted as a lack of respect of their maturity.

CONTRIBUTIONS OF THE RESEARCH AND LIMITATIONS

This community study painted a picture of the Dominican adolescents' multiple worlds, highlighting the key factors in each world that become borders, boundaries or bridges for the students as they move between their worlds. The study contributed to the literature by filling a gap in the research: there are very few studies about the fastest growing type of immigrant, transnational or binational immigrants. There is also a lack of research on secondary students, particularly secondary level language minority students, and very few studies that explore students' perspectives and compare them with established theories on minority school performance.

Being a single site case study of a narrowly defined population of Dominican adolescents, this study can be expanded upon in a variety of ways. One of the limitations of the study was the lack of a control group. Future studies could compare Dominican teenagers in different communities. While some of their distinctive cultural traits attracted me to Dominicans as a group for in-depth study, I chose Dominicans as an example of one recent Hispanic immigrant group. Throughout my study, I highlighted factors that appear to be unique to Dominicans and factors that Dominicans most likely share with Caribbean, Hispanic and other ethnic groups. While it was beyond the scope of the study to conduct an in-depth comparison, a study that compares Dominican teenagers with other ethnic groups would be of great value in identifying general versus distinctly Dominican influences.

CONCLUSIONS

There are a number of practical implications emanating from the study. It is the task of U.S. schools to provide a more welcoming school climate via programs such as mentoring, "homerooms" that match students with a mentor-teacher, culturally responsive pedagogy, curriculum, counseling, and community programs that focus on career goal-building, and school accommodations for binational immigrants. U.S. educators need to build trust and improve communication with parents of Dominican and other immigrant students. U.S. schools can break down racial borders by encouraging social interaction and moving against school-based segregation in the form of academic tracking. Finally, schools should offer long-term, two-way bilingual programs, more flexible scheduling as well as articulation with adult education and community colleges for older adolescent immigrant students.

Dominican students, like other immigrant students, encounter many differences between the Dominican and U.S. educational systems. These differences have an impact on how they adjust to their new school world. U.S. educators who are aware of these differences will tend to be more sensitive towards their immigrant students.

REFERENCES

Bourdieu, P., & Passeron, C. (1977). *Reproduction in education, society, and culture.* London: Sage.

D'Amato, J. (1993). Resistance and compliance in minority classrooms. In E. Jacob & C. Jordan (Eds.) *Minority education: anthropological perspectives.* (pp. 181-207). New Jersey: Ablex Publishing Corporation.

Eldering, L. (1997). Ethnic minority students in Netherlands from a cultural-ecological perspective. *Anthropology & Education, 28* (3), 330-350.

Ellis, R. (1985). *Understanding second language acquisition.* Oxford: Oxford University Press.

Erickson, F. (1993). Transformation and school success: The politics and culture of educational achievement. In E. Jacob & C. Jordan (Eds.) *Minority education: anthropological perspectives.* (pp. 27-52). New Jersey: Ablex Publishing Corporation.

Escobar, G. (1999, May 14). Dominicans face assimilation in Black and White. *The Washington Post.* Pp. A3, A22.

Fernandez-Kelly, M.P., & Schauffler, R. (1994). Divided fates: Immigrant Children in a restructured U.S. economy. *International Migration Review, 28*(4), 662-689.

Gibson, M.A. (Ed.). (1997). Ethnicity and school performance: complicating the immigrant/involuntary minority typology [Theme issue]. *Anthropology & Education, 28* (3).

Grossman, S. (1998). *Listen to us: Dominican teenagers' perspectives on education.* Unpublished manuscript.

Grossman, S. (2001). "Soy Dominicano:" The multiple worlds of the Dominican adolescent. Michigan: UMI Dissertation Services.

Krashen, S. (1988). Providing input for acquisition. In P.A. Richard-Amato. *Making it happen: interaction in the second language classroom.* (pp. 330-342). New York: Longman (Reprinted from *Principles and Practice in Second Language Acquisition,* 1982, 58-73).

Lopez, N. (1996). "Diploma, GED, no diploma, same job": The meaning of dropping out for Dominican students. (Sociological Abstracts Accession Number 96S32346). New York: American Sociological Association.

Lucas, T. (1993). *Applying elements of effective secondary schooling for language minority students: a tool for reflection and stimulus for change.* Washington, DC: NCBE Program Information Guide Series #14.

Lucas, T. (1997). *Into, through, and beyond secondary school: critical transitions for immigrant youths.* U.S.A.: Center for Applied Linguistics.

Luna, E., Gonzalez, S., & Wolfe, R. (1990, July/August). The underdevelopment of educational achievement: mathematics achievement in the Dominican Republic eighth grade. *Journal of Curriculum Studies, 22* (4), 361-376.

Minicucci, C., & Olson, L. (1992, Spring). Programs for secondary limited English proficient students: a California study. *NCBE Focus: Occasional Papers in Bilingual Education, Number 5.*

Ogbu, J. (1995a, March). Community forces and minority educational strategies: a comparative study. Berkeley, CA: University of California, Department of Anthropology.

Ogbu, J. (1995b). Cultural problems in minority education: Their interpretation, and consequences - Part one: Theoretical background. *The Urban Review, 27* (3), 189-206.

Ogbu, J., & Simons, H.D. (1998). Voluntary and involuntary minorities: A cultural-ecological theory of school performance with some implications for education. *Anthropology & Education Quarterly, 29*(2), 155-188.

Ortiz, D.L. (1996, Winter). Male Hispanic high school dropout dilemma: Self-reported perceptions. *The Journal of Educational Issues of Language Minority Students, 18*, 35-45.

Phelan, P., Davidson, A. L., & Yu, H.C. (1994). Navigating the psychosocial pressures of adolescence: The voices and experiences of high school youth. *American educational research journal, 31* (2), 415-447.

Phelan, P., Davidson, A. L., & Yu, H.C. (1998). *Adolescents' worlds: Negotiating family, peers, and school.* New York: Teachers College Press.

Portes, A., & Rumbaut, R.G. (1996). *Immigrant America: A portrait* (2nd ed.). California: University of California Press.

Rumbaut, R.G. (1994). The crucible within: ethnic identity, self-esteem, and segmented assimilation among children of immigrants. *International Migration Review, 28* (4), 748-795.

Suarez-Orozco, M.M. & Suarez-Orozco, C. (2001). *Children of immigration.* Cambridge, MA: Harvard University Press.

Valdez-Pierce, L. (1991). *Effective schools for national origin language minority students.* Washington, DC: The Mid-Atlantic Equity Center.

Valverde, S. (1987). A comparative study of Hispanic high school dropouts and graduates: Why do some leave school early and some finish? *Education and Urban Society, 19* (3), 320-329.

Waters, M.C. (1994). Ethnic and racial identities of second-generation Black immigrants in New York City. *International Migration Review, 28* (4), 795-820.

PART 3.

ATTITUDE IN THE CLASSROOM

CHAPTER 10.

> *Pages 319 - 344*
> Disruptive Behaviour Inside A Jamaican Classroom
>
> *Loraine D. Cook*
> Department of Educational Studies, University of the West Indies, Mona, Jamaica.

CHAPTER 11.

> *Pages 345 - 386*
> Learning Patterns of Caribbean Boys in the Secondary School
>
> *Hyacinth Skervin*
> University of Cincinnati, Ohio, OH, USA.

CHAPTER 12.

> *Pages 387 - 402*
> Does disruptive classroom behaviour make adolescent Caribbean students more popular or less popular with their peers?
>
> *Tony Bastick*
> Department of Educational Studies, University of the West Indies, Mona, Jamaica.

PART 3

CHAPTER 13.

Pages 403 - 432
Reading Comprehension, Attitudes to reading and Locus of Control beliefs of African-Caribbean students: A Jamaican-UK study.

Jossett Smikle
Department of Educational Studies, University of the West Indies, Mona, Jamaica.

CHAPTER 14.

Pages 433 - 456
An Analysis of Jamaican Technical High School Students' Attitudes to Technical and Vocational Education

Anita Thomas-James
University of Technology, Jamaica

and

Kola Soyibo
Department of Educational Studies, University of the West Indies, Mona, Jamaica

CHAPTER 10

THE IMPACT OF DISRUPTIVE BEHAVIOUR ON THE TEACHING LEARNING PROCESS: A CASE STUDY FROM A JAMAICAN CLASSROOM.

LORAINE COOK

ABSTRACT

This case study explores disruptive behavior as a factor that contributes to the underutilization of instructional time in the teaching-learning process. The study involved a mixed ability grade eight class from a traditional co-ed high classroom. The class population was 39 students: 21 males and 18 female students. The student culture of the school was stable and lent itself to high academic achievement.

The study discusses the various kinds of disruptive behaviour that teachers and students encounter in this specific classroom and their impact on the teaching – learning process in the classroom. Corrective measures at the macro-level and micro-level are also outlined.

INTRODUCTION

Studies have demonstrated that the "amount of time that students are engaged in instructional activities vary from less than 50% in some classes to more than 90% in others" (Jones & Jones, 1998, 233). Therefore, the aim of effective classroom management strategies is to minimize inappropriate or disruptive behavior in the classroom in order to facilitate the two main goals of the classroom: Teaching and learning. Disruptive behavior can be defined as "behavior that works against effective teaching and learning" (Brown, *2001*, 116). Disruptive behavior ranges from noise making to fighting and violence. However fighting and violence are not part of the student culture of the observed school owing to the social and economic backgrounds of the students. As such, disruptive behavior was restricted to talking, noise making, students leaving their seats without permission, fidgeting and lateness to class.

When students are disruptive it cuts into instructional time because the teacher has to take time out from teaching to correct the student (s). The following teacher expressed this about a child who was continuously disruptive in class:

> "Carol is restless, awkward and often very noisy...
> I can get a lot more done when Carol isn't there"
> (Furlong, 1984, 150).

Disruptive behavior is also contagious because one child's negative action can have a multiplier effect on the classroom climate, where the entire class reacts disruptively to the initial misbehavior. Mr. Smith's experience in his English class illustrates this:

> Holly's frequent out-loud quips, gestures, and facial contortions evoke laughter among her peers in Mr. Smith's ...English class. Mr. Smith finds that occasional clowning is humorous and a healthy diversion from work. However, Holly's clowning has become so frequent that it is impeding class progress (Cangelosi, 1988, 272).

Zeidner (1986) noted that " classroom disciplinary problems appear to have plagued school teachers and administrators from time immemorial and will most likely continue to do so in the near future with unrelenting severity" (p.69). It is important for teachers to recognize that teaching is not only an academic process but it is also a social process (Hargreaves, 1972, 248). Education takes place in a social environment in which the facility of instruction and learning is affected by the matrix of social values held by students and teachers within the context of the classroom environment. It is important that classroom teachers understand the psychosocial dynamics of the age group they are teaching at different grade level in the school system and the hidden or unconscious expectations of their students.

Various theories by Dreikurs, Coopersmith, Erikson, Elkind and Glasser, and Maslow have been employed to understand student behaviour. However, this study will examine two of these theories and their potential contribution in enlightening classroom management: First, Erickson's: Psychosocial

Development theory will be used to investigate the development stage of grade 8 students and second Elkind theory on the three contracts between adults and children will be employed to understand the expectations of educators and students

This paper is divided into four main sections. Section 1 is the literature review and theoretical overview. In section 2, I shall address the issue of methodology, using the context of a grade 8 classroom. Section 3 shall examine the findings from the study and the final section shall discuss the recommendations that ensued.

SECTION 1

DEVELOPMENT STAGE OF GRADE EIGHT STUDENTS

As young people develop they will experience various levels of emotional and physical changes. Each of these levels contributes to the determination of the emotional and psychological responses of each student to his/her social environment. It is therefore important that the academic staff and leadership within a school be cognizant of the stage theories of development. Erikson's theory on the developmental stages of adolescence is relevant to understanding the developmental stage of grade 8 students.

Erikson's theory outlines eight stages. However, stages 1V and V deal specifically with adolescence. The eight stages are: Stage I: trust versus mistrust (birth – 18 months); Stage II: autonomy versus doubt (18 months – 3 years); Stage III: initiative versus guilt, (3 years – 6 years); stage IV: Industry versus Inferiority (6 years – 12 years) ; Stage V: identity versus role confusion, (12 years – 18 years) and Stage VI: Intimacy versus isolation, young adult (Slavin , 1997, p.53).

The relevant stages to this study are stages IV: Industry versus inferiority (6 to 12 years) and stage V: Identity versus role confusion (12 to 18 years). During these stages the question of "Who am I ?" is very important (Slavin, 1997, p.53). Erikson describes stage V as a stage when young adolescents search for a sense of identity. Jones & Jones (1988) noted that during the initial phase of stage V, ages 11 to 13, "there is a dramatic increase in self-consciousness and a lowered self-esteem. Young adults feel on stage, as if everyone is observing them" (p.43). At this stage, as the students move from grade 7 to grade 8, their ability to consider abstract ideas and to better understand the concepts of past and future increases, and they begin to view the world more critically and subjectively (Jones & Jones, 1998, p.43). Adolescents at this stage, start developing a basic need to scrutinize ideas, rules and decisions critically. They are likely to question the practical relevance of concepts taught. Additionally they may question why they must complete their homework or follow a rule that does not apply to adults in the same environment.

Students in grade 8 " are often testing their new personal, physical and cognitive skills by challenging rules or adult behavior that they view as illogical or indefensible" (Jones & Jones, 1998, p. 44). Metz (1978) also noted that eighth graders were:

> more articulate, display remarkable moral insight and moral compassion. They would take stands and refuse to yield a point even at some costs to themselves. But half an hour later the same children might engage in a childish prank without thought of its consequence (p.69).

These questions and behaviours may arise because the young adults have no clear sense of what is appropriate for favourable reactions from adult.

Whereas every teacher can attest to the submissiveness and trust of seventh graders, eighth grade classes " are difficult places in which to practice authority but excellent places to see issues of authority made explicit" (Metz, 1998, p. 70). This was confirmed in my discussions with the sampled school's guidance counselor; throughout the years as guidance counselor she observed that seventh graders coming into a new environment tend to be more submissive and more pliable than eighth graders.

Jones and Jones (1998) noted that it is in the early (age 13 yrs.) and mid-adolescent (ages 14-16yrs.)

period that students start testing their new sense of power and control by challenging the rules and structures of the adult world. During this time adolescents need clearly articulated structures and the support of adults who are strong and "flexible enough to be involved openly in discussing questions adolescents have about subject matter, teaching techniques, and school rules and procedures" (p. 44).

TEACHERS' INFLUENCE ON STUDENTS BEHAVIOR IN THE CLASSROOM

Teaching involves understanding students. However, before teachers can understand students they must understand the role and the expectations placed on teachers or students. Jones and Jones (1982) cited Elkind's theory of relationship between children and adults. Elkind describes the relationship between adults and children in terms of patterns of implicit contracts. He proposed three basic contracts:

- Responsibility – freedom ;
- Achievement – support; and,
- Loyalty – commitment (p.45).

The responsibility – freedom contract refers to adults who sensitively monitor the child's level of emotional, intellectual and social development in order to provide opportunities for the exercise of responsibility and appropriate freedom (Jones & Jones, 1998, p. 45).

The achievement – support contract refers to adults gauging their expectations according to age – appropriate achievements and providing the necessary resources (e.g., personal and material) to help students reach expected goals.

The loyalty – commitment contract refers to the contract pattern that deals with the expectations of adults that are due to the adults' input (time, effort and energy), where children will be expected to respond with loyalty and acceptance of the adults. Elkind emphasized that children's needs are met when the contracts change in response to their personal and cognitive skills. The contracts are mutually exclusive, in that they are indexed to the stages of development. These changes occur primarily in response to the children's needs as they develop (p.45). Adults, however, frequently transgress these contracts; such transgression causes stress in youngsters who most time respond with disruptive behavior. During this period of identity crisis, or role confusion, these contracts are either being violated or established.

Several studies in Jamaica (Evan (2002), Brown (2002) and Yusuf-Khalil (2002)) have demonstrated teachers' violation of the "achievement – support contract" in the Jamaican classroom by their failure to provide the emotional support to students to facilitate the expectations placed up on them. Brown (2002) in her research noted that:

Teachers' discussions or conversations with students usually related to academic work. But whether the teacher was admonishing, informing or correcting, the tone was often hostile, uncaring, sarcastic or disrespectful (p. 128).

Jones & Jones (1998) commented that when adults respond with criticizing or giving up on the student, rather than discussing and understanding the problem, contract violation occurs (p.46). Such violation does have tremendous negative repercussions on students' behavior in the classroom.

Brown (2002) noted in her study, *Inside A Jamaican Classroom*, that the students in her sample "felt that they had ability and should do well. What they needed was for teachers to motivate them and help them achieve. In their view this was not happening". (pp. 129 – 130).

SECTION 2
METHODOLOGY

The research method took the form of interviews (structured and unstructured), participant observation and survey.

SAMPLING FOR INTERVIEWS

STUDENTS

In a class of 39 students, the sample size of the students for interviews was 8 - 20% of the population (Gay 2000, 134). The students interviewed were chosen through quota sampling; 4 students were chosen from the group of students who had the highest grade point average ranging from grade point average 82-88 in the previous term and 4 other students were chosen from the group with the lowest grade point average (from 53-64) also from the previous term. The school provided this list. The interviews were structured in that the students were asked specific questions.

TEACHERS

Eight teachers out of ten were interviewed. The interviews with the teachers were semi structured in that there were a few prepared questions but for most part it was unstructured in format. The interviews with teachers were conducted in the semi-privacy of the staff room at a time convenient to them. Interviews with teachers lasted between ten and twenty minutes.

PARTICIPANT OBSERVATION

I observed ten classes over a two-week period. For three of the ten instructional sessions, I was the teacher responsible for organizing work for the students and monitoring their interaction. To minimize observer biases the problems experienced by the grade eight students were examined using various techniques; non-participant observations, participant observation, interviews that were recorded on tape and field notes.

SOCIOMETRIC STUDY

This is the study of interrelationships among group members (Hopkins, 1998, p.431). The main reason for carrying out a sociometric study with grade 8A was to identify the leaders in the group; students who have the potential to be effective form captains. Teachers could work along with such individuals to minimize disruptive behaviour in the classroom.

SECTION 3
FINDINGS

GENERAL PERCEPTION OF GRADE 8A

Seven teachers out of eight agreed that grade 8A, relative to the other grade 8 classes, exhibits disruptive behaviour that hinders effective teaching and learning. The following teachers echo the concern of most teachers for this specific grade:

> **Teacher B:** "This class is definitely a problem class"

> **Teacher M**: "Behaviour- wise they are a problem. They take a long time to settle down. Even after waiting for them to settle they are still inattentive. There are constant interruptions. They are indisciplined…"

Students also expressed concern about the disruptive behaviour of the class.

> **Student 3:** "I enjoy the ___ class but sometimes we are enjoying what we are learning, then all of a sudden we have to stop, because of disruptive behaviour."

> **Student 18** also expressed: "They are all smart. It's just that they waste time a little bit more".

STUDENTS' DEFINITION OF DISRUPTIVE BEHAVIOUR

Students' understanding of the term disruptive behaviour reflects not only their moral awareness and insight but also their knowledge of what is acceptable behaviour and what is unacceptable behaviour in the classroom. To the question "What do you understand by the term disruptive behaviour"? The following students replied:

> **Student 22 :** "When one person makes noise and every other person finds it funny, then the whole class gets involved".
>
> **Student 38:** "When you don't listen to anyone. When you think oh well I don't need this. when you are rude".
>
> **Student 3:** "Disruptive behaviour is talking to other students while the teacher is talking".
>
> **Student 21:** "When the teacher is talking and someone starts talking that disrupts the class. If the person beside you is trying to listen and you are talking to the person".

On my first encounter with the class I noted that during the icebreaker a certain group of students was frequently engaged in chatting sessions which were disruptive to the teaching-learning process. On several occasions I had to request for their listening ear. At one stage I told the talkers that if they persisted I would have to send them outside. It was only then that they quieted down.

THE KINDS OF DISRUPTIVE BEHAVIOUR THAT OCCURRED IN THE CLASSROOM

The types of disruptive behaviour observed in the classroom were:

- Fidgeting (e.g., two boys were twirling a wire about 12" in length during class time – observation) ;
- Walking around the classroom without permission from the teacher; within one class more than three students were out of their seats at the same time without permission (observation) ; and,
- Chatting, one student reported this weakness as a compulsive disorder, as he is unable to restrain himself (student 21).

In my observation of the 8 teaching sessions that took place in the grade 8A classroom, at no time did a teacher arrive to find an orderly class, where students were seated in their respective seats, with their books and relevant material prepared for work. Instead, before the start of all classes in the grade 8A classroom, several students could be seen on the corridor engaged in pranks and antics; while inside the classroom there was the usual pandemonium with students chatting away in small groups (observation). It took most classes at least five minutes to settle down after the teacher's arrival.

THE PERVASIVENESS OF DISRUPTIVE BEHAVIOUR

There is a general consensus among students and teachers that not all the students in grade 8A were disruptive in their behaviour.

Teacher H noted: "You have leaders in the class who are not leading the class in the right direction".

Teacher S expressed: "It is not really a problem class. You just have individuals that give problems within the class. Those same individuals do very little work".

Teacher U also noted: "There is definitely disruptive members in the class".

Students who were interviewed highlighted certain students who were disruptive. These students behaviour tended to have a ripple effect on the climate of the classroom. They would say a joke and the majority of the class would respond with laughter. For example, two boys started slapping each other in the face and the entire class stopped their work and started behaving as if they were at the stadium (observation).

It is important to note that the three students whose name came up repeatedly as disruptive during classes share a mutual bond (see the only triangle for boys on the Sociogram –appendix).The sociogram study also confirmed that the two students who were functioning as class monitors were not influential among their peers, in other words they were not the stars in the social interactions for the class. It was the form teacher who had selected the class monitors.

DO STUDENTS BEHAVE DISRUPTIVELY IN ALL CLASSES?

Similar to P. Brown (2002), I also observed that students were not disruptive with every teacher. They were disruptive only in some classes. On the 2001.05.28 I noted in my field notes:

As I approached grade 8A there was unusual silence coming from the classroom. I wondered at that point if they were out of the classroom or if they were doing some major test. However as I approached the classroom I observed that they were not doing a major test (this was confirmed when I inquired from the teacher later). Every student was in his/her seat, with each pair of feet under the desk; with their backs against the chair and their face towards the front of the class. There was absolute silence.... (observation).

In response to the question "Why were you students so quiet ?" Several students replied,

"It's Miss U".

" What about Miss. U?", I inquired One student quickly replied on behalf of the nodding heads, "we are quiet because of Miss. U. She is strict and whatever she says she means. If she says she is going to give you a detention, then she is going to give you a detention. She gives detention to anyone who breaks her rules."

An Elkind interpretation would suggest that teachers who are attuned to sustaining and respecting the boundaries of contractual relationships (rather than fostering a relaxed posture towards them)

will in turn find those sentiments reciprocated by the students.

In my interviews with students, the names of five teachers were repeatedly mentioned as teachers who are able to maintain discipline in the classroom. It was observed that these teachers interaction with their students was laced with politeness. As Elkind pointed out, "when we are polite to children, we show in the most simple and direct way possible that we value them as people and care about their feelings" (http://teach.fhu.edu/technology/PSY306/elkind.html). These teachers seemed to have combined firmness with politeness. The students were also very much aware of the teachers who can be pushed and those who will not allow students to push them beyond a boundary point.

STUDENTS' PERCEPTION OF THE CONSEQUENCES OF DISRUPTIVE BEHAVIOUR

Students believed that disruptive behaviour is short circuiting their learning, and taking away the joy of learning. The following confirms Gray and Richer's (1988) statement, that students require lessons free from disruption (p.1).

Student 3 expressed her frustation: "Two weeks ago Miss. H had to send us to the Dean. The teacher wasn't able to teach us the topic. We spent the rest of the time with the Dean".

Student 18 expressed that: "In my (Miss R.) class they were just doing it to make a joke and they don't realize they are wasting their time and other people's time. The entire class is now in detention for making noise. When the students keep talking they hold us back".

Student 21 was asked, "What subject do you like the least?" The reply was "M" because I miss a lot of lessons and I am sent out a lot".

Eating in the classroom is against the school rules, however, student # 7 observed that because of disruptive behavior this happens very frequently

"Most of the time why we end up eating in class is because we do not have enough time in break. Like say, it is the same disruptive behavior that cause it, because we get held back in class, so by the time we go to buy lunch it is time to return to classes".

Based on the above accounts, it seems clear that teachers' response to the problem is also perpetuating the problem. For student 21, he does not like subject " M" because he is not able to understand the information since he is constantly being sent out of the classes. This in itself will result in the student being bored with the subject, which in turn will lead to a disengaged mind, and consequently to idleness and repeated disruptive behavior.

As Evans (2001) pointed out, when students failed to understand what was being taught, they become frustrated and quickly find ways to express their frustration.

The fact that students felt that the punitive consequences of disruptive behaviour is short circuiting their academic progress implies that the adults' response of persistent removal of students from the classroom is a violation of the teachers' contractual responsibility of achievement – support. Rather, it is important for teachers to understand why students misbehave and as such promote the mutual fulfillment of the implied terms in the achievement – support contract.

For student 7, the teacher's behaviour had the following consequences:

- The reduction of time for lunch break and the diminution of instructional time for the subsequent subject; and,
- Eating during class, which is contrary to the school rules and which adversely impacts upon effective teaching and learning.

METHODS OF TEACHING AND DISRUPTIVE BEHAVIOUR

Several writers (e.g., Grey & Richer, 1988) have pointed out that certain methodologies can stimulate misbehaviour. However, in my observation, I have found that methods did not affect how students behaved as much as the students' perception of the teacher. I observed three of the teachers who students believed had the least control over the class. These teachers varied their methodology, by using activities and group work; this still did not minimize the disruptive behavior in the class. I did observe however that these teachers did not offer any incentives to the students when they completed their work (such as grading the activity). As the Guidance Counsellor pointed, "these students need incentives and rewards".

SECTION 4

RECOMMENDATIONS

Recommendations can be carried out on two levels: at a macro level – institution wide and at a micro level – class specific.

MACRO - LEVEL

1. The rules outlined in the school's handbook for students and parents do not state the required behaviour of students during the interval previous to the start of an instructional session . Such a rule is needed to provide guidelines for students' behaviour . This will have a positive effect on instructional time.

Suggestion for the above rule:

> Before teachers arrive for their classes students are required to be on time and seated with their books and other relevant materials on their desk in preparation for class.

The form captain could enforce this rule.

2. A workshop should be planned and implemented by the Guidance Counsellor to assist teachers in understanding disruptive behaviour in the classroom

and the various behavioural modification techniques that a teacher can exercise.

3. Reciprocal arrangements could be encouraged among colleagues (Gray and Richer, 1988). This involves colleagues observing students in each other's classes and offering suggestions. Each member of the teaching profession cannot exist as an island; teamwork is essential, similar to that employed within the medical profession. When a doctor cannot diagnose the complaints of the patient help is solicited from other professionals in the field for the good of his/her patients.

4. The grade supervisor could co-ordinate meetings between parents and teachers of the class, so those parents are aware of their children's conduct at school, and are able to work with the school in the development of their own children.

5. Punishment should be aimed at individuals who are the initiators and perpetuators of disruptive behavior. Teachers need to reduce the amount of class punishment that is presently handed out as this has a serious impact on the instructional time of those who are motivated to work.

MICRO-LEVEL

Based on interviews, observation and sociometric study (see appendix: 5) the present form captains have a low degree of social influence and are therefore ineffective in maintaining order in the classroom. It is recommended that:

1. The students and not the Form Teachers should select Form Captains. Teachers need to recognize that informal leaders contribute to the class and sustain its culture (Hargreaves, 1972, 236). If students with a high degree of social influence are disruptive in their behavior then an adult (teacher or guidance counselor) needs to work closely with such students.

From the sociogram, it can be noted that student 7 is the only boy with a high degree of social influence whereas 27 & 33 are the two girls who have a high degree of social influence (see appendix:5). However, student 7 is not connected to any other student in the sociogram. In other words, he did not reciprocate those who selected him.

It is also important to note that the present form captains (students 23 and 14) have a low degree of social influence This is not surprising because when the classroom was in its state of pandemonium, the presence of the form captains was not felt. In fact, on one occasion, the female form captain was just reading a book in the midst of the noise; also, in response to the question, " Are you functioning as the form captain?" She replied:

N,. not really, I don't like getting people in trouble.

At the beginning of this research I seriously felt that the class should be divided in 9th grade.

Subsequently I have changed my perspective. I believe, as one teacher also indicated that they should stay together so that "they can see themselves evolve within the group".

The members of the class who are being consistently disruptive should be required to work with the guidance counsellor, the grade supervisor and the dean of discipline, over an agreed period of time.

CONCLUSION

Erikson and Elkind actually complement each other in giving a clear understanding of the dynamics of teacher-student relationship and its effect on behaviour in the classroom. Erikson's stage theory depicts the psychosocial developmental stages of individuals, and explicitly explains the developmental needs of individuals. Elkind fleshes out the substance of these developmental needs in the contractual obligations of specified by the three types of contracts. For example, the developmental stages of a child at stages V and V1 may require the adult in his/her contractual relationship to be more explicit about the terms of the relationship, therefore lubricating the child's transition through the identity confusion stage.

As such it is important for schools and classroom teachers to communicate explicit expectations for student behaviour as well as the penalty associated with breaches.

When the social process within the classroom is stable, a comfortable climate is created where a high percentage of students can spend their time engaged in planned activities in order to master basic skills. It is the social process that equips students with the necessary social skills to effectively function within a group and eventually society; social skills such as "the ability to listen and seriously consider the suggestion of others, to express disagreement in a friendly way and to develop self discipline and responsibility" King et al. (2000).

An in disciplined classroom creates stress both for teachers and students. It is therefore important for both teachers and students to be educated about the causes, consequences and solutions for disruptive behaviour. Teachers should not believe that disruptive behaviour is beyond their control, rather, they should always explore solutions that can be implemented. It is unfortunate that in our society individual teachers are expected to function as lone rangers; no one teacher has the answer to every problem that arises in the classroom. It is therefore important for teachers to develop team spirit towards the classroom, so that if there is disruptive behaviour in the classroom that one teacher cannot handle, then those who are not experiencing the same problem can assist.

REFERENCES

Becker, H. S. (1984). Social – Class Variations in the Teacher –Pupil Relationship. In A.Hargreaves and P. Woods (Eds.), *Classrooms & Staffrooms : the Sociology of Teachers and Teaching.* (pp. 98 –107) . Milton Keynes , England : Open University Press.

Brown, P. (2001). Student behaviour and teacher- student relationship at a secondary high school for boys. In H. Evans, *Inside Classrooms* (pp. 116 –131). Kingston, Jamaica : Faculty of Arts and Education (U.W.I.).

Congelsoi, J. S. (1988). *Classroom Management Strategies: Gaining and Maintaining Students' Cooperation.* New York: Longman Inc.

Dewey, J. (1944). *Democracy and Education.* United States: Macmillan Company.

Evans, H. (2001). Teaching and Learning in the All – Age School. . In H. Evans, *Inside Classrooms* (pp. 133 –143). Kingston, Jamaica : Faculty of Arts and Education (U.W.I.).

Farrant, J.S. (1980). *Principles and Practice of Education.* (2nd ed.). Essex, United Kingdom : Longman House.

Furlong, V. J. (1984). Interactions sets in the classroom: towards a study of pupil knowledge. In M. Hammersley & P. Woods (Eds.). *Life In School: The Sociology of Pupil Culture* (pp. 145 –160). Milton Keynes, England: Open University Press

Gay, L.R. (2000). *Educational Research: Competencies for Analysis and Application.* (6th ed.). New Jersey: Prentice – Hall, Inc.

Gray, J. & Richer, J. (1988). *Classroom Responses To Disruptive Behaviour.* London: Macmillan Education Ltd.

Hargreaves, D.H. (1972). *Interpersonal Relations and Education.* London : Routledge & Kegan Paul Ltd.

Hopkin, K.D. (1998). *Educational and Psychological Measurement and Evaluation.* (8th ed.). Needham Heights: Allyn & Bacon.

Jones, F.J., & Jones, L.S. (1998). *Comprehensive Classroom Management.* (5th ed.). Needham Heights, Mass.: Allyn and Bacon.

King, R., Morris, P., Morrisey, M. & Robinson, P. (2000). *Social Studies through Discovery.* Kingston, Jamaica : Chalkboard Press.

Khalil –Yusuf, Y. (2001). What school is like for high and low achievers. In H. Evans, *Inside Classrooms* (pp.97 –115). Kingston, Jamaica : Faculty of Arts and Education (U.W.I.).

Metz –Haywood, M. (1978). *Classrooms & Corridors : The Crisis of Authority in Desegregated Secondary Schools.* United States: University of California.

Musaazi, J. C. S. (1982). *The Theory & Practice of Educational Administration.* London: Macmillan Ltd.

Slavin, R. E. (1997). *Educational Psychology: Theory and Practice.* (5th ed.). Needham Heights, United States: Allyn & Bacon.

Smith, R. (1985). Freedom & Discipline. London, United Kingdom: George Allen & Unwin.

Zeidner, Moshe. (1986). *The Relative Severity of Common Classroom Management Strategies: The Students Perspective.* (This article was obtained from the U.W.I. School of Education Documentation Center).

LORAINE COOK

CHAPTER 11

LEARNING PATTERNS IN SECONDARY SCHOOL BOYS

HYACINTH SKERVIN

ABSTRACT

This study examines learning behaviors in the classroom that can be associated with gender identities in the male student. The topic is linked to the wider issue of the growing disparity between the academic achievement of secondary school boys and girls. Previous studies have focused on the effect of social and economic factors on male learning behaviors. That boys demonstrate a preference for individual work, for learning experiences and activities that allow them flexibility in their thinking and allow them to apply new learning are some of the findings in this study.

BACKGROUND

One of the arguments in support of the view that there is improvement in the academic achievement of female pupils has been linked to global economic trends. In a survey of one hundred and twenty countries that examined the influence of economic globalization on gender equity in secondary schools, Ilon (1998) found that existing conditions of schooling have changed in favor of girls. This means in general that there now exist more access and opportunities for girls in schools. This significant change is reflected in higher gross enrollment ratios for girls both at the secondary and primary school levels. The logic of her argument is based on the reality of global economic dynamics that has seen a shift from domestic production and markets to external production and markets over the last two decades in rich and poor countries alike. Whereas the degree of shift varies among countries, the pattern of shift continues in them similarly. It is not only that more countries are being pulled into the play of the global economy but also increasingly the various sectors of their economy are becoming intricately linked to the global market place. This expresses itself usually in the framing of policies that tend to link education to new kinds and ways of production. It is reportedly linked for instance to the growth of vocational and service educational programs in schools and to educational programs that are intended to respond to market conditions. The inclusion of information technology education at all levels of the formal education system and the attention that nations are giving to the broadening of capacities for participation in formal education and training are noted policy programs.

It is these major thrusts in education that have been associated with increasing female participation and developing countries have been experiencing their share in the worldwide trend. Global development agencies such as the World Bank, UNESCO and their partners for example encourage and support more government and private investment in primary, secondary and tertiary education in developing countries. Latin American and Caribbean governments are reported to be among the largest recipient of this assistance in recent years. The intent is to raise quality and improve efficiency as well as social benefits. Although commending general growth in educational opportunities in the region, reports from the World Bank since the 1990's indicate that more aid allocations are directed at influencing curriculum reform through intervention projects. These are intended to improve local technological skill needs by integrating information technology into the curriculum and introducing other technology programs (Leach & Little 2001, p 378; World Bank Review 1995 and Reports 1999, 2000). As it is for ethnic minorities and other indigenous groups, a gender sensitive educational curriculum is also a priority particularly at the school level. In this increasing attention is being given to the educational needs of girls and boys equally through such partnership programs as cost-sharing to encourage higher enrollment and more opportunities to earn bursaries that reward participation and achievement. As the review emphasizes, today's Bank funds are used less for buildings and more for other educational inputs so that the narrow project focus of the past is increasingly giving way to a broad sectored approach.

TRENDS IN FEMALE SCHOOL PARTICIPATION

Ilon's assertion of an association between female school participation and economic trends has its base in the first-generational human capital-modernization theory postulated by Alan DeYoung (1992). The theory represents a deviation from traditional views about female participation in schooling. Determinants in the traditional views were classified as socio-cultural and were specific to localities. These include parent' education and religious customs. Now it has been found that government policy and increase in government funding have become the main determinants of female school participation. Are there ramifications from this infusion of female students in secondary school education? It is a logical argument that because of the tendency towards more equitable distribution of male to female students that there has been a deeper change impact on the structure and implementation of the school curriculum? Or alternatively, since the structure of any curriculum that is understood to be responsive to labor market changes that result in greater female participation, could it be that this structural change is also more suited to the educational interests of female students than it is for male students? Thirdly, and as a consequence of the second, are instructional approaches in secondary schools likely to be biased towards female students thereby providing male students with not as strong instructional support. Would this have an impact on the quality of male students' academic achievement?

The questions are relevant to recent research on student achievement. Particularly since the 1990s, research indicates that general patterns of academic achievement in the secondary school increasingly tend to favor girls. The trend in disparity is widening enough to be a cause of concern among educators and educational policy makers nationally and internationally. The basic concern is that boys are under-performing and are at risk of becoming disadvantaged (OECD 1998 and Columbia University 1998). International reports from organizations such as the World Bank (1993) indicate that female pupils are achieving equally or surpassing males in secondary school achievement. Such evidence is strongest in regions such as the Caribbean (and parts of South East Asia) where secondary and tertiary enrollment and grade attainment for female pupils to male pupils have been closer to a ratio of 2:1(Parry, 1996 and Handa 1995). The research also indicates higher visibility in the choices and performance of females outside of their traditional gender-identified subject clusters and accrues this to heightened awareness and modern educational policy initiatives that widen curricula subject areas. Although much of the latter kind of research has been conducted in developed countries, international comparisons suggest girls' improvement in performance spreads generally across curriculum subject areas while males tend to perform in a traditional narrow selection of clusters involving usually the physical sciences and technical studies (OECD 1998 in Collins, Kenway & McCloud 2000, July). In the British

Isles for instance, where girls are generally outperforming boys at both the ordinary and advanced levels secondary school examinations. This result is purported to be a widening trend at every level of the National Curriculum and in all subjects but the sciences and mathematics (OFSED Report 1998, August).

Patterns in the USA generally conform to these disparities. But further studies indicate that boys are lagging behind girls for all ethnic groups and in all subject areas except science and mathematics (Kleinfeld, 1999). More recent reports from a longitudinal study of the NAEP completed in 1996 on these two subjects show that the difference in the performances has narrowed considerably since the 1990s. Other research shows that boys are disproportionately represented in remedial special education class and in other educational impairment at a ratio of 2:1 (NCES, 1994). Further, a 1996 Halpern study also claims that boys are over-represented at the lower ability end of many distributions.

But conclusions about gender achievement gaps that are based on these findings are varied and the gaps in achievement are attributed to different causes. Halpern (1996) blames inherent neurological and psychological differences as opposed to biased treatment in the learning setting. The NAEP (1996) and Kleinfeld (1999) studies discount sex differences in classroom participation and interaction claiming that they have little impact on academic achievement. Two Australian comparative studies (1998; 2000, July) and the Kleinfeld report concur that poorer achievement does not influence life chances of males as males usually have more options than females for educational achievement outside of the traditional learning environment such as the secondary school. In effect, male students have less incentive to improve their performance in the traditional secondary school. Other research such as the UNESCO 1996 report are more insistent that academic under-achievement of boys as well as girls extends to the world of work and ultimately to social exclusion (in Collins, Kenway & McCloud 2000, July; UNESCO 1996). Another suggests that the predominance of female teachers in the schools and the introduction of more coursework and modular exams tend to suit girls better and are therefore contributing factors to boys' disaffection towards learning (Sukhnandan, Lee & Kelleher, NFER 2000). Such lack of affectation should be compounded from constraints imposed by a traditionally narrow educational selection and flexibility among male students.

These arguments suggest at least three different areas that can be explored in further research. The first that those neurological and psychological differences in males can be the basis for ways of learning that is peculiar to boys. The second is that other factors such as personality have possible influences on learning and achievement in boys. A third suggestion is that boys are likely to make choices, have preferences, and show inclination or disinclination to learning in accordance with their inherent differences.

The research questions for this study were accordingly generated from these ideas and were stated as follows:

1. What particular ways of learning can be identified in the male secondary school student?
2. What are the specific characteristics of these learning dispositions?
3. How are these characteristics reflected in the choices, preferences and inclinations of male students in a typical learning setting such as the classroom?

The purpose of the study was to describe patterns of relationships on four but linked personality factors that influence learning and achievement. The factors were students'- attitude, motivation, performance and perceptions about learning. They were examined in relation to the specific contexts of the classroom and therefore involved classroom factors such as the students' courses of study, their classroom interaction during instruction and learning and their thinking in regard to their own learning experiences.

The study combines both qualitative and quantitative research techniques and was an exploratory one for two reasons. It sought to identify patterns of learning behaviors in the male student using variables that were directly related in the classroom and variables that were implicitly related to classroom discourse. It sought to identify these behaviors with a view to their use in subsequent research on male underachievement in the secondary school.

Theories relating to attitude formation, motivation and social interaction provide the theoretical framework for the study. Research on the relationship involving the three personality attributes of attitude personality and self-perception shows that students' attribution for academic success has a strong influence on their "subjective statement of affect" and that their motivated behavior or effort towards tasks reflects their achievement expectations for the future. Demonstration of these personality behaviors within a situational context such as the classroom is a modern approach to studying the interaction of personality and situational influences.

THEORETICAL CONTEXT FOR THE RESEARCH

The assertions that modern educational policy initiatives have widened curricula and practice that have favored female participation and performance over boys suggest that school curricula is likely to be more partial to female interest and therefore less preferred by male students. This in turn can be expected to result in such a claim as attitudinal and motivational theorists as Pervin (1980) and Bandura (1982) have espoused, that there will be low attitude and motivation in boys towards learning a curriculum in which they have little interest. The 1996 UNICEF funded research project in the Caribbean, which was conducted by Parry, lend support to this view. Parry generally argued that male gendered responses in classrooms are informed by cultural expectations that translate into pedagogical relationships.

He further argued that classroom interaction is informed by socio-economics and other constraints so those gender identities are socially constructed and historically shifting. The better academic achievement among female students can therefore be viewed as the result of a cultural dynamic which time has come leaving behind their male colleagues in its wake. Moreover, if the cultural expectations are now higher for female students as a result of current economic dynamics and changing curricula, then the resulting pedagogical relationships in the classrooms that are contributing to high female academic achievement cannot be expected to favor male pupils as much.

Arguments in favor of inherent or trait differences in males as well as females provide an alternative theory but also underscore Parry's argument. Atkinson, Atkinson and Hilgard (1983) define attitude as likes and dislikes, affinities for and aversions to situations, objects, persons, groups and any other identifiable aspect of the environment including abstract ideas and social policies. They continue that attitudes are expressions consisting of the three components of belief based on cognition, affect that is represented as feeling, and behavior, which is the action, exhibited. The authors' conclude that each component of attitude is predictive of the other and that all three are coherently organized although the basis of the organization is not necessarily logical. The authors contend however, that human beings always strive for consistency between all three and any inconsistency among them motivates the individual to modify or make changes to restore some kind of coherent whole again.

There is therefore a valid rationale for accepting that males students like female students will tend towards common learning behaviors according to how their group identities and various environments dictate. This will produce what White and Tisher (1986) describe as attitude and define as the stable characteristic trait of a person. It constitutes in their view that part of the personality attributed to conditioning by the environment. Attitude is also described as a state that is transitory being consequent on the interaction of the trait and the context in which the individual is placed so that changing the environments will also influence change in attitude. It is this desire and effort to make change or to restore coherence that is the substance of human motivation,,which according to Boeree (2000) becomes the characteristic of the individual as it is directed in the specific context to different ends. Motivation is therefore friable and transferable to what may be of interest at any one time. Its nature suggests a behavior that can be driven by individual as well as group dynamics and because it is inherent can be freely activated or directed to desirable ends.

Research on student motivation in recent years has also focused on other variables. One such variable is attribution, which describes the causes of students' success and failure in school. It has been found especially, that students who believe the learning events that they experience are under their own control are more highly motivated to learn. In contrast, students who believe that they have little or no control over learning events in school are less motivated to learn. Although these findings are associated with research, which studied minority students, the results showed that school achievement correlates highly with measures of locus of control despite the students' abilities and perceptions of their abilities to learn (Wittrock 1986). One implication of these findings is that perception and belief about school and classroom events have impact on students' attitude to learn. Since attitude is indicated by beliefs, judgments and feelings among other traits, then students' high or low motivation are reflective of those beliefs and their perceptions of control or lack of control of their learning processes and events is also a measure of their attitude. It follows then, that any measure of motivation should also be a measure of attitude and the criteria used in judging the quality of students motivation are also by implications judging the quality of their attitude.

Other theories of motivation have also postulated that effort expended on task is a product of the degree to which people expect to perform that task successfully and the value they assign to the reward for successful effort (Good and Brophy 1987). Good and Brophy have therefore identified effort, success and reward as the three-value components that the individual considers to a greater or lesser degree In assigning value to task. The authors liken the motivated student to one who has a tendency to find academic activities meaningful and worthwhile and will try to get the intended benefits from it usually by completing it successfully. The benefits accrued and expended show his or her intrinsic motivation to learn.

Likewise, purposeful learning may be measured by a high degree of interest. Smith and Ragan (1999) associate this interest with attending to what is going on during instruction and choosing to apply effort as a result of it. This interest is also identified in two types being influenced in pattern and importance by the nature of the topic being taught and the learning tasks. The first is identified as individual interest and is conceptualized as an enduring preference for certain topics while situational interest is conceptualized as an emotional state brought about by situational stimuli. Indications and measures of motivation are therefore extended to and reflected in the preference and choice of the learning tasks and topics to which students attend and make purposeful effort to learn. Further, since learning topics and instructional procedures are usually related and designed in accordance with the nature of curriculum subjects, then the quality of student interest in any topic may also reflect the quality of the interest in the curriculum subject and represents another measure of student motivation towards it.

METHOD

The target population was students in a 10th Grade Piadiea class of an urban co-educational secondary high school in the mid-western United States. Grade ten students are considered mature enough to be allowed course specialization and the choice of courses reveal the students' personal goals, interest, and direction beyond school. Lack of clear choices at this level is considered normal and indicates indecisiveness, anxiety, or cynicism about the worth of school to personal goals and ambitions particularly in students at either end of the transition phase of this level of maturity. A co-educational setting was selected for two reasons. Single sex schools are known to experience often higher and more consistent patterns of academic achievement than co-educational schools. Secondly, and consequently, the nature of the challenge to academic achievement can be assumed to be different in competitiveness in grade classes composed of both male and female students.

A sample of six subjects was selected for more detailed examination among the twenty- three males in the class of forty students. The subjects in the study represented a mixed ability group. One of the six was an "inclusion" student who had been transferred from the 10th Grade special education class because of his 'better work'. The grading curve is higher for this student and the high marks for work done are in part intended for student motivation. Another of the six students was gainfully employed every school day for as many hours as he spent in school. The development of critical thinking skills is the distinctive emphasis in the curriculum for a Piadiea class.

The boys were between fifteen to seventeen years of age. One student was substituted in the interview section of the study. Research variables were contextual to the classroom situation and students' learning experiences. The variables were divided into four categories. Each variable category identified specific student behaviors for which data was collected. The variables were:

- Students' attitude towards their curriculum courses of study indicated by their course preferences and the value of importance given to the courses.
- Students' academic performance in the curriculum courses indicated by their grades for the school term that was studied.
- Students' level of motivation indicated by the quality of their classroom engagement with the instructional methods and instructional techniques that were used and the learning task and activities in which they were involved.
- Student' perceptions about their classroom experiences indicated by their opinions about their own learning experiences and learning preferences, their learning expectations and learning goals

Data were obtained from Likert and Semantic Differential Attitudinal surveys, classroom observations, the Teachers' Grade Book, and a Focus Group semi-structured interview with the students. The variable categories are represented in the following data display:

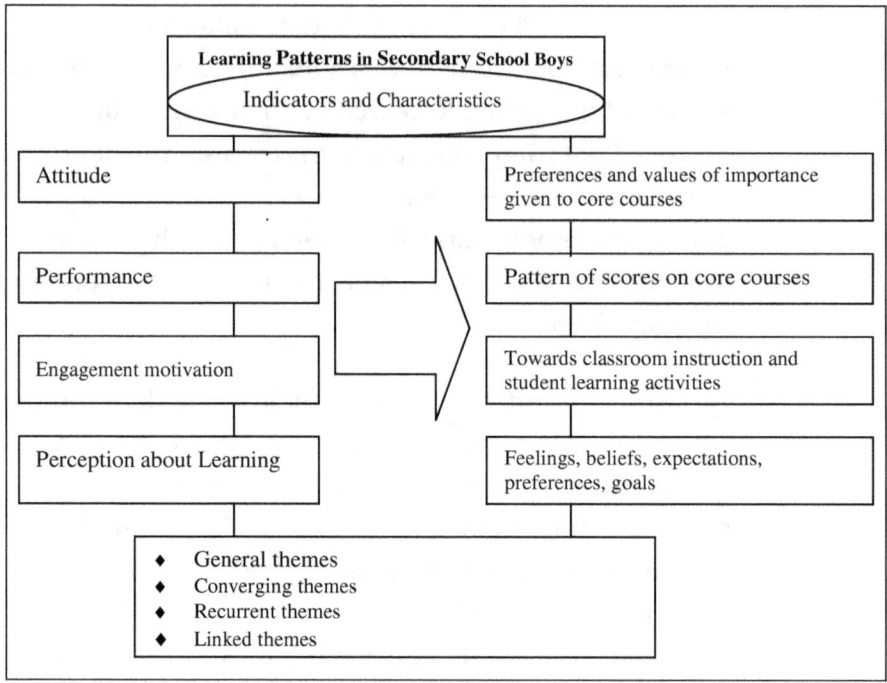

PROCEDURE

The Attitudinal Scale questionnaires that were administered consisted of the list of curriculum courses that Grade Ten students are permitted to study in this school. The response options from 'Strongly Like to Strongly Dislike' on the Likert Scale indicated the degree of preference that could be given each course. Response options from 'Very Important to Not Important' on the Semantic Differential scale indicated the value of importance that could also be given to each course. The response options on the two surveys were scored on a five-point scale. Preliminary analysis of the survey data included a comparison of the responses on the two scales to determine the two and similar curriculum courses that were given highest and lowest preference and highest value of importance respectively. The Teacher's Grade Books were examined to establish the pattern of performance on the four courses that were selected from the attitudinal scale surveys. One classroom observation was done during instructional time for each of the four selected courses. The students' focus group semi-structured interview was tape-recorded. It consisted of the students' opinions in responses to seven open-ended questions about facets of their own learning and their classroom learning experiences. These included reference to instructional procedures, the nature of learning tasks and activities, learning expectations, preferences and goals.

The findings reported in this study identified and described from triangulation any systematic similarities and convergence in the content of themes in each set of data and across the data sets. They identified and described casual relationships within and across the content of themes of the data sets and they conceptualized those relationships as identifiable patterns of learning in the secondary school male.

DATA COLLECTION

Data for this study is comprised of records of the learning behaviors of the six male subjects in the sample. The class because of its size is divided into two groups. The six subjects are shared between the two groups, which are rotated within the time slot for each class. Each record in the data is related to a specific attribute of the subject's behavior that was actively demonstrated in the classroom, was given vocally or was obtained from a documented source.

The first category of behavior examined was the students' attitude towards their curriculum courses of study. Analysis of data included summation of common scores for each course on the Likert and Semantic Scales. Strong attitudinal preference and high value of importance were given to common scores of 5 and 4 respectively. Weak attitudinal preference and low value of importance were given to common scores of 1 through 3. The four core curriculum courses were selected based on these indications and the fact that they were convenient to further usage in the study.

The students' performance scores over the given school term on the four-selected curriculum courses were the second category of behavior that was examined. Scores were graded downwards from 'A' to 'X'. 'F' scores were failing scores whereas 'I' represented incomplete and 'X' represented no record of a score in that particular set of scores for the student. Each course had four sets of grade scores for each student.

The level of students' engagement motivation was the third category of behavior that was examined. Measurements were taken on an Observation Schedule during instructional time for the four selected courses. Five characteristic and sequential behaviors were observed repeatedly with each change of the instructional method, instructional technique, and the assigned student task. These behaviors were recorded as they became evident and when the interactive discourse permitted them. The behaviors in sequential order were the student's demonstrated action in 'preparation for class'; 'paying attention'; 'being on task'; 'staying on task'; and 'completion of task'.

The students' responses to a series of semi-structured and probing questions during an intense interview ware the final category of behavior that was examined. Transcription of the interview included the use of the broad coding sub-categories of attitude; perceptions; learning preferences; learning expectations and learning goals. The content under the themes was further grouped where they appeared similar or related.

ANALYSIS OF DATA

Table 1: Strongest Attitude toward Core Curriculum Courses of Study

Rating	Preference 5 4 3 2 1	Value of importance 5 4 3 2 1
Frequency of Students		
English	2 2 2	5 1
Geometry	1 3 1 1	3 1 1 1
US History	1 2 3	2 2 2
Chemistry	2 2 1 1	3 3

Summary of Attitude	English (%)	Geometry	US History (%)	Chemistry
High preference	67	67		
Low preference			50	50
High value of importance	100	67		
Low value of importance			33	50

Except for English, the evidence from the attitudinal survey showed that the boys had strongest attitudinal preferences for the optional curriculum courses. These included Physical Education and Health Education. English and Geometry were the only two of the core courses for which the boys indicated a strong attitude. A generally weak attitude was indicated for History and Chemistry and the other two of the core courses. The core courses are mandatory for all students in the 10th Grade Paidiea class and therefore the only courses in which all six students participated. The pattern of optional course preferences suggests future research could focus on exploring reasons for the boys' strong attitudes towards these courses. Table 1 indicates how the boys their towards the four selected courses.

Triangulation was useful in arriving at a perspective on why the students had their strongest and contrasting attitudes for the two core courses English and History and also provided some insight into where the learning inclinations tend to lie. The following responses would indicate that reading as well as creative writing are favored activities, while relevance, relatedness to other interest, subject fascination including openness to exploration would bear some evidence of learning expectations and preferences of the students.

(STE-1)   I like to read

(DUS-2)   English is different from whatever you learn because you get like to write, to read....

(MEL-3)   English is all right. I like the stuff that I do. You get to write and not just copy stuff.

(ROD-5)   I don't really like English. It is really not an interesting subject really. I am interested in reading....You have got to learn to speak the grammar, write and such important things.

(DES-6)   You get to do creative things in English. I like to write a lot. I get to write stories and use my imagination cause I have a lot of interaction.

And History

(DUS-2)   Well history, well social studies is my favorite subject...like the time I am in you   don't take it   how you receive it.... And what happen in the past reflect on the future

(MEL-3)   History is hard, almost a subject I hate. It is not open and it is not making the kind of sense so that a lot of people want to sleep in the class

(ERN-4)   I mean, the thing is history is dead. We just sit in our seats and it makes the day long. We just sit there as he talks. It makes it kind of boring when we just sit there and he talks. I find it easier when he is explaining and we are working.

(ROD-5]   Well, I am not really fascinated by history. I don't think it can help me out in my future....But   history, I don't think I will need it too much to get a job.

(DES-6) I like history. I think history is about moments in the past. The history business- I don't know. I think my best year of history was in the sixth grade coming up. We never used textbooks and she was like you are going to have fun, but you will learn, so you are going to remember it-so, she made it fun. It is easy to follow. It is not like you are trying to understand it. It is like you are looking for ways to create it.

The evidence from the students' performance records on these courses did not completely confirm the attitude they held nor the responses they gave in relation to their attitudes during the interview. Chemistry for example, for which a generally low attitude was indicated, had the highest and most consistent set of scores of the all the scores for the students although the only student with the strongest attitude toward the course had the best scores. In contrast, English and Geometry, which were high preference courses, had comparatively lower scores. The pattern of the students performance would suggest that attitude is not by itself a predictive factor in determining how students will perform or will achieve in a given course. However, it may provide the context in which to identify where the learning preference is. In fact, the only one of the six students to indicate high scores and a strong preference for Chemistry also gave in his reason a comparison with another high preference course as:

(RO5) I don't really like English. Its really not an interesting subject really…..I guess when I get older I am interested in science and Chemistry.

Table 2 presents the performance patterns of the students on the four core courses.

Table 2: Pattern of Performance on Curriculum Courses

	English	Geometry	US History	Chemistry
Student 1	B B B B	A B A B	B B C B	A B B B
Student 2	B B D C	C C A D	C C B C	A B A D
Student 3	C B C B	C D B C	B B D C	B B C C
Student 4	B C C B	B D C C	B D D C	B C C C
Student 5	I X F F	F X F C	B A B B	A A B B
Student 6	B B F C	B C C D	B C B C	B C B C

The element of students' engagement motivation provided more detailed insight into the students' attitudes and classroom learning behaviors (See appendix Tables 3, 3a – 6, 6a). Engagement motivation was presented in the form of behavior profiles for each student as he interacted during the class discourse..

Direct instruction and guided inquiry were the teaching methods that were used in sequence in English class s while instructional techniques and procedures involved questioning including prompts at different points during the lesson. These were intended to facilitate students in forming, developing and applying the concept of 'conscience'. Student 1 and student 2 belonged to this group. Table 3 shows the sequence of instruction and activities. A significant portion of the class time for both groups was given to the final writing exercise.

The same instructional procedures and student learning activities continued with group B. Des-, Student 6, was absent from this class. There was more variety to be seen in the interaction and engagement motivation of the other student subjects who were present. In addition, a shorter time was spent elaborating on the class routines and concept teaching. 'Conscience' and its universal themes were also the concepts to be defined, developed and applied. A summary of the classroom interaction and motivation for Group A and Group B is represented in Table 3a of Appendix 1.

The overall patterns of the students engagement motivation seemed stronger when they were given writing tasks and when the writing event was accompanied by teacher questioning techniques that allowed to them to be reflective. There is support for these conclusions in the references that the students made later when commenting on English as a preferred course. They referred to use of imagination, to being creative, to being able to tell stories and to the fact that they are allowed to write "and not just copy stuff". Having their thought processes activated toward ends that they prefer is important to these students. Des- captured this pattern perhaps more than the others in a burst of self-revelation that met with the approval and admiration of his peers. Speaking on his strong preference for English he continued:

(DUS-2) ....It encouraged me to write more. Now I have two poems being published by a poetry company.....I want to use my technique later in life.

As in English direct instruction and guided inquiry were the instructional methods used in history class. Questioning was a common technique throughout the lesson. (See Table 4 in Appendix 1). Following the usual preamble about homework and timeline a two-part question opened the lesson for both group A and B.

> "What is propaganda? What kind of propaganda have you seen in your life"? This was followed by an announcement of the topic for the day's lesson: "Race to Berlin".

This was group B. All four of subjects in this group participated in this initial exercise and received some feedback from the teacher. Mel-Student 3, asked an "excellent" follow-up question before giving his response to the first of the two questions. Ern- student 4, and Des- student 6, also had responses to the first question. Ern-student 4, gave 'advertisement' as an example in his response to the second question and. Rod-5 also gave an "outstanding" example of second. There was the feeling that there was much variation in this class. The pace was fast and changed to different activities regularly. Subjects participated actively and almost always consistently. It does not explain for this group however, why history is not a highly preferred or highly valued course of study. The boys were especially responsive to the questions and the teacher's approach. They drew from their experiences considerably and extended discussions or draw parallels from areas that were perhaps unexpected. To think of 'victory bonds' as an example of propaganda to change people's minds; and the poster message that "we are the greatest" despite all other social problems to the contrary was not overlooked by Dus-2 (student 2) who cited similar contradictions in the present age. He opines further:

> "...but I thought I never had to take history any more but now I have a negative perception of US history. But there is another different kind of history that is there to be seen".

The teacher's method and procedures as well as the student patterns of behaviors were virtually identical with group A. That is, the students volunteered responses except that the boys were extremely animated in this class especially when relating their experiences (some public, some personal) of propaganda. They spoke of their observations and conclusions.

Overall, the students' participation in history class showed evidence of consistent engagement motivation up to the point where they began each task (See table 4a in Appendix 1). Less consistency was observed when they did not all continue or persist with their writing tasks though none of these activities had to be completed in class. They demonstrated instead different types of distraction. But generally, the content of what they were doing seemed important as the subjects among the other males in both class groups dominated the rather animated discussions and gave all the responses to the questions that were asked. The pattern of the students' engagement motivation would suggest that the boys are inclined to learning activities in which real life scenarios from their own experiences or which they can appreciate vicariously play a part. They are also inclined to learning activities that allow them to analyze those scenarios against their own knowledge and viewpoints. There were indirect references to these preferences in stating some of their perceptions of what history is and should be

(MEL-3)   History is hard. Almost a subject I hate because it is really that. Not open and it is not making the kind of sense.....

(RUB-2)*   (substituted for student 1) History can tap into a couple of things. History can tap into English, you know what I am saying. History is like...without history you would not have geometry. You need to base history in what is going on.

(DES-6)   ...It is not like you are trying to understand it is like you are looking for ways to create it.

It should be noted however, that the interest and enthusiasm that the students showed might have been compromised by the fact that the posters were oriented towards males. That is, they bore images of mostly males. Secondly, the students were learning about a war, in particular World War 11 where the fighters were mostly men.

Direct instruction was the instructional methodology used in Chemistry class but techniques varied to include a teacher-led discussion, lecture and use of multimedia. Student's activities included the interactive discussions, note taking, laboratory assignment review, worksheet exercise and observation of a video presentation (See sequence of instruction in Table 5 in Appendix 1). The class took place in a classroom and not a chemistry lab although there were stimulus materials around the room. This was group B. The teacher discussed the mandatory chemistry lab session for "Friday's" class. The lab exercise would be about Freddie's Fish Farm. An interactive 'warm-up' session followed in which students provided for discussion a term (theoretical) or a context (real life experience) in which chemistry or reactive chemicals had some kind of detrimental effect. The topics discussed in this group were red eyes as an effect from ganja smoking and differences in the effects of ganja smoking and crack inhalation. The students were expected to volunteer their contributions to the discussion. Only Mel-3 did. The other students exhibited a range of non-scholarly behaviors during the time including being highly talkative.

The order of the lesson was reversed for group A. The teacher-led warm-up discussion on the reaction of salt water on metals and prescriptive glasses occupied the first part of the lesson. This was followed by a discussion on the video-related worksheet ahead of the presentation of the video documentary. This group A was much quieter although there were more girls than boys in this class but the other boys asked more of the questions just as in group B. There was also more teachers input and greater application of the subject material being applied to real life situations. Ste-student 1 and Des-student 2, were virtually passive learners in this class. Their participation involved very little besides occasional writing and a single request for clarification when an application was implied with respect to the warm-up topic.

The video presentation seemed an interesting technique. It had most of the students absorbed and responding - at least initially. But it left an important question as to why the motivation was not sustained over the entire period. It also left possible questions then about how useful was the application of an all-inclusive instructional methodology as is the Piadeia to numerically based courses of study or whether the teacher's style or the length of the video had an influence. Interest was more sustained in the second group. The group showed similar and perhaps more intensity in the degree of interest and input into the discussions and over the entire session of the presentation. The curiosity was high among this group and for this the question was whether the time of day and the point at which the video was introduced in the lesson had anything to do with the contrasting behaviors of the subjects and their respective colleagues.

The only evidence of consistency in the students' engagement motivation in the two groups was that they appeared for class and that they paid attention to what was done at each stage of the lesson (See table 5a in Appendix 1). Their on task behavior was consistent only when they were taking notes and except for one student when working on the worksheets and interest in the application of learning was not sustained either. The group however showed the highest and more consistent set of scores across the group for this subject. It is s left to conjecture whether the it is the teacher's grading curve or the boys success in working on their own is responsible for this better performance in a subject to which they that they do not generally have a high attitude or show strong class motivation.

Mrs. H....., the teacher, thought her students were not motivated, and claimed this accounted for their restless and distracting behaviors. But their performance did not bear this out. Conjecture suggests that independent work had a role to play in the students' performance since this is the only course of study in which the students regularly complete independent work as lab assignments and the subject for which they also articulated a strong learning preference. Their response to the following follow-up question suggest this:

(IN)   So do you like group work then?

(ERN-4)   Yeah (not very convincing) but it will be a little bit easier.

(ROD-5)   I don't so much like working in groups. I work better as an individual.

(RUB-1)*   Me too. (The others "Yeah") Yes. That's right.

(DES-6) Sometimes a group can hinder you back. Sometimes in groups ..like I can be ahead three pages but I have to wait up for my group members so that we are on the same page. I don't want to work with people that much but if I have to then I have to make sure that my group members are on the same page (The others nodded their agreement).

Direct instruction in along with instructional techniques involving questioning, demonstrations, and application was the only instructional method used in this geometry class. Each procedure was conducted in interactive session with the two class groups. Student activities included an introductory problem solving exercise, concept development and note taking and a final problem sheet based on application of the new concepts learnt (See table 6 in Appendix 1).

Students spoke casually with the teacher before the time scheduled for the beginning of the lesson. Rapport with students seemed good. There were stated rules for math class on the chalkboard and the classroom walls had a variety of stimulus materials. The teacher (routinely) had written the day's agenda and warm-up question to one side of chalkboard that students attempted to answer before the lesson officially began.

This was group A. The students were given twelve minutes of time, calculators and writing paper to solve the two warm-up questions written on chalkboard.

Students asked questions of teacher and of each other as they solved the problems. The teacher moved around the room helping those students who ask for help. Ste- listened keenly while Des interacted with other students regularly. Students volunteered the responses to the questions in an orderly manner and the boys in particular affirmed their correct responses with each other by giving the 'high five'. These problems also had to be completed for entry into the work sheet.

Concept teaching with the aid of dictionary, example and non-examples was the first procedure in the new lesson. It also involved the efforts of all the students in rephrasing then writing down their definitions of concepts that included: surface areas, prism and types of prism- for example, the lateral and oblique.

The teacher's technique was one of continuous and active involvement with students during which he provided the opportunities for clarification, for immediate answering of questions and attending to the students' difficulties in completing task. An immediate application of concept learnt and regular feedback relating to how the boys were doing their task seemed important in sustaining their interest in learning.

The evidence showed that engagement motivation was maintained throughout the lesson except for short lapses from task at the beginning and during the final problem solving activity by several of the subjects. But the students generally reverted to their tasks. Des-

perhaps expressed why the enthusiasm seemed so high for almost all members of the subject group and for the class in general:

(Dus-2) This is what...., say look at Mr. S? He teaches geometry. I don't like geometry but sometimes he does things that trying to make geometry fun that make me want to take geometry because he uses jeopardy games, some form a quiz or he uses like different portfolio that includes some kind of jeopardy, or you build some kind of project-and that a lot of kids like to do. So it is the way he teaches it. It is the way you teach different subjects. No subject is boring".

> Mr.S— himself said his approach (he thought) had contributed to this enthusiasm, in that he had allowed the students increasing amounts of freedom as they were able to use it responsibly and he created activities that they could enjoy. His perceptions were that the students were rather constrained at the beginning of the school year when they came to him and their grades were generally low. He had seen improvements since.

Learning behaviors in this class suggest that subjects showed the strongest evidence of engagement motivation when they were seeking to understand concepts, concept examples and when they were required to apply the concepts in calculating the measurements of different surface areas on the problem sheet. They indicated this as they remained on task, asking multiple questions and provided extended answers to teacher questions during feedback times in the class.

BOYS THINKING ABOUT THEIR OWN LEARNING

Did the students consider the courses they were learning and the way in which they were learning them within their best interest if they are to acquire a worthwhile education?

The students had comments concerning the courses that they were doing and about how they were conducted to suggest that they had concerns about their learning environment. In fact, 10 Piadiea students take the same weekly and daily schedule of core courses every day and are allowed to complete the related assignments at their own discretion although within bounded timeframes. This arrangement seemed quite banal and the surmising was borne out when the students were asked it there was anything they would like to see changed or added to the way they were learning in school and in the way they felt about their education. There was a general opinion that the curriculum was restricting in that students were not 'given the chance' to do the courses and things that they liked to do nor to the extent that they would have liked to do it. In addition, Dus-student 2, thought:

> "The school should stop to find out what we think about our education before they think like giving us these exact(ing) homework".

> "They should find out first what we want to do before they give you two hours of homework because the same that we are going through is not what they are going through" (a reference to

less time for other things that he would like to do).

He feels he should be allowed to do more courses for which he can get extra credit. (A view towards college may be an influence in the thinking of this student). Ern-student 4, shares the same feeling.

"Extra classes", he says.

"They should let us do things like classes which benefit you".

Mel-student 3, thought there was just too much homework and more of the same kind of homework. He thought like Rod-student 5, that he should be allowed to do computing as a full course. Rod felt he should be doing:

"...Some program like computer program that can help you in life" (The latter is a frequent and important reference for Rod).

SUMMARY OF RESULTS

GENERAL FINDINGS

General and Recurrent Themes

1. Applicable and useable of learning
2. Relevance of learning to the here and now
3. Open learning- that is, open to creative thinking, writing and (content) exploration
4. Learning that provides functional skills in life
5. Independent learning (individual interest)

Linked Themes

A   1 Application and usable learning

3 Open learning- that is, to creative thinking, writing and subject (content) exploration

5 Individual learning (individual interest)

B   2 Relevance of learning to the here and now

4 Learning that provides functional (life) skills

5 Individual learning (and individual interest)

The pattern of learning in this study suggests that the manner of instruction and nature of the learning experience have a stronger influence than subject preferences in determining the learning behaviors of boys. The most consistent and highest set of scores involved the only course in which the boys were allowed to pursue truly independent work and independent inquiry. Yet chemistry represents one of the courses for which the boys did not indicate an especially strong preference. It likewise represented the only subject for which the boys had a female teacher and therefore does not confirm the suggestion that boys are disinclined towards learning if the teacher is female. It could suggest however, that the low preference by itself that was indicated for this subject and in part the seemingly poorer quality of the boys' classroom behavior might be related to this fact (See in this study Sukhnandan, Lee & Kelleher, NFER 2000).

Particular learning behaviors were also expressed in a preference for teaching and learning that allow the boys to use their imagination, to be creative and to be able to relate stories. That is, the boys appeared to prefer instruction and learning tasks that provide for flexibility in their thinking an act in which they seemed to have taken considerable delight and this was reflected in a higher level of motivation where this was allowed in all four classes. The boys' strong preference for English especially, may be related to these characteristics of the English class, since traditionally boys are not inclined to favor English with a strong preference (See in this study OECD 1998 in Collins, Kenway & McCloud 2000, July). Teacher-questioning techniques that allowed the boys to be reflective accompanied the writing events in that class. It was also strongly evidence in the history class when the boys responded well to learning activities in which real life scenarios that either involved their own experiences or experiences that they could appreciate vicariously played a part. The boys tended to analyze those scenarios against a combination of their own knowledge and viewpoints. This preference also has inherent in it an inter-play of use of the boys' imagination, creativity and the opportunity to relate stories.

The boys also showed evidence of a stronger motivation when they were seeking to understand concept and apply concepts for instance, in the level of attention given to the calculation of the measurements and to the writing exercises. That is boys seem to favor the application of learning and the independent use of new learning to create their own learning product.

CONCLUSIONS

This study indicates that there are distinctive patterns to male pupil learning and suggests that the opportunity to learn in their preferred ways might have a more positive impact on their academic performance. The study also suggests that the method and process of instruction can be designed to facilitate the learning patterns and specific learning preferences in boys. The study shows for example, that desirable learning behaviors in boys may be more easily encouraged if the application of learning is an integral part of the learning experience.

Instruction that makes the learning event relevant to male real life experiences and to the things in which they have immediate interest also seems basic to male patterns of learning. It also generally supports the preference for use of the imaginations and "creative genius" in learning while representing the most measurable component of their learning expectations. To base learning in "what is going on" as one subject puts it, is to make it not only relevant but also to make learning open to all or as many inputs and experiences as possible. It is also to facilitate more ways of learning the different courses of study and provides more opportunities for students to create their own original learning product.

DIRECTION FOR FUTURE RESEARCH

Evidence of identifiable patterns of relationships from the results of this study are useful in providing ideas about learning behaviors and subsumes ideas about learning preferences in secondary school male students. The ideas provide information about identifiable and measurable facets of male pupil learning that can be used in further investigation. This may include investigation to determine the degree to which these facets of male pupil learning behaviors are accommodated in current instructional practices and whether the degree of accommodation has a direct bearing on male pupil achievement patterns. Further, the findings in this study suggest a need to replicate the study - firstly with a larger sample population and secondly, with other secondary grades. Similar results would imply possible generalizations of the findings to other school populations.

REFERENCES

(1998). Part 111, Achievement, assessment and evaluative learning, *Doing Comparative Education: Three Decades of Collaboration 5th Ed.* Selected works, (New York: Teacher's College, Columbia University).

Atkinson, L. P., Atinkson, R. C., & Hilgard, E. R., (1983). *Introduction to Psychology.* 8th Ed. (New York: Harcourt Brace Jovanovich Publishers).

Bandura, A., (ref. in Wittrock 1986 ed.) In: Adaptive teaching to individual differences among learners, *Handbook for Teaching and Research.* 3rd Ed. (New York: MacMillan Publishing Company).

Boeree, G. C., (2000). *Personality Theories: The Ultimate Theory of Personality* http://www.ship.edu/negboeree/conclusions/html

Collins, C., Kenway, J., & McCloud, J., (2000, July). *Factors Influencing Performance of Males and Females in School and Their Destinations after Leaving School.* (Commonwealth of Australia: Deakin University, University of Australia).

DeYoung, A., (1992). *Children and Resources: Human Capital Theory, Modernization Theories and the School. In: Economics and American Education* (New York: Longman).

Foster, V., (1998). *Gender, Schooling a Achievement and Post-School Pathways: Beyond Statistics and Populist Discourse* (Australia: Australian Council for Commonwealth Department of Education).

Good, T. L., & Brophy, J. E. (1987). *Looking in Classrooms.* Harper and Row. Publishers, New York.

Halpern, D.,1996 in: Nowell, A., & Hedges, L.V., (1998). Trends in gender differences in academic achievement from 1960 to 1994: an analysis of differences in mean, variance, and extreme scores. *A Journal of Research,* 39 (nl-2).

Handa 1995). The impact on education, income and mortality on fertility in Jamaica, *World Development,* 28 (1) 178-186.

Ilon, L., (1998). The effects of international economic trends on gender equity in schooling, *International Review of Education*, 44 (4) 335-356.

Kleinfeld, J., (1999, Winter). Student performance: males versus females, *The Public Interest*, 34 (1).

Leach, F. E., & Little, A. W., (2001). *Education, Cultures and Economics: Dilemmas for Development* (New York: Falmer Press).

NAEP 1996 in: Kleinfeld, J., (1999, Winter). Student performance: males versus females, *The Public Interest*, 34 (1).

NECS 1994 in: Kleinfeld, J., (1999, Winter). Student performance: males versus females, *The Public Interest*, 34 (1).

OECD 1998 in: Collins, C., Kenway, J., & McCloud, J., (2000, July). *Factors Influencing Performance of Males and Females in School and Their Destinations after Leaving School.* (Commonwealth of Australia: Deakin University, University of Australia).

Pervin, L. A., (ref. in Wittrock 1986 ed.) In: Adaptive teaching to individual differences among learners, *Handbook for Teaching and Research. 3rd Ed.* (New York: MacMillan Publishing Company).

Parry, O., (1996). In one ear and out the other: unmasking masculinities in the Caribbean classroom, *Sociological Research Online*, 1 (2). http//www.socresonline.org.uk/1/2/2.html

Smith, P., & Pagan, T., (1999). *Instructional Design* (New Jersey: Prentice-Hall).

Sukhnandan, Lee & Kelleher, (2000). *An investigation into gender differences in achievement, Phase 2: School and classroom strategies* (United Kingdom: National Foundation of Educational Research {NFER}).

White, R. T., & Tisher, R. T., (in Wittrock, 1986 ed.). In: Research on natural sciences, *Handbook for Teaching and Research.* 3rd *Ed.* (New York: MacMillan Publishing Company).

Wittrock, M. C., (1986 ed.) In: Students' thought processes, *Handbook for Teaching and Research.* 3rd *Ed.* (New York: MacMillan Publishing Company).

(1993). *Access Quality and Efficiency in Education* (World Bank Country Study).

(1999). *Educational Change in Latin American and the Caribbean* (World Bank Group).

(2000). *Caribbean Education Strategy* (World Bank Group).

(1996). *Learning: The Treasure Within* (UNESCO Publishing). .

(1998). *Reviews of Research on Gender and Achievement: Recent Research on Educational Performance,* United Kingdom: OFSTED).

(1996). *Trends in Academic Progress* (USA: National Assessment of Educational Progress {NAEP}).

CHAPTER 12

DOES DISRUPTIVE CLASSROOM BEHAVIOUR MAKE ADOLESCENT CARIBBEAN STUDENTS MORE OR LESS POPULAR WITH THEIR PEERS?

TONY BASTICK

ABSTRACT

Teachers of Caribbean students, particularly of adolescent male students, frequently experience social management problems in their classrooms. What these students see as 'normal' spontaneous social interactions is often viewed as lack of self-regulatory behaviour by their teachers, educational psychologists and school counsellors. This chapter considers the inter-group dynamics related to self-regulatory behaviour of adolescents in the classroom. It investigates whether this 'problem' behaviour is being socially promoted by making the perpetrators more popular with their peers or whether it is being socially inhibited by making the perpetrators less popular with their peers. To answer these questions three sub-scales of Humphrey's (1982) Children's Perceived Self-Control

Scale were administered to 18 classes of Jamaican adolescents students (N=717). In addition, same-sex popularity and opposite-sex popularity were assessed for each student using in-class sociometric nominations and ratings. Results showed that females had significantly higher self-regulatory control than males (p<0.005) and that those students, both male and female, who resisted aggression and stayed on task were more popular with the opposite sex (p<0.005). The utility of these results is that peer-popularity and sexual attractiveness are strong modifiers of adolescent behaviour that may be utilised to promote pro-social behaviours.

INTRODUCTION

Police crime statistics show that Caribbean adolescents, as a group, are associated with social violence and disruptive behaviour both in the Caribbean and in major urban centres in Britain, Canada and in the United States. Teachers of Caribbean students, particularly of male students, frequently experience social management problems in their classrooms. What these students see as 'normal' spontaneous social interactions is often viewed as lack of self-regulatory behaviour by educational psychologists and schools counsellors. This chapter considers the inter-group dynamics related to self-regulatory behaviour of adolescents in the classroom. It investigates whether this 'problem' behaviour is being socially promoted by making the perpetrators more popular with their peers or whether it is being socially inhibited by making the perpetrators less popular with their peers. It is important for class teachers as well as educational psychologists to know whether 'spontaneous social interaction' or 'higher self-regulatory control' is being reinforced by peer-group popularity so that this knowledge might be used to reduce these problem behaviours.

Although there is very little published research that investigates relations between self-control and popularity, it has been postulated that self-control is a personal competency that can promote health and adjustment in children (Bukowski, Hoza, & Boivin 1993), and many studies have found that popular children have fewer behavior problems than rejected children (Frentz, 1991; Munsch, & Kinchen, 1995). Hence, this research investigated aspects of self-control that might contribute to popularity. Self-control is referred to in the literature as self-regulatory behavior (Wentzel, & Asher, 1995) and in a review of the literature on social competence at school in 1991 Kathryn Wentzel concluded that self-regulatory behaviors explained links between socially responsible behavior and peer popularity. Interpersonal aggression is one of the most overt forms of lack of self-control in classrooms and this has been linked to low peer popularity by Coie and Dodge (1988) and Coie, Dodge, and Kupersmidt, (1990) who found that rejected children, particularly boys were more aggressive than children of average popularity and that the most popular children were the least aggressive. Fabes and Eisenberg (1992) similarly found that it was the least popular children who were most involved in incidences of anger.

Adolescence is a developmental stage when children are more aware of their same-sex and opposite-sex peer popularity. It has been widely found that such peer pressures influence adolescent behavior (Santor, Messervey, & Kusumakar 2000). For example, in an eight-year longitudinal youth study Susan Giancola (2000) found that the influence of an adolescent's peer group explained student behavior throughout the high school years better than any other variable. Hence, it is particularly important to know if self-control promotes or detracts from adolescent popularity. However, there has been little recent work investigating relationships between self-control and classroom popularity. It could be hypothesised that adolescents who display controlled self-regulatory behavior are perceived by their peers as boring, lacking in excitement and less 'fun' than their freer more spontaneous classmates. Alternatively, social responsibility, dedication to study and on-task behaviors might make a student more popular among his or her classmates. This study used (i) a traditional sociometric measure based on Coie, Dodge, and Coppotelli's (1982) conceptualisation of sociometric status as dependent on the relatively independent dimensions of liking and disliking, and (ii) Humphrey's (1982) Children's Perceived Self-Control (CPSC) Scale, to discover whether self-regulatory behavior contributed to, or detracted from, same-sex and opposite-sex popularity of adolescents in the classroom.

METHOD

The unit of study was the intact adolescent class. Fourteen schools were chosen at random from secondary schools in Jamaica. Principals and teachers from these schools agreed to the administration of the research instruments to 18 intact classes of adolescent students. The number of students in each class ranged from 35 to 49 with a median of 40. In all, 320 male and 397 female black grade 9 students participated in the study. The inter-quartile range of their ages was 14-15 years ages with a media age of 14 years 7 months.

INSTRUMENTS

Students were given code numbers and guaranteed that their individual responses would be held in confidence. They then completed the 11 questions of the CPSC scale shown in Figure 1. These questions contribute to three sub-scales of self-control: Interpersonal Self-Control (ISC) questions 1-4, Personal Self-Control (PSC) questions 5-7, and Self-Evaluation (SE) questions 8-9, with reported test-retest reliabilities of 0.63, 0.63, 0.56 respectively and 0.71 for the whole instrument (Humphrey, 1982).

Figure 1: The 11 questions comprising the Children's Perceived Self-Control (CPSC) Scale

1. If someone bothers me when I'm busy I ignore him/her.
2. When the teacher is busy I talk to my friends.
3. When someone pushes me I fight them.
4. I think about other things while I work.

5. It's hard to keep working when my friends are having fun.
6. It's hard to wait for something I want.
7. I make mistakes because I work too fast.
8. I know when I'm doing something wrong without someone telling me.
9. If my work is too hard I switch to something else.
10. After I do something it's hard to tell what will happen next.
11. It's hard for me to finish my work if I don't like it.

The original CPSC instructions for dichotomous responses were modified to elicit more discriminating and involving responses. The original instructions were:

"Below are eleven statements. Please consider each in terms of whether it is usually true for you or not. Answer each according to the following scale.
1 = Usually yes
2 = Usually no
____ 1. If someone bothers me when I'm busy I ignore him/her." etc.

The modified instructions were:

"The following sentences are about you. For each sentence (i) If you Agree you are like it says then circle the A. If you Disagree it is like you then circle the D. (ii) Then write a number on the line, from 0 to 9, to show how strongly you agree or disagree.

0-1 means 'slightly agree/disagree'
2-3 means 'agree/disagree a little'
4-5 means 'mostly agree/disagree'
6-7 means 'strongly agree/disagree'
8-9 means 'very strongly agree/disagree'

A D ___ If someone bothers me when I'm busy I ignore him/her." etc.

In addition each subject completed the following modified form of the traditional sociometric classroom questionnaire (SCQ).

"In the columns below, print the names of the two students in this class who you like the best, and mark how much you like them from 0-9 (1 meaning 'like them just a little' - 9 meaning 'like them the maximum')

Print First name | Print Last Name | Like them 0-9

In the columns below, print the names of the two students in this class who you like the least, and mark how little you like them from 0-9 (0 meaning 'do not like them at all' - 9 meaning 'I dislike them the most')

Print First name | Print Last Name | Like them 0-9

Their nominations and ratings were used to calculate the three popularity scores.

ANALYSIS

Figure 2 is a schematic illustrating how the three popularity scores for each student were derived from the nominations and ratings they received on the SCQs from their peers.

Figure 2: Schematic illustration of how peer nominations and ratings were coded to produce three popularity variables.

	Student #	Nominations received by students											
		Males							Females				
		1	2	3	4	5	.	.	36	37	38	39	40
Nominations given by students — Males	1												
	2			8		-7				-4		9	
	3			**1** Male to Male					**2** Male to Female				
	4												
	5												
	.												
	.												
	.												
Nominations given by students — Females	36	-6		4		-5						8	
	37			**3** Female to Male					**4** Female to Female				
	38												
	39												
	40												
Popularity 1 Same sex 2 Opp sex 3 Total		Sum quadrant 1 Sum quadrant 3 Sum quadrants 1+3							Sum quadrant 4 Sum quadrant 2 Sum quadrant 2+4				

'Likes' were coded as + and 'dislikes' were coded as -. In Figure 2 for example, student number 2 nominated student number 3 with a rating of 8 for 'like' (coded 8), nominated student 5 with 7 for 'dislike' (coded -7), nominated student 37 with 4 for 'dislike' (coded -4) and nominated student 39 with 9 for 'like' (coded 9). The students' numbers were sorted vertically and horizontally with males followed by females so that quadrants 1 and 4 held same-sex nominations and quadrants 2 and 3 held opposite-sex nominations. The coded ratings in the relevant columns were summed to give the three popularity scores awarded to each student numbered horizontally. Similar calculation procedures, and interesting graphic representations, can be found in standard textbooks on measurement and assessment in teaching indexed under 'Sociogram' or 'Sociometry', (e.g. Linn & Gronlund, 1995, pp. 181-184; Mehrens & Lehmann, 1973, 196-200).

To counteract the possibility that some classes were more expressive than others in awarding higher nominations, the three popularity measures were standardized within each class as the unit of study. For each popularity measure, students in the top quartiles were labelled the 'most popular' and students in the bottom quartiles were labelled the 'least popular' students. 'Most' and 'least' popular students on each of the three popularity measures - total popularity, same-sex popularity and opposite-sex popularity - were compared on their mean scores for the 11 questions, the three sub-scales and the complete CPSC scale (see Table 1).

RESULTS

The positive coding of 'Agree' responses and the reverse coding of responses to Q1 and Q8 in Figure 1 shows that the larger scores on these CPSC questions indicate less perceived self-control. Table 1 shows the mean ratings for the least (n=161) and most popular (n=161) students on each of questions, on the three subscales and on the total scale. These least and most popular groups were derived from quartiles 1 and 4 of the total popularity nominations, both same-sex and opposite-sex combined.

Table 1 Mean ratings of lack of perceived self-control for most and least popular students

n=322			Total Popularity		
Questions			Least	Most	Sig
ISC	Q01		-1.670	-2.300	0.356
	Q02		1.340	0.025	0.053
	Q03		-2.520	-4.380	0.002 **
	Q04		1.520	-0.150	0.017 *
PSC	Q05		3.410	2.540	0.194
	Q06		2.580	2.260	0.633
	Q07		3.010	1.830	0.070
SE	Q08		-4.390	-5.170	0.169
	Q09		0.620	-0.120	0.297
-	Q10		1.630	1.300	0.615
-	Q11		2.840	1.600	0.065
Sub-scales					
	ISC		10.889	10.497	0.002 **
	PSC		11.568	12.541	0.080
	SE		7.821	7.648	0.084
Total					
		CPSC	25.967	25.806	0.000 **

It is noticed from Table 1 that, although the differences were only statistical significant for Q3 and Q4, it can be seen from Figure 3 that there was a consistent pattern of the least popular students having less perceived self-control on every question. These differences accumulated to give a significant difference on the ISC sub-scale and on the total CPSC scale.

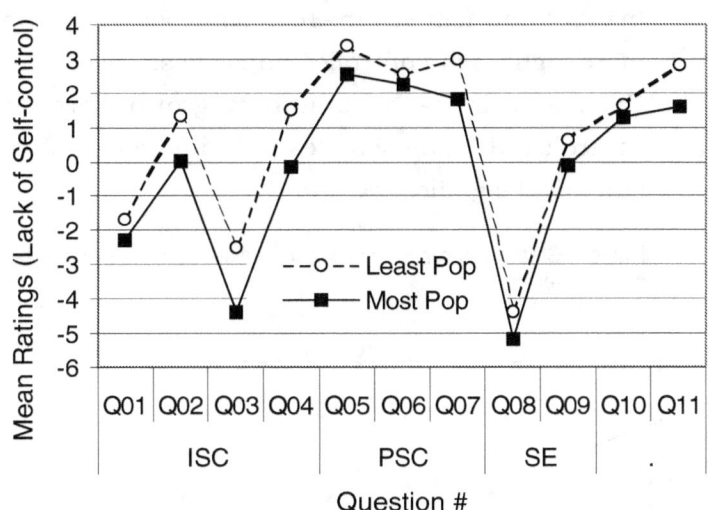

Figure 3 Mean ratings of most and least popular students on each question.

There was also a large difference in the means of perceived self-control for males and females with the mean for males at 8.34 (n=309) compared to the mean of females at 0.22 (n=380, p<0.0005). An ANOVA, however, showed no statistically significant interaction between sex and popularity (F=0.003, p=0.954).

There were no significant differences in mean self-control scores of popularity groups based on negative nominations (dislikes). However, there were significant differences in self-control associated with positive opposite-sex nominations. The mean self-control of the students nominated as most popular by the opposite sex (n=151) was significantly higher than the mean self-control of the students liked least by the opposite sex (n=164) (F=7.915, p=0.005). Interestingly, as illustrated in Figure 4, there was no significant popularity-sex interaction (F=0.004, p=0.951) indicating that males (n=153) and females (n=162) both positively nominated more highly self-controlled opposite sex peers. Although, the males in each popularity group were less self-controlled than the females, this difference did not reach statistical significance.

Figure 4: Greater self-control of males and females who were more popular with the opposite sex

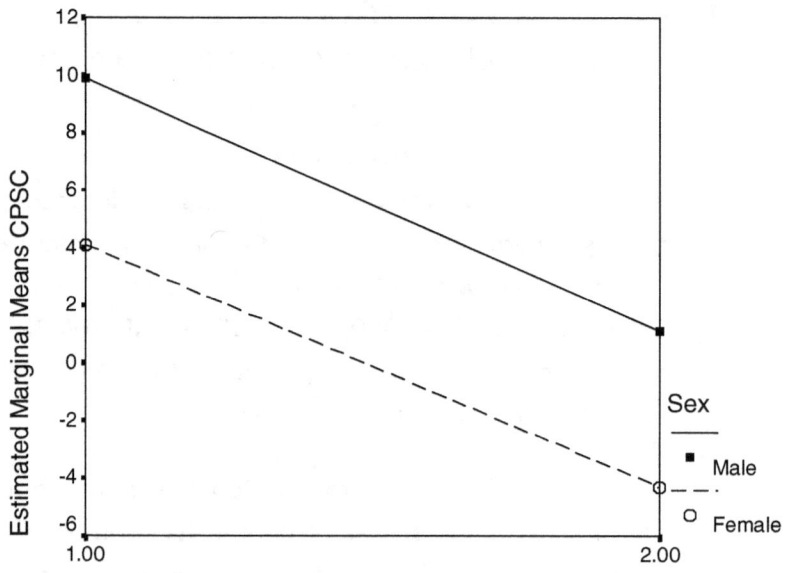

A similar analysis for same-sex popularity gave different results, illustrated in Figure 5.

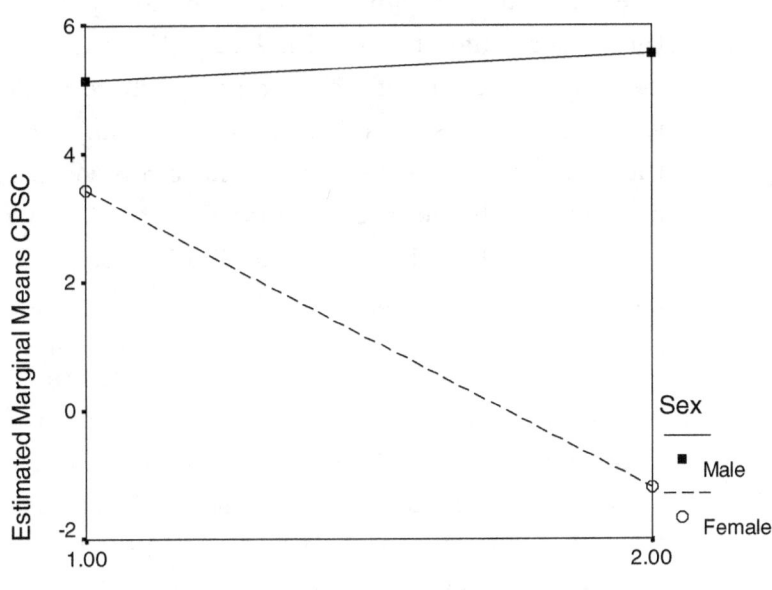

Figure 5: Girls with greater self-control nominated in same-sex popularity

Although these differences are not statistically significant, it is interesting to note that in this sample the girls preferred other girls who were more self-controlled, but this was not so for the boys. Self-control of 'most' and 'least' popular male groups nominated by other males was low and showed little difference.

DISCUSSION

The CPSC results from this study confirmed those of Laura Humphrey (1982) in showing that these Jamaican males had lower perceived self-control than females. It is encouraging to note that adolescents with higher self-control, particularly higher interpersonal self-control (ISC) were more popular with their peers than those with less self-control. This is particularly encouraging in Jamaica where adolescent violence is of considerable concern. A possible limitation that must be mentioned is that these pro-social results are typical of higher socio-economic status (SES) groups and this study did not control for the socio-economic background of the respondents.

The most significant markers of peer popularity in this study were restraint against personal aggression, question 3 and on-task behavior, question 4. This first finding was consistent with earlier studies (Coie, & Dodge 1988; Coie, Dodge, & Kupersmidt, 1990; Fabes & Eisenberg, 1992). As other studies cited have shown the power of peer pressure to alter adolescent behavior, perhaps then we can now look to this as a possible influence on the reduction of aggression and increase in on-task behavior among Jamaican adolescents. Most notable were the results showing that adolescents with greater perceived self-control were significantly more popular with the opposite sex, both for girls and for boys. It is known that adolescent students who receive many positive nominations on sociometric measures dated more frequently (Franzoi, Davis, & Vasquez-Suson, 1994). As the need to be attractive to the opposite sex is a major component of peer pressure and motivator in adolescence it is a considerable modifier of adolescent behavior. Hence, further replication and use of these results could be a powerful natural influence for increasing some pro-social adolescent behaviors.

REFERENCES

Bukowski, W. M. , Hoza, B., & Boivin, M. (1993). Differences and Consistency between Same-Sex and Other-Sex Peer Relationships during Early Adolescence. *Developmental Psychology, 29*(2), 255-63.

Coie, J. D., & Dodge, K. A. (1988). Multiple sources of data on social behavior and social status in the school: A cross-age comparison. *Child Development, 59*, 815-829.

Coie, J. D., Dodge, K. A. & Coppotelli, H. (1982). Dimensions and types of social status: A cross-age perspective. *Developmental Psychology 18*, 557-571.

Coie, J. D., Dodge, K. A., & Kupersmidt, J. B. (1990). Peer group behavior and social status. In S. R. Asher & J. D. Coie (Eds.), *Peer rejection in childhood.* New York: Cambridge University Press.

Fabes, R. A., & Eisenberg, N. (1992). Young children's coping with interpersonal anger. *Child Development, 63*, 116-128.

Franzoi, S. L., Davis, M. H., & Vasquez-Suson, K. A. (1994). Two social worlds: Social correlates and stability of adolescent status groups. *Journal of Personality and Social Psychology, 67*, 462-473.

Frentz, C. (1991). Popular, Controversial, Neglected, and Rejected Adolescents: Contrasts of Social Competence and Achievement Differences. *Journal of School Psychology, 29*(2), 109-20.

Giancola, S.P. (2000, April). *Adolescent Behavior Problems: Peer Pressure "Is" All It Is Cracked Up To Be*. Paper presented at the Annual Conference of the American Educational Research Association, New Orleans, LA.

Humphrey, L. L. (1982). Children's and teachers' perspectives on children's self-control: The development of two rating scales. *Journal of Consulting and Clinical Psychology, 50,* 624-633.

Linn, R. L., & Gronlund, N. E. (1995). *Measurement and Assessment in Teaching.* (7th Ed.). Upper Saddle River, NJ: Merrill.

Mehrens, W. A., & Lehmann, I. J. (1977). *Measurement and Evaluation in Education and Psychology.* (4th Ed.). Fort Worth, FL: Harcourt Brace.

Munsch, J., & Kinchen, K. M. (1995). Adolescent Sociometric Status and Social Support. *Journal of Early Adolescence, 15*(2), 181-202.

Santor, D. A., Messervey, D., & Kusumakar, V. (2000). Measuring Peer Pressure, Popularity, and Conformity in Adolescent Boys and Girls: Predicting School Performance, Sexual Attitudes, and Substance Abuse. *Journal of Youth and Adolescence, 29*(2), 163-82.

Wentzel, K R,. & Asher, S. R. (1995). The Academic Lives of Neglected, Rejected, Popular, and Controversial Children. *Child Development, 66*(3), 754-63.

Wentzel, K. (1991). Social competence at school: Relation between social responsibility and academic achievement. *Review of Educational Research, 61*(1), 1-24.

CHAPTER 13

READING COMPREHENSION, ATTITUDES TO READING AND LOCUS OF CONTROL BELIEFS OF JAMAICAN STUDENTS IN PRIMARY AND SECONDARY SCHOOLS

JOSSETT LEWIS-SMIKLE

INTRODUCTION

Developing children's concepts of responsibility concerning reading comprehension presents fundamental and significant challenges to the teacher of reading. Perhaps that is why so many students at both the primary and secondary levels underachieve in this area. Unless children are cognizant of their responsibilities in learning to read, they may not extend the necessary efforts that complement both the cognitive and emotional factors involved in the development of reading comprehension. The interrelationship of self-responsibility, attitudes to reading and reading comprehension typically are theoretically complex and important.

Social learning theory proposes the theoretical framework for the concept of self-responsibility. From the early 1960's research relating to the extent to which individuals accept responsibility for events that occur in their lives have been gaining much prominence in social psychology (for example, Crandall et al, 1965; Rotter, 1966; Chance, 1972; Findley and Harris, 1982; Rath, 1991; Slavin, 2000). This psychological construct, termed locus of control belief, is a personality trait that concerns whether people attribute responsibility for their failures or successes to internal or external factors (Slavin, 2000). Individuals who accept responsibility for their successes and failures are said to be internally oriented; conversely those who perceive that others (for example, teachers, peers, classroom environment) are responsible for their successes and failures, are said to be externally oriented. This theory has been elaborated to include causal dimensions - the perceived reason(s) why an incident occurred. Weiner's attribution theory identified four major causes that individuals generally select for success and failure events - ability, effort, task difficulty, and luck.

A child's motivation and attitude will give the power to focus on the reading material. Literacy development reports (for example, Wilson, et al, 2001) stress the necessity to be aware of pupils' reading attitudes especially as they relate to enjoyment and utiliitarian purposes. It is important for literacy professionals to note that pupils' attitudes toward reading are conceptualized as multidimensional (Lewis and Teale,

1980). These researchers proposed a three-dimensional model which distinguishes three different aspects of reading attitude - "Individual development", "Utilitarian" and "Enjoyment", and suggest that an individual may have different beliefs and feelings about reading. This model is supported by the theory that attitude is divided into three components - affect (or emotion), cognition (or belief) and behaviour (action tendencies).

Although research literature documents a number of studies carried out in relation to reading comprehension of Jamaican children there is a scarcity of material relating to attitudes to reading. Generally, it is recommended that investigations be conducted in this neglected area - the conjunction of cognitive and affective variables. There is also a scarcity of material relating these areas to locus of control beliefs relevant to these pupils. It is quite probable that inclusion of this variable in investigating pupils' reading comprehension could lead to a better understanding of the problem they experience. Eventually this could give an indication of how best to proceed with intervention programmes aimed at enhancing reading comprehension, improving attitudes to reading and developing a more internal locus of control belief in relation to reading comprehension.

Underachievement in reading comprehension in Jamaican schools is evident. This is documented historically, and more recently. Roughly one-third of the pupils leaving primary and entering secondary schools cannot read adequately (Craig, 1972). A study conducted by the examination section of the Ministry of Education, revealed that two-thirds of grade six pupils had scores considered to be below acceptable levels in English Language skills and similar problems are being detected in the secondary schools (UNESCO Report, 1983). More recent report also acknowledges the existence of this problem. The estimate from studies done in the Ministry of Education and Culture and the University of the West Indies is that thirty percent of primary school leavers have not learnt to read at a functional level equivalent to the grade 3 level (Wilson, et al, 1994). This is an ever present problem which also manifests itself when Jamaican pupils reach adolescence and leave school without attaining proficiency in Language Arts skills in which reading Comprehension is an essential component.

The Caribbean Examination Council (CXC) and the Secondary School Certificate (SSC) national assessment reports attest to the low performance in the Language Arts over the years. This low performance is attributed to varying problems including deficiency in reading comprehension.

The need to improve pupils' reading standards is recognized as central to education. Reading comprehension is highlighted in this research, as reading to derive meaning is a central concern in schools. The focus is on the stages where readers start to extend beginning reading, and also where they read to gain new understanding. According to Pumfrey's (1991) adaptation of Chall's model these stages fall within the 7-13 age range (see Figure 1). Children ages 9, 11 and 13 were used in this research.

Figure 1: Reading Development Model

AGE	STAGE
0-5 years	**(1) PRE-READING** The child develops spoken language and becomes aware of the use of symbols to represent objects and events. Metacognitions concerning nature of literacy are developed. The child recognises that speech can be represented by letters, words, phrases, sentences, etc. Awareness of the concepts and labels used in connection with text is expanded.
5-7 years	**(2) LEARNING TO READ** Learns to associate letters and sounds. Uses these skills to construct the meaning of textual material. Over learning of skills ensues.
7-9 years	**(3) EXTENDING BEGINNING READING** Reading simple books and other textual materials centered on familiar themes continues. Earlier skills become overlearned and thus automated. Speed of reading increases and range of materials encountered extends.
9-13 years	**(4) READING TO GAIN NEW UNDERSTANDINGS** Access to new fields of knowledge is extended through reading.
13-18 years	**(5) APPRECIATION OF EVIDENCE AND ARGUMENTS** Can read and appraise the strengths and weaknesses of contrasting view-points on a range of issues.
18+ years	**(6) CONSTRUCTION AND RECONSTRUCTION OF UNDERSTANDINGS** Judgments concerning a widening range of literary genres and authors are made. The reader's knowledge, beliefs and values are challenged, revised and extended.

A study of groups of pupils in Kingston and St. Andrew, Jamaica is employed in this research. The aims are to examine the patterns of relationship between reading comprehension and attitudes and motivation to reading in relationship to age related variables and gender. The study seeks to describe pupils' performance on various instruments. Specifically, it will identify relationships between demographic variables and factors amenable to change that can help to improve pupils' reading comprehension and develop positive attitudes and a high motivation to reading. It will also illuminate important similarities and differences between the genders and levels of schooling that will enable implications for development in pedagogy to be considered.

MEASURES USED

Reading Comprehension
- Suffolk Reading Scale
- Irwin Reading Comprehension

Reading Attitude
- Teale and Lewis Reading Attitude Scale "Individual Development"; "Utilitarian"; "Enjoyment".

Locus of Control Beliefs (Self-responsibility)
- Intellectual Achievement Responsibility (IAR) Scale.
- Total Internal Scale (I-total);
- Internality for Success (I+); (Accepting responsibility for successful events, for example high performance in reading comprehension).
- Internality for Failure (I-); (Accepting responsibility for one's failure, for example, low performance in reading comprehension).
- Attributions to Effort (Ie); Attributions that are Undifferentiated (caused by Factors other than effort, for example, ability,
- Interest (Iu).

SAMPLE

A sample of 1,236 pupils from 10 primary and 13 secondary schools, ages 9, 11 and 13 years old, were randomly selected and tested on all the measures used in the survey. Table 1 gives a breakdown of the sample by gender, school-type and year group.

Table 1: Sample of Pupils by Gender, School-Type and Age-Group

AGE (YRS)	SCHOOL-TYPE	MALE	FEMALE	TOTAL
9	Primary	197	209	406
11	Primary	181	212	393
13	Secondary	204	233	437
Total		582	654	1,236

Different types of secondary schools are represented proportionately.

FINDINGS AND DISCUSSION

READING COMPREHENSION

Data are presented on the mean scores, as obtained on the Suffolk Reading Scale and the Irwin Reading Comprehension, for age-group, gender and school-type. These tests measure similar constructs.

Table 2: Mean and Standard Deviation for Reading Comprehension – Age-Group

	READING COMPREHENSION							
	Suffolk Reading Scale				Irwin Reading Comp.			
	Raw Score		Standardized Score		Raw Score		Grade Level	
AGE-GROUP (YEARS)	X	SD	X	SD	X	SD	X	SD
9 (N=407)	34.8	9.8	86.7	10.0	14.3	6.8	3.8	1.8
11 (N=392)	39.5	9.3	86.4	10.1	30.5	9.2	7.1	1.8
13 (N=437)	40.1	14,0	82.4	12.4	30.6	12.4	6.9	2.4

Reading comprehension increases with age on the raw score measures (Table 2). Analysis of variance shows that on both measures the mean difference is significant from 9 to 11 years ($p<0.01$) but not from 11 to 13 years. The procedure for break-down analysis t-test follows that suggested by Lewis (1971). The pattern is different on the Suffolk standardized measure and the Irwin grade level. On the Suffolk standardize measure the younger pupils score higher with a significant difference between ages 11 and 13 ($p<0.01$) but not between ages 9 and 11. In terms of mean grade level, 9 year-olds are reading at grade 4 (normal level); 11 year-olds - grade 7 (1 grade level above the norm), and 13 year-olds - grade 7 (1 grade level below the norm). It is thus indicated that reading comprehension for these pupils increases up to age 11, but not between age 11 and 13 years. Overall the main point is that after age 11 reading comprehension remains stable. Given these findings it is not surprising that the 13 year-olds have larger standard deviations than the younger pupils. This could be as a result of the varying abilities of the different categories of secondary school pupils and the effects of different curricular. This remains a hypothesis, as there could be other explanations.

Generally, reading comprehension increases with age (Saracho, 1983), but this condition may be altered depending on the level of motivation, and the structure of the curriculum in the different school contexts. In the Jamaican education system the primary ages of schooling is focussed on the examinations to gain entry to secondary school (Grade Six Achievement Test - G.S.A.T.) which culminates at age 11 when pupils sit this examination.

The G.S.A.T. effect could serve to stimulate pupils' performance up to age 11. It is not surprising that there is a decline after this age (the end of primary school). In the secondary schools pupils do not do reading as a "classroom subject". Content area teachers, regrettably,

do not generally see themselves responsible for enhancing pupils' reading comprehension. From a long involvement in the system it is the author's knowledge that the tendency is to avoid the challenge. It is possible that other causal mechanisms are involved. At the secondary stage pupils need to be given more time to learn through the process of self-discovery, but will also need some direct instruction (Fielding, 1990).

In terms of gender groups females generally gain higher reading comprehension scores than males (Table 3). Findings will vary depending on cultural background. In the Jamaican context, females tend to outperform males (Wilson et al, 2001).

Table 3: Mean and Standard Deviation for Reading Comprehension - Gender

	READING COMPREHENSION							
	Suffolk Reading Scale				Irwin Reading Comprehension			
	Raw Score		Standardize Score		Raw Score		Grade Level	
GENDER	X	SD	X	SD	X	SD	X	SD
Males (N=582)	36.7	12.4	84.6	11.6	23.2	12.2	5.6	2.5
Females (N=654)	39.0	10.5	85.5	10.6	27.0	12.4	6.3	2.5

The type of school pupils attend have both psychological and educational effects on self-image and reading comprehension, respectively. The performance of pupils who attend the newly upgraded secondary schools can account, in part, for the low overall performance of secondary pupils (Table 4).

Table 4: Mean and Standard Deviation for Reading Comprehension Showing Interaction Between Gender and School-Type Specifying Different Categories of Secondary Schools

		READING COMPREHENSION							
		Suffolk Reading Scale				Irwin Reading Comprehension			
		Raw Score		Standardize Score		Raw Score		Grade Level	
GENDER	SCHOOL-TYPE	X	SD	X	SD	X	SD	X	SD
Male	Primary (N=378)	36.2	10.2	86.5	10.4	20.9	10.8	5.2	2.4
	Secondary High (N=83)	49.6	9.7	90.9	12.4	37.3	7.6	8.1	1.0
	Technical High (N=19)	48.5	7.4	88.4	10.0	37.1	5.1	8.1	0.5
	Comprehensive (N=7)	41.7	6.4	81.0	7.2	34.3	7.8	7.9	1.1
	Upgraded Secondary (N=95)	24.3	10.6	71.3	2.8	16.4	1.0	4.2	2.5
	Primary (N=421)	37.0	9.2	86.6	9.7	23.5	11.8	5.6	2.5
	Secondary High (N=117)	49.4	7.0	90.5	10.2	39.4	5.2	8.4	0.8
	Technical High (N=16)	51.6	6.2	91.8	9.2	40.8	3.6	8.9	0.5
	Conprehensive (N=11)	48.0	4.9	87.4	6.6	40.3	3.0	8.5	0.5
	Upgraded Secondary (N=89)	31.1	8.7	72.4	4.2	23.3	9.8	5.7	2.2

The mean grade level at which the different categories of pupils function illuminates the low performance of the pupils attending these schools. In the male category, primary pupils function at a grade 5 level (the norm), newly upgraded secondary school pupils at grade 4 (4 grade levels below the norm); while the other categories of secondary schools function at grade 8 (the norm). In the female category, primary pupils function at grade 6 (1grade level above the norm), newly upgrade secondary at grade 6 (2 grade levels below the norm); while the other types of secondary pupils function at the normal level (grade 8) or above (grade 9) (Table 4). The newly upgraded secondary school effect is therefore an important contributing factor to the low performance of secondary school pupils, especially the males.

READING ATTITUDES

In this study pupils' attitudes toward reading are analyzed in relationship to scores from the Teale and Lewis Reading Attitude Scale which highlights three distinct dimensions - "Individual Development", "Utilitarian" and "Enjoyment". All age groups show similar level of attitude to reading for individual development (Table 5).

Table 5 Mean and Standard Deviation for Reading Attitude - Age-Group

	READING ATTITUDE					
	INDIVIDUAL DEVELOPMENT		UTILITARIAN		ENJOYMENT	
AGE-GROUP (YRS.)	X	SD	X	SD	X	SD
9 (N=407)	35.0	5.0	36.3	5.2	36.0	5.1
11 (N=392)	35.9	4.7	37.5	4.5	36.6	4.5
13 (N=437)	35.5	4.6	38.1	4.4	35.1	5.6

There is no significant difference between any of the groups. When pupils attending primary school are taken together, there is also no significant difference between the mean scores of pupils attending primary and secondary schools on this dimension. Males and females also show similar level of attitudes toward reading on this dimension (Table 6).

Table 6: Mean and Standard Deviation for Reading Attitude – Gender

	READING ATTITUDE					
	INDIVIDUAL DEVELOPMENT		UTILITARIAN		ENJOYMENT	
AGE-GROUP (YRS.)	X	SD	X	SD	X	SD
9 (N=407)	35.0	5.0	36.3	5.2	36.0	5.1
11 (N=392)	35.9	4.7	37.5	4.5	36.6	4.5
13 (N=437)	35.5	4.6	38.1	4.4	35.1	5.6

The difference between the groups does not reach significance. Analyses were done using

break-down analysis t-tests. Attitudes to reading for individual development is related to the belief that reading is a way of developing one's knowledge about self, others and general aspects of life. It is deemed that reading for individual development is an accepted motive for reading thus the commonality among the groups.

In the Jamaican context much focus would be on the "Utilitarian" dimension which relates to belief about reading for school or vocational success. Attitude to reading for utilitarian purposes increases slightly across age groups and between primary and secondary schools (Table 5 and 7). This result is not surprising as children are generally told by teachers and other adult caregivers to learn to read in order to be able to get a good job.

Universally, societal values, the world of work and progression to institutions of higher learning dictate the necessity of reading for utilitarian purposes.

Table 7: Mean and Standard Deviation for Reading Attitude - School-Type

	READING ATTITUDE					
	INDIVIDUAL DEVELOPMENT		UTILITARIAN		ENJOYMENT	
SCHOOL -TYPES	X	SD	X	SD	X	SD
Primary (N=799)	35.4	4.9	36.9	4.9	36.2	4.8
Secondary (N=437)	35.5	4.6	38.1	4.4	35.1	5.6

Male and female pupils show similar levels of reading for utilitarian purposes (Table 6). Reading for the purpose of obtaining a good job is also a generally acceptable motive for both genders.

Attitudes to reading for enjoyment decrease from age 11 to 13 years and over primary and secondary schools (Tables 5 and 7). Although the difference does not reach significance, it is of educational importance that as pupils move through the educational system, the drive for reading for pleasure appears to diminish. How pupils think and feel about reading for enjoyment might be influenced by the school curriculum. The primary school curriculum engages pupils in direct reading activities. Pupils can, therefore, read for enjoyment and relaxation in these engaged time for reading. Generally, at the secondary level, direct teaching in reading is not done and pupils read mainly to learn in the different content areas. The emphasis is on gaining knowledge for qualifications of some sort; hence, there is not much time to read for enjoyment.

Females portray significantly more positive attitudes toward reading for enjoyment, than do males. This finding concurs with those of other surveys (Lewis, 1990). Generally, females appear to be keener on reading - they choose reading as 'out-of-school activity more than do males.

MOTIVATION

LOCUS OF CONTROL (SELF-RESPONSIBILITY)

Examination of the locus of control variable as measured by the Intellectual Achievement Responsibility (IAR) Scale may increase one's understanding of the motivation of pupils of, for example, different school types, gender and age group. Assertions are made generally, which might not be typical of all classification of pupils.

General tendencies can be noted in Table 8 for all internality scales to increase between 9 and 11 years but decline between ages 11 and 13 years. When analysis is done by school type the mean scores of pupils attending primary and secondary schools are similar (Table 9). Previous research found that older students take less responsibility for their learning (Igoe and Sullivan, 1991). Factors that work to increase pupils' internality from ages 9 to 11 years had ceased to operate between ages 11 and 13 years. Numerous research studies have shown that having an internal locus of control is related to high academic achievement (Slavin, 2000). If higher reading comprehension is to be encouraged, pupils must be helped to accept responsibility for their own progress.

Key to Variables:

I-total   Total Internal Scale
I+   Internality for Success
I-   Internality for Failure
Ie   Attributions to Effort
Iu   Attributions caused by factors bother than effort

Table 8: Means and Standard Deviation for Locus of Control - Age -Group

AGE -GROUP (YRS.)	Locus of Control									
	Itotal		I+		I-		Ie		Iu	
	X	SD	X	SD	X	SD	X	SD	X	SD
9 (407)	24.6	3.7	13.3	2.1	11.3	2.6	11.6	2.2	12.9	2.2
11 (392)	26.5	4.2	14.0	1.9	12.4	2.1	12.5	2.0	14.0	3.1
13 (437)	25.6	3.3	13.7	1.9	11.9	2.3	12.0	2.1	13.6	2.1

Table 9: Mean and Standard Deviation for Locus of Control - School-Type

SCHOOL-TYPES	Locus of Control									
	Itotal		I+		I-		Ie		Iu	
	X	SD	X	SD	X	SD	X	SD	X	SD
Primary (N=799)	25.5	4.1	13.7	2.0	11.8	2.4	12.1	2.1	13.5	2.8
Secondary (N=437)	25.6	3.3	13.7	1.9	11.9	2.3	12.0	2.1	13.6	2.1

Possible reasons for the lack of increased internality of pupils between ages 11 and 13 years could be attributed to the level of parental encouragement, and the quality of interaction with teachers. Although parents generally encourage their children towards academic achievement more emphasis seems to be given up to age 11. There is a desire for children to do well to gain the benefit of subsequent schooling at "good" Secondary High Schools. Reports have shown that the more parents encourage their children's achievement behaviour, the more likely it will be for children to accept self-responsibility for their successes and failures (Katkovsky et al ,1992).

Table 10: Mean and Standard Deviation for Locus of Control - Gender

	Itotal		I+		I-		Ie		Iu	
GENDER	X	SD	X	SD	X	SD	X	SD	X	SD
Males (N=582)	25.4	3.5	13.5	2.0	11.9	2.4	12.0	2.1	13.5	3.0
Females (N=654)	25.7	4.1	13.8	1.9	11.8	2.4	12.0	2.1	13.6	2.1

CORRELATION BETWEEN READING COMPREHENSION AND READING ATTITUDE

Reading comprehension, generally, increases significantly with the three dimensions of reading attitudes. For all categories of pupils - age 9, 11, 13 year-olds, pupils attending primary and secondary schools, and males and females, the strongest relationship is found on the "Utilitarian" dimension (Table 11). The data suggest that school and society continue to emphasize the extrinsic (utilitarian) worth of education, while intrinsic (individual development and enjoyment) aspects are less emphasized. "Read it carefully. You will need to understand it for your examination" is increasingly said by teachers as pupils move upward in the educational system.

Table11: Correlations Between Reading Comprehension and Reading Attitude for all Subjects.

N=1,236	READING COMPREHENSION	
READING ATTITUDE	SUFFOLK (Raw Score)	IRWIN (Raw Score)
INDIVIDUAL DEVELOPMENT	.22**	.19**
UTILITARIAN	.47**	.42**
ENJOYMENT	.20**	.14**

With N= 1,236 for sig. at p=.01 level, r=0.081. (**significant at .01 level)

CORRELATION BETWEEN READING COMPREHENSION AND LOCUS OF CONTROL BELIEFS

Reading comprehension, generally, increases with internality. When Internality for Success (I+) and Internality for Failure (I-) were compared for all groups the stronger correlation with reading comprehension are on the Internality for Success scale (Table 12). Although both acceptance of responsibility for success and the acceptance of responsibility for failure facilitate reading comprehension, the emphasis is on the former. This finding seems to be an effect of teachers, and parents' perceptions of how to motivate children. There is willingness by children to accept responsibility for success but less ready to do so for failures in reading comprehension. (This is true of adults also). The balance between internal and external locus of control beliefs for both successes and failures in reading comprehension is dynamic and delicate. The teacher also accepting responsibility for pupils' progress in reading comprehension parallels accepting responsibility for both successes and failure by the pupil. In terms of attributions to effort (Ie) and attributions that are undifferentiated (Iu), the stronger relationship is with Iu, indicating that more attention is given to attributions to factors other than effort.

Table 12: Correlations Between Reading Comprehension and Locus of Control for all Subjects

N = 1,236	READING COMPREHENSION	
LOCUS OF CONTROL	SUFFOLK (Raw Score)	IRWIN (Raw Score)
Itotal	.24**	.30**
I+	.29**	.32**
I-	.16**	.21**
Ie	.14**	.17**
Iu	.26**	.32**

With N= 1,236 for sig. at p=.01 level, r=0.081. (**significant at .01 level)

CORRELATION BETWEEN READING COMPREHENSION AND LOCUS OF CONTROL BELIEFS

Reading comprehension, generally, increases with internality. When Internality for Success (I+) and Internality for Failure (I-) were compared for all groups the stronger correlation with reading comprehension are on the Internality for Success scale (Table 12). Although both acceptance of responsibility for success and the acceptance of responsibility for failure facilitate reading comprehension, the emphasis is on the former. This finding seems to be an effect of teachers, and parents' perceptions of how to motivate children. There is willingness by children to accept responsibility for success but less ready to do so for failures in reading comprehension. (This is true of adults also). The balance between internal and external locus of control beliefs for both successes and failures in reading comprehension is dynamic and delicate. The teacher also accepting responsibility for pupils' progress in reading comprehension parallels accepting responsibility for both successes and failure by the pupil. In terms of attributions to effort (Ie) and attributions that are undifferentiated (Iu), the stronger relationship is with Iu, indicating that more attention is given to attributions to factors other than effort.

Table 12: Correlations Between Reading Comprehension and Locus of Control for all Subjects

N = 1,236	READING COMPREHENSION	
LOCUS OF CONTROL	SUFFOLK (Raw Score)	IRWIN (Raw Score)
Itotal	.24**	.30**
I+	.29**	.32**
I-	.16**	.21**
Ie	.14**	.17**
Iu	.26**	.32**

With N= 1,236 for sig. at p=.01 level, r=0.081. (**significant at .01 level)

IMPLICATIONS FOR THEORY

Two major affective and motivational variables are examined in relationship to reading comprehension. In general we have:

Figure 2: Inter-relationship between Reading Comprehension, Reading Attitude and Locus of Control Beliefs

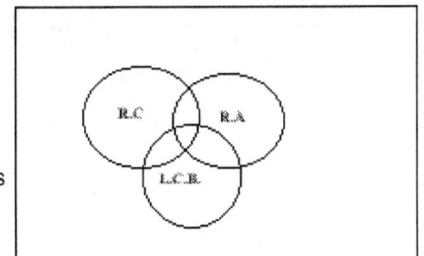

R.C.   Reading Comprehension
R.A.   Reading Attitude
L.C.B.   Locus of Control Beliefs.

The methodology adopted was intended to plot changes in the relationship between these variables in respect of gender, age group and school-type. It could not establish causality. Similarities and differences in patterns across gender, age group and school-type, point to complex processes that will affect interrelationships of all three variables. Put simply, high attainments in reading comprehension, positive attitudes to reading and internal locus of control beliefs are mutually supportive. This is a confirmation of the importance of simultaneously considering all three aspects.

IMPLICATIONS FOR CLASSROOM PRACTICES

It is necessary for the reading curriculum to take the affective and motivational areas into consideration when developing reading programmes. Different aspects of attitudes and locus of control beliefs are correlated with reading comprehension- high reading comprehension is associated with positive reading attitudes, and internality.

The direction of causality is unlikely to be unidirectional. If we take reading comprehension, attitudes to reading and locus of control beliefs, it is possible to identify how teachers, parents and pupils themselves can improve each of these. If, however, as has been shown in this research, all three variables are positively correlated, then the case for adopting educational methods that integrate these variables and also parents, teachers and pupils, would appear to be justified. Thus strategies involving the interrelationships of these areas to improve reading comprehension at age 9, 11 and 13 years, by teachers parents, and/or pupils, or any combination of persons are presented as suggested by previous research.

On theoretical grounds, teaching methods and material that capitalize on enhancing motivated time on task with a significant other using self-selected material in which success is highly likely, is to be encouraged. We must identify approaches that integrate success in reading and understanding text (thus ensuring high attainments, positive attitudes and internal locus of control beliefs):

self-selection of material - positive attitudes and internal locus of Control beliefs.

self-pacing - high attainments, positive attitudes, and locus of control beliefs. With control in his/her own hands, the pupil is likely to "own" responsibility for progress.

Significant other - positive attitude

- Teachers along with pupils can select reading materials, and reading comprehension activities that are of interest to pupils. It was found that pupils demonstrated more willingness to read and comprehend more readily where the material was more interesting to them (Wilson et al, 2001). Pupils will display more positive attitudes where reading materials are of interest to them. It is also likely that they will become intrinsically motivated.

- Paired reading has been gaining prominence, as a way of improving pupils' reading comprehension. Different variations involve teachers, parents, and pupils. (Although most times direct interaction involve parents and pupils, teachers direct these activities via workshops and seminars).

In the above situations, cognitive, affective and motivational factors are utilized. Children will most likely get the feeling that significant others are interested in their reading performance. This intrinsic reinforcement has been found to promote positive attitudes and internality.

Other forms of paired reading include **peer-tutoring** and **cross-aged tutoring** (pupils tutoring other pupils). This methodology creates more within school time for reading. In addition, it is likely that this one-to-one setting facilitates a higher level of intrinsic motivation than the normal classroom teacher/class setting for both tutors and tutee - tutees may be motivated to aspire to the level of their peers (tutor).

Implications for development in pedagogy can be considered.

•   Pupils need to be helped to become more aware of the intrinsic value of reading for meaning (individual development and enjoyment) as they progress through the educational system. At present the focus of reading comprehension is largely based on extrinsic value (utilitarian).

•   Special attention given to pupils' education by both the home and the school can yield positive effect on reading comprehension, reading attitude and locus of control orientation. The 11 year-olds (pupils being prepared for examination to gain entry to secondary schools) perform at comparable level to, or higher than their older counterparts in reading comprehension attainments. They also show the most positive attitudes toward reading for individual development and enjoyment, and all areas of self-responsibility.

• Homes and schools need to implement programmes to boost, for example, male pupils' beliefs in the value of reading for enjoyment.

• More pupil participation in classroom reading comprehension activities is required.

• There is the need to examine the structure of secondary education with a view to increasing pupils' self-responsibility for academic progress, and raising their level of reading comprehension attainments - particularly in the newly upgraded secondary schools (formerly New Secondary). It is important that the low achieving pupils are not segregated from their peers, in terms of the type of school that they attend. In a parallel study carried out with a British sample, where a comprehensive secondary school system exists, reading comprehension, positive reading attitude and self-responsibility increase as the individual matures.

REFERENCES

Chance, J. (1972) 'Academic correlates and maternal antecedents of children's belief in external or internal *control* of reinforcement. In: J. Rotter, J. Chance and E. Phares (Eds.) *Application of a Social Learning Theory of Personality,* pp.163- 179. New York: Holt, Rinehart & Winston.

Craig, D. (1972) *'Report of the Esso Grant Project'*. Institute of Education, University of the West Indies, Mona.

Crandall,V., Katkovsky, W. & Crandall B. (1965) 'Children's belief in their own control of reinforcements in intellectual-academic achievement situations'. *Child Development,* 31, pp.91-109.

Fielding, E. (1990) 'Reading in the Content Areas: the importance of choosing appropriate level texts'. *Reading,* 24, 3, pp.179-184.

Findley, M. & Harris, C. (1983) 'Locus of Control and Academic Achievement: a literature review'. *Journal of Personality and Social Psychology,* 44, 2,pp. 419-427.

Igoe, A.& Sullivan, H. (1991) 'Gender and grade-level differences in student attributes related to school learning and motivation'. (Eric Document Reproduction Service) ED 333044.

APPENDIX
THE MEASUREMENT INSTRUMENTS

Lewis, D.G. (1971) *The Analysis of Variance*. Manchester: Manchester University Press.

Lewis, J.I. (1990) 'Attitudes to and Attainments in reading of pupils at multicultural innercity primary schools in Manchester'. Unpublished M.Ed. Dissertation. University of Manchester, Center for Educational Guidance and Special Needs.

Lewis, R. & Teale, W. (1980) 'Another look at secondary school students' attitudes Toward reading'. *Journal of Reading Behaviour*, 12, 3, pp. 187-201.

Pumfrey, P.D. (1991) *Improving Children's Reading in the Junior School: Challenges And Responses*. London: Cassell Educational Ltd.

Rath, K. (1991) 'The social integration of pupils with SEN in junior mainstream School'. Unpublished M.Ed. Dissertation. University of Manchester, Faculty of Education.

Rotter, J. (1966) 'Generalized expectancies for internal versus external control of Reinforcement'. *Psychological Monographs*, 80, (1, No. 609).

Saracho, O. (1983) 'Cognitive style and Mexican American children's perceptions of Reading'. In: T. Escobedo (Ed,) *Early Childhood Bilingual Education: a Hispanic perspective*. London: Teachers College Press.

Slavin, R.E. (2000) *Educational Psychology: theory into practice*. Boston: Allyn and Bacon.

U.N.E.S.C.O, Report (1983) *'Development of Secondary Education'*. Ministry of Education, Jamaica .

Wilson, D.G., Coy, P. & Mitchell, I. (1994) 'Concept Paper for Revision of LMW Language Arts Series'. University of the West Indies, Mona.

Wilson, D. G., Smikle, J.I., Grant, N. (2001) 'Using Children's Literature to Improve Literacy Skills in Early Primary Grades: A Study of the Literature-Based Language Arts Project - 1998-2000. University of the West Indies, School of Education, Mona.

READING COMPREHENSION

(A) SUFFOLK READING SCALE

The Suffolk Reading Scale was designed to measure reading comprehension at three different levels. The levels are so structured that progress can be monitored across levels. The item format is multiple choice sentence completion., for example, "The fuel most cars use is_____(petrol, kerosene oil, electricity, coal)".

(B) IRWIN READING COMPREHENSION

The Irwin Reading Comprehension Test was designed to analyse objectively, pupils' reading comprehension.

The test is divided in ten sections, each of which requires pupils to demonstrate different reading comprehension skills. The format is mainly multiple choice (both sentences and passages).

READING ATTITUDE

TEALE AND LEWIS READING ATTITUDE SCALE

The Teale and Lewis Reading Attitude Scale was developed out of the need for an instrument to measure different dimensions of reading attitude instead of overall reading attitude. Research has shown that instruments that seek to measure overall reading attitude may not reveal important information that could facilitate curriculum development and classroom practices.

This scale consists of thirty-three items – three 11-item, which was designed to measure different dimensions of reading attitude – Individual Development, Utilitarian and Enjoyment. Individual Development is illustrated by statements such as, "People who read are usually interesting people." Utilitarian is exemplified by statements like:

> "A person who cannot read well will have trouble doing the everyday things involved in life", and is related to pupils' beliefs about reading for school or vocational success.. The Enjoyment dimension taps the affective domain and is demonstrated by statements like: "Reading just does not appeal to me".

THE INTELLECTUAL ACHIEVEMENT RESPONSIBILITY (IAR) SCALE.

The Intellectual Achievement Responsibility(IAR) Scale.was designed specifically for school-aged pupils. It was devised to produce scores for Internality for Success (I+) and Internality for Failure (I-). It also assesses Attribution to Effort (Ie) and Attributions that are Undifferentiated (Iu) (caused by factors other than effort).

The items in the scale are characteristic of academic achievement situations likely to take place in pupil's everyday experiences. These items are constructed to sample an equal number of positive and negative events and each poses one internal and one external response as the reason for a particular event to take place. For example:

POSITIVE ITEM:

"When you do well on a test at school, is it more likely to be

(a) because you studied for it,

or

(b) because the test was especially easy?"

NEGATIVE ITEM :

""When you have trouble understanding something in school, is it usually

(a) because the teacher didn't explain it clearly,

or

because you didn't listen carefully.

CHAPTER 14

AN ANALYSIS OF JAMAICAN TECHNICAL HIGH SCHOOL STUDENTS' ATTITUDES TO TECHNICAL AND VOCATIONAL EDUCATION

ANITA THOMAS-JAMES
& KOLA SOYIBO

ABSTRACT

This study determined whether or not (a) the attitudes of selected Jamaican technical high school students towards technical and vocational education (TVE) were positive, and (b) if there were significant differences in their attitudes linked to their gender, grade level and school location. The sample, which was randomly selected from six Jamaican technical high schools, consisted of 310 students (150 boys, 160 girls, 146 tenth graders, 164 eleventh graders, 160 students and 150 students from rural and urban schools respectively). A questionnaire on students' attitudes to TVE that the authors developed was used for data collection. Results indicated that most of the students had highly positive attitudes towards TVE; while there were no significant differences in their attitudes towards TVE based on their gender, grade level and school location; and, there was no relationship between each of the students' three independent variables and their attitudes to TVE.

INTRODUCTION

Technology could be defined as " a body of knowledge and the systematic application of resources to produce outcomes in response to human needs and wants" (Savage & Sterry, 1990: 20). A Committee on Technology Education (1993), that the Minister of Education for Trinidad and Tobago appointed, adopted as the definition of technology "the systematic application of knowledge and resources to satisfy needs and wants and extend human capabilities" (p. 2). Technology education can therefore be defined as a programme of education that is capable of enabling a person to acquire the knowledge and skills to design, construct, test and evaluate devices and products that can satisfy human needs, and assist in solving human problems through practical research. The Trinidad and Tobago Committee on Technology Studies (1993: 2) defined technology education as "a comprehensive action-based programme concerned with the nature of technology, its impact on individuals, society and the environment, and which develops proficiencies in technological design, problem-solving, research and evaluation".

Unesco (1980) defined technical and vocational education (TVE) as the connecting links between the school system and the employment market, which means that the developments in TVE are intimately linked to the general trends in the economy and the labour market and are particularly susceptible to the effects of technological change, the speed of which will probably be affected by its social acceptance. But historically, in many nations including the Anglophone-Caribbean nations and other third world countries patterned on the colonial educational systems, TVE has for long been accorded a low status in contrast to academic education (Watson, 1994). Wallace (1985) reported that TVE in England, (a) had no place in the selected grammar schools, (b) had a lowly place in the secondary modern schools, and (c) had been struggling for space in the comprehensive schools and that technical colleges were established after 1945 for those students who had failed to gain entrance to the grammar schools.

This system of selection was adapted in some Anglophone-Caribbean nations. For example, Morris (1994) observed that some Jamaican students were allowed to enter technical schools after their failure in the common entrance examination (CEE) which was abolished in 1997. Prior to the abolition of the CCE, Jamaican students were admitted into the technical high schools from the all-age schools after passing the technical entrance examination. With the introduction of the Grade Six Achievement Test (GSAT) in 1998, some of Jamaican students who pass the GSAT or the Junior High School Examination/ Grade 9 Achievement Test are admitted into technical high schools where they spend 5 years before they graduate. Some of those who pass the Junior

High School/Grade 9 Achievement Test are admitted into technical high schools where they spend 3 years before graduation. The technical entrance examination was abolished in the year 2001. All-age schools are post-primary schools to which students who failed the CEE or do not obtain satisfactory marks in the GSAT are sent instead of the traditional high schools. Similar trends are manifest in other English-speaking Caribbean nations. Be as it may, many individuals (including parents and students) in many Caribbean nations and elsewhere, regard TVE as inferior to academic education because it carries a certain stigma related to manual labour.

The historical low-status of TVE was described by Lewis and Lewis (1989) cited in Morris (1994) when they stated that Caribbean governments so often only see TVE as a solution to the problem of school leaver employment. For this reason, they contended that TVE is ill-directed, under-resourced and fails to take into consideration local variations. Layton (1986: 18) identified three main reasons why until comparatively recently, technological education has been only a marginal contributor to general education in many countries: (a) First, the association of technology education with vocationalism and with preparation for a specific occupation has encouraged a view of it as antipathetic to liberal education. In the USA and the UK technology in the curriculum of general education was seen as a means of confining working-class children to working-class jobs. (b) A second consideration, in countries with a capitalist economy, is that technology education, if it were to be developed much beyond a study of the principles of science applicable to the practice of a trade or industry, might expose to public scrutiny critical components of technique on which the economic success of the industry depended. (c) Thirdly, technology has frequently been portrayed in a subservient and dependent role in relation to science. This perception of technology as merely applied science has been widely promulgated despite the existence of much empirical evidence which refutes it. Furthermore, Young (1993) reported that regardless of the content of vocational subjects, vocational qualifications are judged by employers and university admissions tutors as inferior. Hence, vocational education runs the risk at all times of being seen as an illegitimate extension of the concept of education and vocational schools are similarly viewed (Lillis & Hogan, 1983).

It is a generally held view that a multi-skilled, technically proficient workforce is needed to transform Jamaica's productive sector to match current realities and that this can only be achieved if the government allocates more resources for the development of various TVE programmes. But, Morris (1994) reported that whereas governments and donor agencies had often promoted TVE and training as a means of achieving a wide range of socioeconomic objectives, the World Bank, which in the 1960s and 1970s had supported such a programme at the secondary level, had by the mid-1980s decided that this type of programme was ineffective.

In an attempt to improve the relatively unfavourable public image of TVE and the provision of TVE, the Jamaican Government outlined its policy perspective in the Ministry of Education Five Year Development Plan (1990-1995) that the Planning Institute of Jamaica (1991) published. Based on this plan, specialised vocational/technical training is expected to be provided at all levels of education: pre-primary, primary, secondary and post-secondary levels in private and public institutions. The public institutions fall under the Ministry of Education and the Ministry of Youth and Community Development. However, most of the emphases in TVE are placed on secondary and tertiary institutions. Three vocational schools (two in agriculture, one in Home Economics) offer specialised vocational education for three and two years respectively to 15-year-old students from all-age schools; the technical high schools and new secondary schools (now called upgraded secondary schools) provide education with technical/vocational bias; the secondary or traditional high ("grammar") schools are mainly academic with limited vocational subjects while the comprehensive high schools (founded in the 1970s as junior high schools) offer academic and vocational subjects. As of the year 2002, there were 14 technical high schools in Jamaica each of which had a well-equipped library, science laboratory, technical/vocational education workshop/laboratory and a state- of-the-art computer laboratory. Indeed, some of these schools prepared their students to sit the Caribbean Advanced Proficiency Examination (GCE Advanced Level equivalent) in mathematics, science and arts subjects as well as in TVE subjects such as Information Technology, Communication Studies and Technical Drawing. TVE is offered at the tertiary level at the University of Technology (UTech), College of Agriculture and four Community Colleges. One of the many defects in the 5-year plan is that the system is fragmented with training programmes being carried out by numerous agencies without any effective approach to the overall coordination (Morris, 1994).

In Jamaica, a network of public and private institutions develop and implement training programmes in TVE. The Human Employment and Resource Training (HEART) Trust/NTA is one of the public institutions that operates under the Jamaican Ministry of Education to provide training programmes for the TVE. It assists in implementing the following programmes: school leavers' programme, the Learning for Activity Programme (LEAP), crafts training programme, community-based training projects, collaborative training initiatives, pre-vocational remedial education programme and the coordination of TVE programmes in seven academies. Similarly, the Jamaican Ministry of Youth and Community Development implements its vocational training and development programmes through the following: its non-formal education division, seven vocational training centres, four youth camps, the Jamaican-German Automotive School, community-based training projects, collaborative training initiatives and pre-vocational remedial education programme.

It was considered pertinent to find out whether or not Jamaican high school students who were offered TVE had positive or negative attitudes towards it because we were not aware of any studies which had been published on it in respect of Jamaican 10th and 11th grade students, while international studies on the subject are relatively rare. Soyibo (1989) carried out a study on the attitudes towards technical education of 247 Ordinary National Diploma (OND) and Higher National Diploma (HND) students randomly selected from two polytechnics in Lagos, Nigeria. He found out that many of the students displayed highly positive attitudes towards technical education; there were no statistically significant differences in the attitudes of the OND and HND students on the one hand and the science and social science students on the other, while the males exhibited statistically significantly positive attitudes towards technical education than the females. On the other hand, Prime (1994) found no significant difference in the overall attitudes towards technology education of first year, purely academic students and specialized crafts/pre-technician course students in a comprehensive high school in Trinidad

Several international studies have reported that males exhibited significantly positive attitudes towards science than females (e.g., Catsambis, 1995; Forrest, 1992; Third International Mathematics and Science Study, TIMSS, 1997) especially during middle and high school years (e.g., Hammrich, 1997). Similarly, many international studies have shown that students who exhibited significantly positive attitudes towards science significantly outachieved their counterparts who displayed less positive attitudes in science tests (e.g., Freedman, 1997; Ledbetter, 1993). Some local studies have also recorded positive, statistically significant relationship between students' attitudes to science and performance in specific science subjects. For example, Field (1998) and Soyibo and Hudson (2000) recorded a positive, statistically significant relationship between Jamaican 10th and 11th graders' attitudes to biology and biology achievement respectively, while Stockhausen (1998) reported a positive, statistically significant relationship between Jamaican 9th graders' attitudes to integrated science and performance in the subject ($r = .70$). Partly because of these findings, we considered it worthwhile to investigate the extent to which selected Jamaican 10th and 11th graders in some technical high schools exhibited positive attitudes towards TVE as well as find out if there were any significant correlations among their attitudes towards TVE and gender, grade level and school location.

We conjectured that many of this study's subjects would display positive or favourable attitudes towards TVE. This is because many of them were admitted to the technical high schools when they passed the technical high school entrance examinations for 13-year-olds, or because some of them failed to gain admission into the traditional high schools which offered mainly academic disciplines. In other words, having to study TVE subjects to a few of them, was Hobson's choice. It was also considered worthwhile to determine if there were statistically significant differences in the students' attitudes to TVE linked to their gender, grade level and school location because some studies have shown that these variables accounted for significant differences in secondary school students' attitudes to science and science achievement (Beaumont-Walters & Soyibo, 2001; Forrest, 1992; TIMSS, 1997; Field, 1998).

This study, therefore, sought to determine if (a) the attitudes towards TVE that a sample of Jamaican high school students exhibited were positive or not, (b) there were significant differences in their attitudes towards TVE linked go their gender, grade level and school location, and (c) there was a significant relationship between each of the three variables and the students' attitudes towards TVE.

This study sought to answer the following research questions:

1. Were the students' attitudes to TVE positive or not ?
2. Were there statistically significant differences in the students' attitudes towards TVE linked to their gender, grade level and school location ?
3. Were there statistically significant relationships among the students' gender, grade level and school location and their attitudes towards TVE?

SAMPLE

The sample comprised 310 students (146 tenth graders, 164 eleventh graders; 150 boys and 160 girls, aged 16-17 years) randomly selected from three urban and three rural technical high schools in Jamaica.

INSTRUMENTATION

A 30-item attitudes to TVE questionnaire, with a 5-point response and 6 indicators, that the authors developed, was used for data collection. The 5 responses were as follows: Strongly Agree (SA), Agree (A), Undecided (U), Disagree (D) and Strongly Disagree (SD). The names of the indicators and what they were meant to measure were as follows:

- ***Interest and enjoyment of TVE:*** This indicator was used to measure the extent to which the students enjoyed/had interest in TVE.
- ***Beliefs about TVE:*** This assessed the students' opinions/beliefs about who should study TVE and their parents/guardians' beliefs about TVE as well.
- ***Career interest in TVE:*** This measured the degree to which the students desired to make a career in TVE subjects.
- ***Usefulness of TVE:*** The extent to which the students considered TVE to be useful or not useful to them and the society was measured with this indicator.
- ***Motivation towards TVE:*** This assessed whether or not the students were motivated to study TVE in their schools.
- ***Social implications of TVE:*** This assessed the students' opinions about whether employers, and the society in general accord respect to students/graduates of TVE.

Each indicator had five items, 2 or 3 of which were positive or negative items. Overall, 16 of the items were stated positively, while 14 were stated negatively. The positively stated items were scored as follows: SA = 5, A = 4, U = 3, D = 2, SD = 1. The scoring was reversed for the negatively stated items. Any omitted item was scored 3. The maximum score on each indicator was 25, while 150 was the maximum score on the entire instrument. In the Appendix are specimen items on each of the six indicators. The questionnaire had an internal consistency or a Cronbach alpha coefficient of .77 and alpha coefficients ranging from .46 to .78 for each of the six indicators/scales The questionnaire was considered to have a satisfactory internal consistency reliability coefficient because Evans (1985) stated that instruments that have reliability coefficients of .75 and above are considered good and acceptable in educational research. Details about the instrumentation are available from the authors.

Table 1: Means and Standard Deviations on the Indicators (N=310)

Indicator	Mean	SD
Interest and enjoyment	20.74	3.21
Beliefs	20.08	2.54
Career interest	21.13	2.91
Usefulness	20.52	2.95
Motivation	19.33	3.12
Social implications	20.24	2.79
Total	122.04	17.52

Maximum score on each indicator = 25

RESULTS AND DISCUSSION

The first purpose of this study was to find out whether or not the students' attitudes to TVE were positive. Table 1 data suggest that most of the students have highly positive attitudes towards TVE considering their mean score on each of the six indicators. The table also indicates that their mean score on motivation towards TVE is slightly lower than their mean scores on the other five indicators, while their mean score on career interest is the highest. Further analyses of the students' responses on the "motivation" indicator revealed that many of them were dissatisfied with the TVE equipment and facilities that were available in their schools although many of them indicated that they enjoyed going to TVE classes and would encourage more students to pursue TVE courses. Note that the equipped status of the TVE workshops/labs etc. of the technical schools mentioned earlier was a recent development.

The overall finding that many of the students had highly positive attitudes towards TVE was expected. This might be due to the fact that (a) most of them indicated that TVE would enable them to secure jobs more easily, (b) they opted to attend technical high schools *ab initio* either by their own choice or otherwise, and (c) a significant number of them could have responded in ways that would please the researchers (Evans, 1985). It could be argued that different results would have been obtained if the study had been conducted in traditional high schools. While this argument seems logical and might turn out to be true, we were unable to access any empirical evidence in support of the assertion. As stated earlier, Prime (1994) found no significant difference in the overall attitudes towards technology education of first year, purely academic students and specialized crafts/pre-technician course students in a comprehensive high school in Trinidad. Furthermore, that this study's subjects' attitudes towards TVE were highly positive receives an indirect support from Soyibo's (1989) finding that a sample of Nigerian polytechnic students displayed highly positive attitudes towards technical education.

Table 2: Means, Standard Deviations and F-Test Comparing Students' Overall Attitudes By Gender, Grade Level and School Location

Variables		n	Mean	SD	F
Gender	Males	150	121.61	11.45	
	Females	160	122.41	11.04	0.86
Grade level	10	146	121.55	11.39	
	11	164	122.42	11.09	0.93
School location	Rural	160	121.43	9.60	
	Urban	150	122.66	12.60	1.32

Maximum score = 150

The second purpose of the study was to find out if there were statistically significant differences in the students' attitudes towards TVE linked to their gender, grade level and school location. The data in Table 2 indicate that the mean attitudes scores of the subjects towards TVE, based on each pair of the three independent variables, are fairly similar and highly positive. It was therefore not surprising that the 3-way analysis of variance (ANOVA) computed on their mean scores revealed that there were no significant differences in the subjects' attitudes to TVE linked to differences in their gender, grade level and school location. These findings imply that, irrespective of their gender, grade level, and school location, many of the subjects displayed highly positive attitudes towards TVE. These findings were unexpected as we had conjectured that the attitudes of the boys, 11th graders and urban students would be statistically significantly more positive than those of the girls', 10th graders' and rural students' respectively. Sadly, we were unable to access any previous studies with which this study's findings could be directly compared. Some of the possible reasons for the absence of significant differences in their attitudes linked to the three independent variables have been stated earlier. Indeed, further analyses showed that there were no significant differences in the subjects' attitudes towards TVE on each of the six indicators based on the three independent variables and when the 10th and 11th graders were compared based on their gender. In all cases, the students indicated the highest positive attitudes towards the "career interest" indicator and the lowest positive attitudes on the "motivation" indicator. It would seem that most of the students displayed the highest positive attitudes towards the career interest indicator as they were likely to have decided to study specific aspects of TVE subjects as their life-long careers. On the other hand, it would seem that the lowest rating they gave the "motivation" indicator does imply that many of them were not motivated to study TVE subjects in their schools. The reasons for this finding could not be explained from this study's data. As many of them were likely to have been admitted to their schools because of their performance in the technical entrance examinations, one would have expected them to have displayed a fairly high intrinsic motivation to study TVE subjects.

The third purpose of the study was to find out if there was a statistically significant relationship between the students' (a) gender, (b) grade level, and (c) school location and their attitudes towards TVE. Pearson's product-moment correlation coefficients were computed (Table 3).

Table 3: Pearson's Correlation Coefficients Relating Students' Attitudes to Science to their Gender, Grade Level and School Location

	Gender	Grade Level	School Location
Attitude	.04	.04	.06

The data in Table 3 suggest that there is no relationship between each of the three independent variables and the students' attitudes towards TVE. These imply that the students' attitudes to TVE were highly positive regardless of their gender, grade level and school location. These findings substantiate the data in Table 2 and the results of the ANOVA discussed earlier. Hence, other variables that were likely to account for significant differences in the students' attitudes to TVE, which were not investigated in this study, should be identified and explored in future studies on this topic. Such variables might include differences in students' cognitive abilities, subject preferences, learning or cognitive styles, socioeconomic backgrounds, teachers' qualifications and teaching experience and different types of high schools (e.g., technical, traditional, upgraded, and comprehensive).

CONCLUSIONS AND IMPLICATIONS

As expected, many of the students showed highly positive attitudes towards TVE. This is an interesting finding because, as demonstrated in the literature reviewed, the common belief in many parts of the world is that TVE carries a certain stigma associated with manual labour. But this common perception does not appear to have been internalised within this study's sample. Future studies should determine whether or not grades 10 and 11 Jamaican technical high school students who show highly positive attitudes towards TVE would perform significantly better on specific TVE subjects' tests (e.g., metal work, woodwork, information technology, and clothing and textiles) than their counterparts who display negative or less positive attitudes towards TVE. This suggestion seems pertinent as the findings of some local and international studies on the relationship between students' attitudes to science and their science performance were mixed. For example, while some local studies have recorded positive, statistically significant relationship between students' attitudes to biology and biology achievement (e.g., Field, 1998; Soyibo & Hudson, 2000), and students' attitudes to integrated science and performance in the subject (e.g., Stockhausen, 1998), some studies recorded no relationship between students' (a) attitudes to biology and biology performance (e.g., Crooks & Soyibo, 2002; Dobson, 1994), (b) attitudes to chemistry and chemistry performance (e.g., Thompson, 2000), and (c) attitudes to integrated science and their performance in the subject (e.g., Soyibo & Pinnock, 1998). On the other hand, many international studies have shown that students who exhibited highly positive attitudes to science tended to perform statistically significantly better in science subjects than those who displayed less positive attitudes towards science (e.g., Forrest, 1992; Freedman, 1997; Ledbetter, 1993; TIMSS, 1997). However, some international studies have also recorded no significant differences in students' science achievements linked to differences in their attitudes to science (e.g., Keeves & Morgenstern, 1992). Moreover, we are not aware of any studies that have been published or conducted on the relationship between high school students' attitudes to TVE and their performance on tests set on specific TVE disciplines. As there were no significant differences in the students' attitudes to TVE linked to differences in their gender, grade level and school location, future studies should find out whether or not these variables could account for differences in the students' performance on tests set on specific TVE disciplines. To amplify and validate the findings of this study, further research, using larger sample sizes and other variables needs to be conducted.

Gallagher (1994) contended that teachers make a difference in students' attitudes and persistence in science. Consequently, students who perceive that their teachers enjoy science and are skilled in instruction are more likely to continue in science than students who are taught in a more impersonal classroom environment. For these reasons, future studies should explore the link between Jamaican technical high school teachers' level of enthusiasm towards the teaching of TVE subjects and their students' attitudes towards TVE and performance on tests on TVE subjects.

REFERENCES

Beaumont-Walters, Y. & Soyibo, K. (2001). An analysis of high school students' performance on five integrated science process skills. *Research in Science & Technology Education,* 19, 133-145.

Catsambis, S. (1995). Gender, race, ethnicity, and science education in middle grades. *Journal of Research in Science Teaching,* 32, 243-257.

Crooks, J. & Soyibo, K. (2002). Relationships among Jamaican preservice teachers' demographic variables and science knowledge. In T. Bastick & A, Ezenne (Eds.), *Sociology of Education: Research in the Caribbean* (pp. 117-128). Kingston: Educational Research Centre, University of the West Indies, Mona, Jamaica.

Dobson, S. (1994). *A comparison of Jamaican high school students' conceptions on nutrition and reproduction.* Unpublished MA thesis, University of the West Indies, Mona.

Evans, K. M. (1985). *Attitudes and interest in education.* London: Routledge and Kegan Paul.

Field, D. M. (1998). *Relationships among students' factors and their biology achievement.* Unpublished MA thesis, University of the West Indies, Mona, Jamaica.

Forrest, G. M. (1992). Gender differences in school science examinations. *Studies in Science Education,* 20, 87-122.

Freedman, M. P. (1997). Relationships among laboratory instruction, attitude toward science and achievement in science knowledge. *Journal of Research in Science Teaching,* 34, 343-357.

Gallagher, S. A. (1994). Middle school classroom predictors of science persistence. *Journal of Research in Science Teaching,* 31, 721-734.

Hammrich, P. L. (1997). Yes, daughter, you can. *Science and Children,* 34, 20-24.

Keeves, J. P. & Morgenstern, C. (1992). Attitudes towards science: Measures and effects (pp. 122-140). In J. P. Keeves (Ed.), *The IEA study of science III: Changes in science education and achievement: 1970-1984.* New York: Pergamon.

Layton, D. (Ed.) (1986). *Innovations in science and technology education.* Vol. 1. Paris: Unesco.

Ledbetter, C. E. (1993). Qualitative comparisons of students' constructions of science. *Science Education,* 77, 611-624.

Lillis, K. & Hogan, D. (1983). Dilemmas of diversification: Problems associated with vocational education in developing countries. *Comparative Education,* 19(1), 89-105.

Morris, H. A. (1994). New developments in technical and vocational education: The output of the educational system and the problem of employment. Mimeograph. University of the West Indies, Mona, Jamaica.

Planning Institute of Jamaica (1991). *Jamaican five year plan (1990-1995)*. Kingston: Jamaica.

Prime, G. M. (1994). The need for the development of a curriculum for technology education in Trinidad and Tobago. *Caribbean Curriculum*, 4, 47-63.

Savage, E. & Sterry, L. (1990). *A conceptual framework for technology education*. Virginia: International Technology Education Association.

Soyibo, K. (1989). A comparison of selected Nigerian polytechnic students' attitudes towards technical education. *Journal of Science Teachers Association of Nigeria*, 26, 68-75.

Soyibo, K. & Hudson, A. (2000). Effects of computer-assisted instruction (CAI) on 11th graders' attitudes to biology and CAI and understanding of reproduction in plants and animals. *Research in Science & Technological Education*, 18, 191-199.

Soyibo, K. & Pinnock, J.(1998). Relationships among some factors and students' integrated science knowledge. *Journal of Education & Development in the Caribbean*, 2, 153-157.

Stockhausen, N. (1998). *Relationships among some students' factors and performance in integrated science*. B.Ed Study. Department of Educational Studies, University of the West Indies, Mona.

TIMSS (1997) *Third international mathematics and science study*. Washington, D.C.: US Department of Education.

Thompson, J.(2000). *Effects of student practical work on Jamaican tenth graders' understanding of electrolysis.* Unpublished MEd project, University of the West Indies, Mona.

Trinidad and Tobago Committee on Technology Studies (1993). *Report.* Port of Spain: Ministry of Education.

Unesco (1980). *Technological change and trends in technological and socioeconomic development. Trends and development of technical and vocational education.* Paris: Unesco.

Wallace, R. G. (1985). *Introducing technical and vocational education.* London: Macmillan.

Watson, K. (1994). Technical and vocational education in developing countries: Western paradigms and comparative methodology. *Comparative Education,* 30, 57-68.

Young, M. (1993). A curriculum for the 21st century. *British Journal of Educational Studies,* 41, 3, 57-69.

JAMAICAN STUDENTS' ATTITUDES TO TECHNICAL AND VOCATIONAL EDUCATION

Appendix: Specimen Items on the TVE Questionnaire

Indicator	Item #	Statement	Type
Interest and enjoyment of TVE	1	It was my own choice to attend a technical high school.	+
	4	I will not advise anyone to attend vocational classes.	−
Beliefs about TVE	7	Students who do well in vocational subjects may also do well in academic subjects.	+
	6	Bright students should not do vocational courses.	−
Career interest in TVE	11	Vocational education is important to my future.	+
	13	I do not want to do any job that requires vocational education.	−
Usefulness of TVE	20	Vocational subjects are useful to the society.	+
	19	Studying vocational subjects is a waste of time	−
Motivation to TVE	22	I am always happy to go for vocational education classes.	+
	21	I often get bored in vocational education classes.	−
Social implications of TVE	30	Employers are very happy to employ students who have completed vocational education courses.	−
	29	People think that I am dull because I do vocational courses.	+

ANITA THOMAS-JAMES AND KOLA SOYIBO

NOTES ON CONTRIBUTORS

TONY BASTICK
EDITOR

Tony Bastick has an abiding interest in developing, through his teaching and research, each individual's personal creative contributions to our appreciation and quality of life. He has been fortunate in living and working in many different cultures and universities around the world, having over the last thirty years held substantive positions in universities in the U.S., South Pacific, U.K., Australia, Asia and the Caribbean. It is these pan-national and inter-cultural experiences that help to enrich the original perspectives he brings to his research in assessment and evaluation. His first degree, in Mathematics, was awarded by the University of Exeter in England; his Ph.D. in Education and Psychology is from Brunel University of West London. Since October 1997 he has been with the Department of Educational Studies at the University of the West Indies in the Caribbean and can be contacted at their Jamaica campus through tbastick@uwimona.edu.jm.

AUSTIN EZENNE
EDITOR

Austin Ezenne received his Ph. D. degree in Educational Administration from the University of Wales, Cardiff, United Kingdom. He taught for over twenty-five years in Nigerian Universities before joining the University of the West Indies as a consultant in

Educational Administration. He has published a number of books and has many articles in learned journals. His research interests are in Educational Administration and Planning, Educational Leadership, Financing of Education, and Human Resource Development in Education. He is a member of the British Society for Research Into Higher Education (SRHE), British Educational Leadership, Management and Administration Society, (BELMAS), the Association for Supervision and Curriculum Development (ASCD, USA) and the Jamaica Association for Human Resource Development, (JATAD).

MAXINE HENRY-WILSON

INTRODUCTION

The Hon. Maxine Henry-Wilson is Minister of Education, Youth and Culture for Jamaica. She was born in Manchester, Jamaica and attended Vaz Preparatory School, St. Andrew High School, the University of the West Indies, Mona, and Rutgers State University, New Jersey, United States. Mrs. Henry-Wilson is the holder of two Masters degrees - one in Public Administration and the other in Public Policy. She has taught at St. Hugh's High School in Kingston and the University of the West Indies, Mona. The Minister is married and has one child.

NOTES ON CONTRIBUTORS

ZELLYNNE JENNINGS

FOREWORD

Zellynne Jennings has Masters degrees from universities in the United Kingdom and a PhD from the University of the West Indies. She has served as Head of the Department of Educational Studies, UWI, Mona, and as a Professor of Education at the University of Guyana, she also served as Head of the Department of Foundations and Administration. She is a specialist in Curriculum Studies and her areas of research span curriculum innovation and change, programme evaluation, literacy, teacher education and the interface between education and the world of work. She has a number of publications in international journals, including the Journal of Curriculum Studies, Compare, Comparative Education and the International Journal of Educational Development. She is Executive Editor of the Journal of Education and Development in the Caribbean.

BÉATRICE BOUFOY-BASTICK

CHAPTER 1

Béatrice Boufoy-Bastick is a linguist who holds a Master's Degree from the Sorbonne in France and a doctorate from the University of the West Indies in Jamaica.

Her main research interests are in the interaction of culture and second language education, in modern language teaching methodology and in anthropological research methods. She has a wide cross-cultural experience in teaching and researching in Europe, Australia, Asia, the South Pacific and the Caribbean.

INGRID WALDRON
CHAPTER 2

Ingrid Waldron was born in Montreal, Quebec to Trinidadian parents. She holds a Ph.D. in Education from the Sociology and Equity Studies in Education Department at the Ontario Institute for Studies in Education of the University of Toronto (OISE/UT). Her doctoral thesis, African Canadian Women Storming the Barricades! Challenging Psychiatric Imperialism through Indigenous Conceptualizations of 'Mental Illness' and Self-Healing examines the psychological, emotional, mental, and spiritual impact of oppression on African Canadian women, racism in the history, tradition, and practice of psychiatry, African-centred psychology, and African indigenous knowledges in mental health. Her masters thesis, Quebec and the New Racism Theory: A Case Study of the Language and Politics of Identity and its Impact on the Schooling Experiences of Caribbean students in Quebec, is concerned with the impact that exclusionary French language policies have on the schooling experiences of Caribbean students in Quebec.

Dr. Waldron was employed for several years as a research assistant for the Center for Integrative Anti-racism Studies at OISE/UT, where she conducted research on anti-racism education, minority schooling, social justice, and immigration issues. She was also a board member and committee member for several anti-racist and social justice organizations in Toronto, including the Congress of Black Women of Canada, the Urban Alliance on Race Relations, and Across Boundaries - An Ethno-racial Mental Health Agency.

Dr. Waldron has also been involved in human rights work locally and internationally. She worked as an intern in the Mental Health and Substance Dependence Department of the World Health Organization in Geneva, where she developed policy reports on mental health issues in developing countries. She was also a member of the Human Rights, Discrimination and Harassment Task Group at the Toronto District School Board, responsible for helping to draft a new human rights policy for public schools in Toronto. Currently, Dr. Waldron is employed as a Human Rights Officer at COSTI Immigrant Services, where she investigates complaints of workplace racism and sexual harassment.

LORETTA COLLINS

CHAPTER 5

Loretta Collins is an assistant professor of Anglophone Caribbean Cultural and Literary Studies, Postcolonial theory, and creative writing in the English Department, Humanities Faculty, University of Puerto Rico, Río Piedras. Her scholarly articles have appeared in journals, including *Small Axe, Journal of Commonwealth and Postcolonial Studies, Caribbean 2000, Sargasso,* and *Literature and Medicine,* as well as anthologies, including *Sound States: Innovative Poetics and Acoustical Technologies, Religion, Culture and Tradition in the Caribbean,* and *Rastafari in the Global Context.* Her creative writing has been published in journals, such as *The Caribbean Writer, Black Warrior Review, TriQuarterly Review, The Antioch Review, The Missouri Review,* and *Quarterly West,* and collections *Pushcart Prize XXI: Best of the Small Presses, Tri Quarterly New Writers,* and *How Much Earth.*

BEVERLY-JEAN DANIEL

CHAPTER 6

Beverly-Jean Daniel immigrated to Canada at the age of 16 from Trinidad and has worked extensively with Caribbean adolescents in the Canadian School system. She is in the last year the PhD program at the University of Toronto, Ontario Canada where her areas of study include critical teacher education, equity and antiracism pedagogy and Black feminism.

CLARISSA WEST-WHITE

CHAPTER 7

Clarissa West-White received her Ph.D. in English Education from Florida State University's English education doctoral program with minor concentrations in: ESOL, counseling, and multi-ethnic literature. She has taught in rural Gadsden County and in urban Miami-Dade. She has expertise in ESOL, counseling, and multi-ethnic literature and currently teaches literature, writing, and education at Florida Memorial College in Miami,

Florida where she also resides with her husband, Headley, their Pug Cocoa Mocha, and their Cockatiel Carter.

BRENDA J. MCMAHON
CHAPTER 8

Brenda J. McMahon has been a teacher and administrator in a variety of school settings within metropolitan Toronto for the past 20 years. Her research interests focus on marginalized students, student engagement and the personal and emotional transformations students' experience, as they become engaged with and academically successful in schools. She is currently a lecturer in the OISE/UT Initial Teacher Education Program.

DENISE ARMSTRONG
CHAPTER 8

Denise Armstrong has worked as teacher, counselor and principal over the past thirty years. She has taught in a variety of academic settings at the elementary, secondary and tertiary levels in the Caribbean and Canada. Her research interests focus on immigrant students, teacher/administrator transitions and marginalized students. She is currently an instructor with the OISE/UT Initial Teacher Education Program.

SHANA GROSSMAN
CHAPTER 9

Shana R. Grossman was born on August 24, 1965, in Perth Amboy, New Jersey, and is a U.S. citizen. She received her Bachelor of Arts from Tufts University in 1987 and she received a Rotary International Graduate Fellowship to study in the Masters of History and Sociology Program at the Universidad de Costa Rica for the year 1988-1989. She received her Masters in Secondary Education, with a specialization in ESOL/ Multicultural Education, from George Mason University, in 1992, and her Ph.D. in Education from George Mason University in 2001. She taught ESOL Literacy and Government to ESOL students for eight years at a high school in the county of the study.

LORAINE COOK
CHAPTER 10

Loraine Cook's research interests are primarily in evaluating online programs, teachers' locus of control, and in investigating relationships between teachers' intended and actual behaviour in the classroom. She has published articles on Teachers' Locus of control and online course evaluation in the Caribbean context. Currently, she lectures part-time in Social Studies, Educational Psychology and Research Methods at the University of the West Indies while pursuing her Doctoral studies.

NOTES ON CONTRIBUTORS

HYACINTH SKERVIN

CHAPTER 11

Hyacinth Skervin is a graduate of the Department of Education University of the West Indies who is currently pursuing doctoral studies in Teacher Education at the University of Cincinnati, Ohio in the USA. Her doctoral studies are focused on teacher preparation and development in cultural geography education. A former secondary school geography teacher, her interest in the learning patterns of secondary school boys has been motivated by her experience of teaching in an all boys school in the Caribbean where the consistent under-performance of students had become a major concern among teachers. She has plans to continue post-doctoral research in this area following the expressed interest of a cross-section of educators in this pilot study in support of further research to determine ways of improving academic performance among minority male students in particular.

JOSSETT SMIKLE

CHAPTER 13

Jossett Lewis Smikle is a graduate of the University of the West Indies. She received her M.Ed, and her Ph.D. on the development of literacy, from the University of Manchester, U.K. She has served as Head of the Language Arts Department and as Vice Principal at Bethlehem Moravian College, Jamaica., and as Visiting Faculty for the Department of Reading and Language Arts, Oakland University, Michigan, U.S.A. She is a Member of the International Reading Association (I.R.A.) and a Founder member of the St. Elizabeth Reading Association (S.E.R.A.). Currently, Jossett lectures in Language Education and Literacy Studies for the Department of Educational Studies, University of the West Indies, Mona Campus.

ANITA THOMAS-JAMES

CHAPTER 14

Mrs. Anita Thomas-James (B.Ed., M.A., UWI Mona) is currently a lecturer in Educational Administration in the School of Technical and Vocational Education, the University of Technology, Kingston, Jamaica.

KOLA SOYIBO

CHAPTER 14

Kola Soyibo (Ph.D., Leeds, U.K.) is currently a Senior Lecturer in Science Education in the Department of Educational Studies at the University of the West Indies, Mona, Jamaica. He has been in the teaching profession since 1965 and began his university teaching career in 1977 at the University of Lagos, Nigeria.

www.ingramcontent.com/pod-product-compliance
Lightning Source LLC
Chambersburg PA
CBHW071135300426
44113CB00009B/985